D1570614

Acknowledgments

The authors and publisher gratefully acknowledge permission to reprint portions of the following:

"Measuring Media Bias: A Content Analysis of Time and Newsweek Coverage of Domestic Social Issues, 1975-2000." 2007. *Social Science Quarterly.* 88(3):690–706.

"Information Sources and the Coverage of Social Issues in Partisan Publications: A Content Analysis of 25 years of the *Progressive* and the *National Review.*" 2007. *Mass Communication and Society.* 10(1):67–94.

The media are only as liberal as the conservative businesses that own them.

Anonymous

Introduction

Complaints that American commercial news media are partisan or "politically biased" are common. They can be heard almost daily on radio and television talk shows, and found on the internet, in articles and letters to editors in countless newspapers and newsmagazines, as well as in a variety of popular books, reports of media watchdog organizations, and in scholarly publications. The more discussion there is of media bias, the more people believe that such bias exists.[1]

In the case of popular complaints, what is seen as biased coverage is typically material that is discrepant with what the dissatisfied already believe.[2] In particular, people with strong political beliefs tend to view the media as hostile to their outlook.[3] In other contexts, those asserting that the media exhibit a liberal bias tend to explain their findings in terms of an assumed liberal perspective held by the majority of leading American journalists.[4] Those arguing that the news media exhibit a conservative bias tend to explain their findings in terms of the corporate ownership and profit orientation of the media, and media dependence on government, corporations, and other elite sources of information.[5]

Most of such writings are seriously limited. First, they tend to be based on anecdotal evidence; they do not answer the question: biased according to what measure? Second, they often do not differentiate and compare various media organizations. They do not ask the question: more or less conservative (or liberal) than what other specific news sources? Third, they frequently fail to consider the possibility that the bias of a publication or broadcast news organization can vary by issue and can change over time.

The research reported in this book represents our attempt to understand media bias in a way that avoids these difficulties. To do so we focus on two mainstream national newsmagazines, *Time* and *Newsweek*. Using an empirical measure developed for this study, we look at their coverage of four domestic social issues: crime, the environment, gender, and poverty. We compare our findings on *Time* and *Newsweek* coverage of these issues with that of two journals of political opinion, one conservative, the *National Review* and one liberal, *The Progressive*. The study reviews the contents of the four publications over the twenty-five year period 1975–2000. Our reasons for selecting the particular media, issues, method, and time frame are discussed in Chapters 2 and 3. As a consequence of the choices, our conclusions may be neither as sweeping, nor as dramatic, nor as ideologically engaging as those of other studies of media bias. We find this acceptable, and hope our readers will as well.

Defining Media Bias

Discussions of media bias often involve concern with the relative amount of attention, approval, or criticism given particular political actors by a media outlet or by the mass media generally. For example, studies of presidential campaign coverage commonly take such approaches but tend to find little evidence of partisan bias in news reporting.[6] However, other research has concluded that the media are seriously biased in their emphasis on certain politically relevant topics and their systematic avoidance of others. Newsworthiness, from this perspective, is the product of negotiation; parties with greater resources generally have the ability to call attention to their issues, concerns, and events over their opponents' issues.[7]

Our approach to media bias differs from these in its focus on media presentations of certain selected domestic social issues. Examinations of media bias, including those characterized above, commonly make use of the descriptors "conservative" and "liberal." While the terms are notoriously vague and ambiguous, their use should not be abandoned. To do so would make any discussion appear largely irrelevant to the ongoing debate over media bias by disregarding socially meaningful and politically important, though inexact, concepts central to popular political discourse in America.

To retain the terms but avoid equivocal assertions, they are used in this study to refer only to two specific opposing positions on a particular domestic social issue. This involved making two assumptions that eliminated several issues from consideration. First, the issue being discussed could be characterized as a clash of two diametrically opposed positions without distorting the actual social conflict. Second, each of the sides could be labeled as either "conservative" or "liberal" in a way that was consistent with the manner in which we believe elites (politicians and journalists) and the politically interested public tend to understand the terms in the case of the particular conflict. This understanding is hegemonic and "common sense"; it represents a narrow range of perspectives taken on each issue dominant in popular political discourse. There are social issues such as education, social security, and domestic terrorism that do not clearly involve conflict between "conservative" and "liberal" positions. Bias in media coverage of these issues cannot be analyzed readily through the use of the measure described in Chapter 3.

"Common sense" understandings of "liberal" and "conservative" on particular issues can change over time. This was taken into account when specifying the operational definitions of the "conservative" and "liberal" positions on each of the issues whose coverage is discussed in the following chapters. An effort was made to identify the features that defined "conservative" and "liberal" positions on an issue that appeared to be constant over a twenty-five-year period. With few exceptions, our findings indicate the consistency of the definitions of the positions used in this study.

Our use of the labels "conservative" and "liberal" can be illustrated by referring to the issue of abortion. There are a number of positions in the abortion debate ranging from the view that access to abortion should be an unlimited right, to the contention that abortion should be outlawed under any and all circumstances, including cases of rape, incest, and threat to the life of the mother. While recognizing the wide range of views, we are nevertheless willing to make two assumptions. First, a position can be classified as either one that focuses on maintaining existing abortion rights, or as one that focuses on limiting such rights in whatever way or ways. Second, it is consistent with the elite and popular usage to label the first political stance on abortion rights "liberal" and the second stance "conservative."

The power of a publication consists in its ability to signify issues in particular ways. In this study, a publication is considered biased to the extent that it relies on sources favorable to a conservative or to a liberal position on a domestic social issue (SOURCES), and defines the issue in terms of the answer it provides to three questions: "Who or what is potentially wronged and what is the extent of the grievance that defines the issue being discussed?" (COSTS), "Who and/or what is responsible for the grievance that defines the issue being discussed?" (CAUSES), and "What can be done to solve the problem?" (SOLUTIONS).

Why Understanding Media Bias Matters

Any view of the nature of media bias entails a perspective on the nature of "news" itself and on the role that news does play and can play in political life. Some understandings of these topics can promote political cynicism and a disinclination to become involved in any form of democratic political participation. Hopefully, the approach taken in this book provides an empirically based understanding of media bias that supports belief in the value of news media, both mainstream and explicitly partisan, and encourages active engagement in civic issues.

All or almost all of what anyone knows about political affairs is not likely to be the result of direct personal experience. Rather, it is likely to come from direct or indirect contact with media of mass communication. It is the result of reading, listening to, watching, or being told "the news." However, "news is not what happens, but what someone says has happened or will happen."[8] It is stories, and the language used to tell stories about political actors, conditions, and events, and not the actors, conditions, and events in any other sense, that people usually experience. Political language is political reality; there is no other insofar as the meaning of political phenomena to spectators is concerned.[9] "Reality is created or constructed through communication, not expressed by it."[10]

In cases where media audiences simply do not attend to the constructed nature of media accounts of politics, they are likely to label such accounts "news." However, when audiences believe that media are using language to tell stories that express political perspectives they do not share, they are likely to consider the news presentations "biased." However, whether people view media presentations as biased or not, it is experiences with these symbolic materials that shape what they believe, question, or do not believe about political reality.

It is not media recording the occurrence of an event, the actions of a political leader, or the presence of a social condition per se that is likely to prompt claims of bias. Rather, objections tend to focus on particular stories about the subject told by some news organizations and the language they use in telling their stories. Complaints concern the sources of information on which the stories are based and what the stories say about social-political problems, their causes, and their remedies. Political conflict is largely a struggle to win public acceptance of particular meanings of subjects. Consequently, the media play a central role in American politics. Empirical research on media bias can reveal core features of a society's ideological conflicts as well as the extent to which its citizens are offered "conservative," "liberal," and "unbiased" stories from which to choose in a democratic marketplace of ideas.

Overview of the Chapters

We begin our study of media bias with a review of several well-known discussions of the topic—popular, scholarly, and those that seem to fall somewhere in between. Interest in some of these analyses has been limited to the academic community while interest in others has placed them on the *New York Times* best-sellers list. Each of the works offers empirical evidence in support of its claims. At first glance, much of this material is impressive. However, subsequent questioning about its validity, adequacy, and relevance often reduces enthusiasm for the position it is intended to support. Nevertheless, judging from the frequency with which it is cited, each of the books and articles continues to influence the thinking of a vast number of its readers. In assessing evidence of media bias, as elsewhere, ideological investment sometimes overrides commitment to the standards of social science research.

In Chapter 2 we present our reasons for selecting two newsmagazines, *Time* and *Newsweek*, to represent America's mainstream news media. These would seem to be somewhat questionable choices at a time when most citizens get their news from television, when subscription rates to newsmagazines and newspapers are declining, and when new computer-related sources of social and political information are gaining in importance. In the chapter we also explain our selection of the *National Review* and *The Progressive* to represent the country's explicitly conservative and explicitly liberal media whose contents are used to compare with the products of the putatively "unbiased" mainstream news organizations. The selection of the *National Review* would seem to be problematic given the proliferation of conservative "talk radio" programs and the development of a highly popular television broadcast network which is widely seen as presenting a conservative perspective on the news.

In addition to presenting the reasons for selecting the newsmagazines for the analysis of media bias, Chapter 2 considers some of the social forces that have shaped their contents. These include the magazines' organizational histories, the social composition of their audiences, and their relationships to their corporate owners and sponsors. Features of the organizational structures of *Time* and *Newsweek* that have troubled conservative and liberal commentators, and have contributed to their perceptions of media bias also are described.

The third chapter presents the details of and the rationale for our methodological approach to media bias. The methodology is based on the premise that ideological bias is a quantifiable phenomenon. Not all who discuss the topic would be willing to accept this assumption. First, it is incompatible with the view that "biased" material is that which is rejected by an audience because it is incompatible with some firmly held belief or beliefs that they share. In this view, "biased" is equivalent to lacking credibility. Content analysis, by itself, cannot reveal how believable material is to some audiences. Second, the premise is incompatible with the view that "biased" material simply is that which is demonstrably false. Here the standard of acceptability is not compatibility with existing beliefs but verifiability by the standards of empirical research. This approach clearly is more amenable to quantification. For example, a study might be undertaken to determine the percentage of the truth claims present in articles on a particular social issue that appeared within a specified time frame in a newsmagazine that were not supported by empirical evidence. However, this approach presents two problems. First, it is immensely impractical; it would require an enormous amount of research activity to produce results of limited interest. Second, as illustrated throughout this book, concerns over media bias generally have more to do with conflicting constructions of social reality than they have to do with conflicting truth claims.

As noted earlier, our quantitative approach to media bias is applied to newsmagazine coverage of four domestic social issues: crime, gender, the environment, and poverty. Chapter 3 describes the process that was used to select these issues and presents operational definitions of "liberal" and "conservative" positions on each of them.

Following a discussion of technical features of the media bias measure, Chapter 4 presents some of the major findings. These include comparisons of the bias scores obtained by each publication for each of the four social issues, comparisons of the overall bias scores of *Time*, *Newsweek*, the *National Review*, and *The Progressive*, and an assessment of the consistency of the bias scores of each publication's coverage of each of the issues over a period of twenty-five years. The chapter considers the broad implications of the data concerning the bias of mainstream news media in America as well as the limitations of the study.

Several of the works reviewed in previous chapters emphasized the central role information sources, particularly "official" sources, play in determining the bias of news stories. However, data presented in Chapter 4 raise some questions about the extent of that influence. It seems reasonable to hypothesize that, if information sources significantly affect ideological content, then information sources of the *National Review* will differ markedly from those of *The Progressive*. Chapter 5 investigates this hypothesis. Results of the analysis support a view of relationships among sources, partisan publications, the electorate, officials, and the development of public policy that is discussed at the end of the chapter.

During the twenty-five years encompassed by this study, the United States had three Republican (Ford, Reagan, and Bush) and two Democratic (Carter and Clinton) administrations. Major events occurred in each of the issue areas whose coverage is analyzed here. Examples include: defeat of the Equal Rights Amendment (1982), the Three Mile Island nuclear accident (1979), the F.B.I. announcement that the country faced a prevalent drug problem (1982), and

Welfare Reform legislation (1996). Chapter 6 considers the extent to which such historical conditions influence media bias.

In the last chapter, we assess what our data indicate about the role that the media have played in sustaining and promoting political democracy in the United States between 1975 and 2000. We conclude by suggesting some positive functions of media bias. Some bias, at least as we have conceptualized it, might not be such a bad thing after all.

NOTES

1. Mark Watts, David Domke, Dhavan Shah, and David Fan, "Elite Cues and Media Bias in Presidential Campaigns: Explaining Public Perception of a Liberal Press," *Communication Research* 26 (1999): 144–175.

2. Robert L. Stevenson and Mark T. Greene, "A Reconsideration of Bias in the News," *Journalism Quarterly* 51, no. 1 (1980): 115–121.

3. Paul A. Beck, "Voters' Intermediation Environments in the 1988 Presidential Contest," *Public Opinion Quarterly* 55 (1991): 371–394; Russell J. Dalton, Paul Beck, Robert Huckfeldt, and William Koetzel, "A Test of Media Centered Agenda Setting: Newspaper Context and Public Interests in a Presidential Election," *Political Communication* 15 (1998): 463–481.

4. Dale A. Berryhill, *The Media Hates Conservatives: How It Controls the Flow of Information* (Lafayette, LA: Huntington House Publishers, 1994); Bernard Goldberg, *Bias: A CBS Insider Exposes How the Media Distort the News* (Washington, DC: Regency Publishing, 2002); Robert Lichter, Stanley Rothman, and Linda Lichter, *The Media Elite: America's New Power Brokers* (Bethesda, MD: Adler & Adler, 1986).

5. Eric Alterman, *What Liberal Media? The Truth about Bias and the News* (New York: Basic Books, 2003); David Croteau and William Hoynes, *By Invitation Only: How the Media Limit Political Debates* (Monroe, ME: Common Courage Press, 1994); Edward S. Herman and Noam Chomsky, *Manufacturing Consent: The Political Economy of the Mass Media* (New York: Pantheon Books, 1988); Mark Hartsgaard, *On Bended Knee: The Press and the Reagan Presidency* (New York: Farrar, Strauss, Giroux, 1989).

6. Dave D'Alessio and Mike Allen, "Media Bias in Presidential Elections: A Meta-Analysis," *Journal of Communication* 50, no. 4 (2000): 133–157; C. Richard Hofstetter, *Bias in the News: Network Television Coverage of the 1972 Election Campaign* (Columbus: Ohio State University Press, 1976); Marion Just, Ann Crigler, Dean Alger, and Timothy Cook, *Crosstalk: Citizens, Candidates and the Media in a Presidential Campaign* (Chicago: University of Chicago Press, 1996); Thomas E. Patterson, *The Mass Media Election: How Americans Choose Their President* (New York: Praeger, 1980); Thomas E. Patterson and Robert D. McClure, *The Unseeing Eye: The Myth of Television Power in National Elections* (New York: Putnam, 1976).

7. Todd Gitlin, *The Whole World Is Watching: The Mass Media in the Making and Unmaking of the New Left* (Berkeley: University of California Press, 1980); Herman and

Chomsky, *Manufacturing Consent*; Philip Schlesinger, *Media, State and Nation: Political Violence and Collective Identities* (Newbury Park, CA: Sage, 1991).

8. Leon Sigal, *Reporters and Officials: The Organization and Politics of Newsmaking* (Lexington, MA: Heath, 1973), 15.

9. Murray Edelman, *Constructing the Political Spectacle* (Chicago: University of Chicago Press, 1988), 104–105.

10. Dan Nimmo and James Combs, *Subliminal Politics* (Englewood Cliffs, NJ: Prentice Hall, 1983), 3.

Chapter 1

The Media Bias Debate

Reading and listening to popular discussion of media bias certainly suggest that those engaged on both sides of the debate have considerable belief in their positions. Below we look at their major arguments, consider the evidence they offer in support of those positions, and raise some questions about the extent to which their confidence is well placed.

The Conservative Argument

Scholarly research pointing to a liberal bias in mainstream media has focused on survey data concerning journalists' political beliefs, attitudes, and voting behavior and on content analyses of news items that illustrate preferential coverage of liberal candidates and issue positions. Drawing on selective findings from academic research and from conservative foundations and think tanks, popular attacks on the "liberal media" offer a litany of individual examples to demonstrate the presence of such bias.[1]

Liberal Journalists

Among the most frequently cited in both academic and popular criticisms of
"the liberal media" is the claim that journalists are overwhelmingly liberal in
their backgrounds and their political and social beliefs.[2] Since the 1970s,
researchers have been studying the characteristics of American journalists,
finding that as a group, journalists are not representative of the public they
purportedly serve.[3] Johnstone found that elite journalists, those working for the
top news outlets (network television news, top-rated national and regional
market newspapers, and newsmagazines), come overwhelmingly from
privileged backgrounds: most were white, college educated males from socially
and economically successful Northeastern families.[4] Based on interviews with
over 200 journalists, S. Robert Lichter found that "most were raised in upper-
middle-class homes" as "children of professionals" who frequently held college
degrees.[5] Both journalists and media outlets were found to be distributed
differently than the general population geographically: leading journalists and
the most influential news outlets were located in the Northeast, where only a
small percentage of the United States population resides.[6] Since the 1970s, this
distribution has become more representative of the general population, but
Northeastern media outlets continue to be among the most influential.[7] White
males continue to dominate the field, although women and minorities appear
more frequently than in 1971, when Johnstone conducted his survey of the
profession.[8] Lichter, Rothman, and Lichter provide this concise description:

> The media elite are a homogenous and cosmopolitan group, who were raised at
> some distance from the social and cultural traditions of small town middle
> America. Drawn mainly from big cities in the northeast and north central states,
> their parents tended to be well off, highly educated members of the upper
> middle class. Most have moved away from any religious heritage and very few
> are regular church goers. In short, the typical leading journalist is the very
> model of the modern eastern urbanite.[9]

In addition to their liberal upbringing, journalists also have been found
frequently to have personal and prior employment connections to liberal
politicians.[10] Early career positions as speech writers, aides, and campaign
workers for Democratic candidates, appointments to cabinet positions during
presidential administrations which followed or interrupted careers in journalism,
and post-retirement media positions for former Democratic aides are provided as
evidence that journalists are personally liberal. Bozell and Baker compile what
they refer to as the "revolving door" of political jobs with the Democratic party
through which "as of early 1990 . . . 235 reporters, editors, producers, and news

division executives" had passed.[11] Ann Coulter updates this list in 2002 to include media personnel connected to the Clinton administration.[12] Among those listed were Sidney Blumenthal (*New Yorker* correspondent), Thomas Ross (NBC News senior vice president), Strobe Talbot (*Time* bureau chief), and Jack Rosenthal (*New York Times* correspondent).[13] While journalists move between media and political positions with both parties, these authors point to a vast disparity in the numbers of journalists who have connections to the Republican Party and those with Democratic Party credentials.[14] Coulter adds that "Democrat journalists not only far outnumber their Republican counterparts, but outflank them on the ideological spectrum. A surprising number of establishment journalists worked for far-left liberals whose closest counterpart on the right would be the John Birch Society."[15]

"Liberal" journalists are not only liberal in their origins, but also in their voting patterns (Democrats over Republicans) and political leanings (liberal over conservative).[16] Richter et al. examined the voting records of more than 200 journalists and found that they had overwhelmingly voted for Democratic presidential candidates during the 1960s and 1970s and a majority saw themselves and their coworkers as liberals.[17] The voting preference among journalists for Democratic or liberal candidates has been cited as far back as the Roosevelt administration.[18] This voting disparity was cited in the 1972 elections, when over 80 percent of journalists preferred McGovern over Nixon, who won with more than 60 percent of the popular vote.[19] In her best-selling book, *Slander,* political pundit Ann Coulter also points out that "in the 1992 election, a mere 43 percent of Americans voted for Bill Clinton. That same year, 89 percent of Washington bureau chiefs and reporters voted for Clinton."[20]

Research over three decades has also documented a gap in personal beliefs and social attitudes of journalists and the general public.[21] David Weaver and G. Cleveland Wilhoit, who have tracked the profession since the early 1980s, have consistently found that journalists hold more liberal viewpoints than the United States population.[22] In 2004, 35 percent of national journalists polled identified themselves as ideologically liberal, while only 7 percent viewed themselves as conservative, and the national press held consistently more liberal views than the public on homosexuality, morality, and the importance of government-provided aid to those in need.[23] In a 2005 report, The Pew Research Center found that news media personnel were more critical than the general public of the Bush administration's foreign policies and were more likely to think that the war in Iraq was the "wrong decision" and that it hurt the "war on terrorism."[24]

Journalists are also less likely than the general public to place importance on religious beliefs and are less likely to "practice any mainstream U.S. religion than the public at large."[25] Lichter goes so far as to assert that journalists "are united in rejecting social conservatism and traditional norms. . . . Leading journalists emerge from the survey as strong supporters of environmental protection, affirmative action, women's rights, homosexual rights, and sexual freedom in general."[26] Weaver and Wilhoit point out that this gap between the attitudes of journalists and the American people is even more pronounced when you separate journalistic staff from editors/managers who tend to be more conservative.[27]

In his book, *Bias*, also a best seller, Bernard Goldberg argues that liberal bias in the media may be unintentional.[28] Journalists, who are overwhelmingly liberal, don't realize that their views on social issues lie outside of the mainstream. In addition, they only know other liberals, thus contributing to the idea that their views are in line with the rest of the country. Because they are blinded to their own leanings, they don't see their coverage of events as "biased," just factual. Goldberg points out that the liberal bias of the media is not a "dark conspiracy." "The reason we don't identify NOW as a liberal group or Laurence Tribe as a liberal professor . . . is that, by and large, the media elites don't see them that way. . . . When you get right down to it, liberals in the newsroom see liberal views as just plain . . . reasonable."[29] H. Brent Bozell makes a similar argument, quoting Walter Cronkite: "I think most newspapermen by definition have to be liberal. If they're not liberal, by my definition of it, then they can hardly be good newspapermen."[30]

Coverage of Elections and Treatment of Politicians

Media coverage of politicians and elections has been extensively examined for political bias.[31] In their 1990 book, *And That's the Way It Isn't*, editors H. Brent Bozell, founder and chairman of the Media Research Center (MRC), and Brent Baker, director of the MRC, present a compilation of studies illustrating how "the liberal media" give short shrift to Republican/conservative politicians during elections and in congressional coverage. Examinations of general election coverage for 1984 and 1988 found that Republican candidates were more likely to be tagged with ideological labels such as "conservative," "ultra-conservative," or "right-wing" and received more negative coverage in general than their Democratic counterparts.[32] Another study by the MRC showed that during the 1984 Democratic and Republican party conventions, coverage included more interviews with liberal Democrats, who made up a small minority of those holding congressional positions. Republicans were also more likely to be described as conservative or ultra-conservative while Democrats were likely to escape any label at all, giving them the air of being "mainstream" or "middle of the road" in their views.[33] Brady and Ma's study of the *New York Times* and the *Washington Post* further points out that conservative members of Congress "are more often given negative labels . . . while liberals are identified with positive terms."[34]

Other research has compared the tone of coverage of presidential candidates and their running mates. Citing a study by Maura Clancey and Michael Robinson, William Rusher reports that Ronald Reagan received ten times as many seconds of "bad press" as "good press" and that George Bush received a total of zero seconds of "good press" during the 1984 presidential election coverage.[35] In addition, Janet Murphy found that Bill Clinton received more positive coverage than Robert Dole in 1996 election coverage during network television news broadcasts.[36]

Coverage of Social Issues

Coverage of social and political issues also reveals a pro-liberal/anti-conservative bias in mainstream media according to those advancing the conservative argument. The relative emphasis placed on particular issues for coverage, how these issues are covered, and how opposing viewpoints are characterized has been examined. Among these issues are: abortion,[37] homelessness,[38] gun control,[39] gay rights,[40] feminism and women's rights,[41] religion,[42] the environment and nuclear energy,[43] racism/racial discrimination,[44] and government economic policies.[45] The omission or dismissal of conservative perspectives in debates of social issues has been cited as evidence of a pro-liberal media bias. Bernard Goldberg points out that while media outlets frequently interview left-leaning elites, such as NOW leaders on women's issues, conservative voices such as Phyllis Schaffley are either ignored or marginalized.[46] When conservative voices or perspectives are included in the media coverage of social issues, they are more likely to be labeled as partisan than are their liberal counterparts.[47] For example, reporters for leading newspapers and newsmagazines "labeled the conservative Heritage Foundation more than thirty-five times as often as the liberal Brookings Institution."[48]

Goldberg asserts that coverage of homelessness varied across presidential administrations in ways that were not connected to significant changes in the prevalence of homelessness during these periods.[49] News reports on homelessness were common during the first Bush administration, dropped precipitously during the Clinton administration and then rose again after George W. Bush came to office.[50] Sociologist Christopher Hewitt found that media outlets tended to report the exaggerated estimates of the homeless population provided by activist groups and were critical of statements made by both President Reagan and Republican officials on the issue of homelessness.[51]

Goldberg further contends that journalists are afraid of offending minority or traditionally oppressed groups such as women's rights groups.[52] This is because they see themselves as allies to these causes and see it as part of their role as journalists to further their agendas. They therefore cover these issues in ways that will not offend the leaders of these groups. As an example, Goldberg argues that rather than covering AIDS as a tragic disease largely affecting a narrow subset of the United States population (gay men and IV drug users), the media framed AIDS as an epidemic threatening the entire country.[53] Likewise, the "guilt" felt by liberal journalists results in politically correct and biased coverage of race and gender issues.[54] In his work focusing on press coverage of abortion spanning 150 years, Marvin Olasky details a long-term shift from a press which condemned the act to one which served as no more than "a lap dog" for pro-abortion interests.[55] Likewise, Bozell and Baker find that the term "anti-abortion" is used more frequently than "pro-life" in abortion coverage and that liberal and radical environmental groups are rarely labeled as such in news reports. This differential "tagging" of individuals and groups serves to "distort the public's perceptions of sources quoted in 'news' stories."[56]

The personal beliefs of journalists are argued to affect their coverage of other issues as well. According to economist and media critic John R. Lott Jr., we are "inundated with bad news about guns and rarely hear about the benefits."[57] Lott also draws on the attitudes of journalists when explaining the slant in coverage, as more than three quarters of journalists polled in 1985 "wanted more regulations" on handguns "while only half the public supported stricter handgun control."[58] Media coverage is slanted against guns in several ways: omitting or ignoring stories which illustrate the potential benefits of gun ownership and gun use, privileging anti-gun experts and other sources interviewed for stories, and the use of polls to bolster support of gun control and shape public opinion. He points to "newsworthiness" as a factor: crimes involving handguns receive widespread coverage but crimes which do not happen because the perpetrator was thwarted by someone with a handgun don't receive coverage.[59] An analysis of *New York Times* coverage of gun control also showed that during a two-year period, no academics were cited who opposed gun control, only one was cited who asserted that gun control was not related to crime, and twenty were cited who strongly supported increased restrictions.[60]

Dismissing the "lively debate" regarding liberal versus conservative bias, Olasky points out that there is a "more crucial type of bias [that] has been ignored almost entirely"—a bias against Christianity, a rejection of the role of God in events and issues, and a belittling of the importance of faith and spiritual life and of those who profess their faith.[61] It results in what Olasky terms the "spiking of the spiritual," a "consistent downgrading of the Biblical worldview."[62] This hostility toward religion generally and Christianity in particular is seen as connected to the lack of religiosity among journalists themselves. They are, according to S. Robert Lichter, "alienated from traditional norms and institutions" which causes them to "differ most from the general public . . . on the divisive social issues that have emerged since the 1960s—abortion, gay rights, affirmative action, et cetera."[63]

Other Research Models Pointing to Liberal Media Bias

While much of the existing research charging the media with a liberal bias rely on polls of journalists or content analyses, two additional research models have been used to study bias in the mass media. Daniel Sutter offers an "indirect test" of bias by comparing the geographic distribution of circulations for the three national newsweeklies to 1996 presidential voting patterns.[64] Because "consumers desire news consistent with their personal political values" readers will select newsmagazines they believe align with these values.[65] Higher circulation rates in markets where the population hold more liberal values therefore point to a more liberal slant for that publication. Sutter finds that both *Time* and *Newsweek* had high readership in geographic regions which voted for Bill Clinton, while *U.S. News and World Report* had slightly higher circulation in regions which supported Robert Dole.

Groseclose and Milyo computed ideological scores using a measure developed by the Americans for Democratic Action (ADA) for individual articles by counting the references to particular think tanks and policy groups.[66] The resulting values were then compared to ADA scores computed for various congressional officeholders. Based on this score, each media outlet studied was assigned an "estimated ADA score of a member of Congress who exhibits the same frequency."[67] Rather than measuring some abstract notion of "absolute" bias, this tool "measures the degree to which media is liberal or conservative, relative to Congress."[68] Their findings generally support the charges that there is a strong liberal bias in mainstream media (television and newspapers). For example, the "average *New York Times* article is ideologically very similar to the average speech by Joe Lieberman."[69] *Time* and *Newsweek*, the newsmagazines examined in our research described in the following chapters, received nearly identical adjusted ADA scores (66.3 and 65.4 respectively).

Reactions to/Evaluations of the Conservative Argument

Research on the political and social leanings of journalists compares them to other business "elites." Herbert Gans argues that this is unfair and proposes a comparison to more similar professionals such as physicians, teachers, lawyers, and social workers.[70] David Croteau points out that while journalists may hold some social values which are to the left of the general public, their views on economic issues are to their right.[71] He finds that the American people were less supportive of NAFTA; more supportive of tax increases, welfare spending, and environmental regulation; and more likely to believe that too much power was concentrated in the hands of corporations than the journalists polled for the study.

While it is well established that journalists hold beliefs which are to the left of the general public on some social issues and vote for Democratic candidates in higher proportion than the general public, it is not clear that their own personal biases result in a biased news product. S. Robert Lichter and his coauthors admit that "none of this [evidence] proves that media coverage is biased."[72] Patterson and Donsbach provide only limited support for this thesis in their research on partisanship and news decision-making.[73] Herbert Gans and others have argued that while journalists may be liberal, the news production process, including the role of editors and management, results in largely ideologically neutral news content.[74] Alterman and others have also pointed to the influence that management exerts over story content in subtle and not so subtle ways.[75]

Issue selection may also produce different results. Analysis of coverage of social issues such as hunger, the death penalty, and other issues find a conservative bias.[76] David Niven points out that media coverage of the death penalty treats this issue as though the majority of Americans approve of it when polls show this is not the case.[77] Coverage of some domestic and foreign policy issues illustrate how the media may "follow the lead" of official (government/military) sources in their coverage.[78]

Most election/campaign research has also been limited in its focus, examining a single election cycle or the coverage of an issue or campaign within a small sample of media outlets. D'Alessio and Allen's meta-analysis of fifty-nine presidential campaign studies indicates that there is no evidence of systematic bias in either direction.[79] D'Alessio criticizes studies which focus on a single election or coverage of individual candidates or politicians as proof of a coordinated bias in media coverage. Bias, he argues, is the result of two, not necessarily mutually exclusive, mechanisms. It might be a matter of selection perception . . . an example of two people observing the same message or event, but interpreting it differently. . . . Or it could be an example of instance confirmation, of people with various positions finding in the competing message environment specific examples of messages that offend them and then arguing that these messages are representative of the whole.[80]

While a particular candidate or politician may receive more coverage or more favorable coverage during a particular election cycle, it is as frequently a Democrat as a Republican who is treated "more favorably" or who receives more attention from the press. Much of the research in this vein fails to take into account other factors which may be relevant when examining election coverage, such as the relative advantage of incumbents, horse race coverage, and the unequal coverage of unequal opponents.

Political scientist David Niven suggests research which makes fair comparisons in similar situations across parties may be more fruitful than existing research which compares coverage of politicians and candidates across different social, political, and economic climates.[81] Comparing coverage of changes in unemployment and murder rates during Democratic and Republican governorships, Niven finds nearly identical coverage in location, length, and tone of coverage.[82]

Some have argued that it is the public that is biased rather than the media. The perceptions of fairness in coverage is strongly associated with whether that coverage is seen as running consistent or counter to our own beliefs and leanings.[83] This "hostile media effect" has been shown to most influence beliefs about media fairness of coverage of issues or events among those with strong partisan beliefs.[84] Finally, Watts et al. suggest that increasing media coverage of media bias have intensified public perceptions of bias.[85] The ubiquitous charges of media bias themselves may have contributed to the general cynicism that exists toward the media by the public.

The Liberal Argument

Studies concluding that mainstream news media exhibit a conservative bias emphasize the commercial nature of news organizations, and ties between media corporations and the government. Content analyses offered in support of the argument illustrate the status quo–supporting character of news items, the topics that are excluded from presentation as news, the sources that provide the material out of which media organizations construct their accounts of political actors, conditions, and events, and the fragmented structure of news reporting.

Commercial and Political Interests

News content in this country has reflected established business and related political interests since the mid-1800s, when partisan publications were replaced by a commercial press.[86] Those arguing that the media are conservative note that the media system then began operating according to the principles of a "market model." As succinctly characterized by David Croteau and William Hoynes, this involved: conceptualizing the media as private companies selling products rather than as public resources serving the public; understanding the primary purpose of the media as generating profits for owners and stockholders rather than promoting active citizenship via information, education, and social integration; treating audiences as consumers rather than as citizens; encouraging their audiences to enjoy themselves, view ads, and buy products rather than to learn about their world and be active citizens; defining the public interest as whatever is popular rather than diverse, substantive, and innovative content, even if not popular; understanding innovation as a threat to profitable, standardized formulas and diversity as a strategy for reaching new niche markets rather than as central to engaging citizens and to the media's mission of representing the range of the public's views and tastes; seeing regulation as interfering with market processes rather than as a useful tool in protecting the public interest; holding media accountability ultimately to owners and shareholders rather than the public, and measuring media success in terms of profits rather than serving the public interest.[87]

Liberal media critics contend that the commercial nature of the media in general, and the news media in particular, has determined their political role. As Terence Qualter put it:

> Their major functions appear to be to support the system, to uphold conformity, to provide reassurance, and to protect the members of society from excessively disturbing, distracting, or dysfunctional information. The mass media are almost entirely commercial, profit-making institutions. Their raison d'être is the promotion of consumerism, and the development of the secure, confident, materialistic society in which consumerism flourishes.[88]

In their widely cited *Manufacturing Consent: The Political Economy of the Mass Media*, Edward Herman and Noam Chomsky claim that commercial news organizations operate to realize these objectives by producing and distributing *propaganda* on behalf of dominant private interests and the government. In making this argument, they are careful to note that:

> The U.S. media do not function in the manner of the propaganda system of a totalitarian state. Rather, they permit—indeed encourage—spiritual debate, criticism, and dissent, as long as these remain faithfully within the system of presuppositions and principles that constitute an elite consensus, a system so powerful as to be internalized largely without awareness.[89]

Herman and Chomsky propose a "propaganda model" that describes a set of "filters" through which information must pass before it appears in the media as news. These filters include: 1. concentrated ownership and increasing wealth of media corporations that emphasize profit while having little, if any, interest in public service; 2. attentiveness to the interests of commercial sponsors that serve as their primary sources of income; 3. reliance on material provided by the public-information operations of large government and corporate bureaucracies and on "expert" sources, often associated with conservative think tanks, of which these established institutions approve and which they support; 4. "flack"—negative responses to media material that is disapproved by the corporate community in the form of letters, phone calls, petitions, law suits, punitive actions, and the like. Some of this comes from organizations such as the Media Institute and Accuracy in the Media, which are sponsored for this purpose; and 5. "anti-communism" as a major ideological filter. Accusations of being pro-communist (hence anti-corporate-capitalist) mobilizes opposition to actors, policies, programs, and proposals labeled as such.

According to Herman and Chomsky, the filters work so as to produce mainstream media news that supports government and dominant private interests and marginalizes dissent. They offer a set of detailed case studies in support of these claims. Each of these is intended to illustrate a difference in the coverage given the actions of the United States government and/or its client states, and coverage given comparable actions of a nation considered by the United States government as an enemy of the United States at the time (the mid-1980s). The authors document the following: people abused in enemy states were considered *worthy* victims (e.g. a Polish priest murdered by the Polish police), while those treated with equal or greater severity by the United States and/or client states were either ignored or characterized as *unworthy* (e.g. two murdered officials of the Guatemalan Mutual Support Group); elections in third world nations that were client states of the United States were treated as *legitimate* (e.g. El Salvador and Guatemala), while those in enemy states were characterized as *meaningless* (e.g. Nicaragua); United States military interventions in Vietnam, Laos, and Cambodia were described as defending nations from aggression and terrorism and in the interest of democracy and self-determination rather than as war against a largely civilian population to prevent a popularly supported but non-capitalist alternative social order from gaining power.

More recent research also has produced findings consistent with the propaganda model. For example, Gross's study of *New York Times* reporting on the suffering of the Iraqi people between 1996 and 1998 as a result of sanctions, largely imposed by the United States, revealed that the paper emphasized, as did the United States government, Iraq's defiance of the United Nations for the consequences of the sanctions. The actual civilian impact of the sanctions, including more than one million arguably preventable deaths was largely ignored.[90] Luther and Miller found that media coverage of demonstrations before and during the 2003 United States led war in Iraq tended to delegitimate anti-war activity.[91] More generally, Zaller and Chiu's analysis of press coverage of forty-two foreign policy crises, from the 1945 Soviet takeover of Poland to the 1999 conflict in Kosovo, conclude that media operate as "government's little helper" by limiting the range of reported opinion to that existing within the government.[92]

In successive editions of *The Media Monopoly*, Ben Bagdikian has warned about the effects of increasingly concentrated ownership of the nation's newspapers, magazines, book publishers, and television outlets on the news they offer the public.[93] In 1984, Bagdikian identified fifty controlling firms that dominated American media. In the 1997 edition, only ten media corporations, Time; Warner; Disney; Viacom; News Corporation Limited; Sony Tele-Communications, Inc.; Seagram; Westinghouse; Gannett; and General Electric, controlled the ideas and information that reached American citizens. (Subsequently, the 1996 Telecommunications Act not only allowed companies to grow bigger, it allowed companies to dominate a larger share of the industry, thus increasing ownership concentration).[94]

In Bagdikian's view, American mainstream news is heavily weighted in favor of corporate values. This can be seen in the media's propensity to pursue subjects in depth if they involve flaws in the public, tax-supported sector of the political economy, and to exclude stories that portray flaws in the private corporate sector. Examples of the former, provided by other researchers, include media coverage of health care issues,[95] welfare reform,[96] and homelessness.[97] While, on occasion, public service announcements call attention to selected social problems, their causes are identified as individual carelessness, incapacity, bad luck, and so on rather than political policies or corporate activities.[98]

Since 1976, Carl Jensen and his Project Censored have documented the media's consistent failure to report items that suggest corporate malfeasance and the failure of government policies.[99] The following is a brief sample of issues, critical to the well-being of the public that, according to Jensen's research, received little, if any, news coverage:

> 1978: A report of the Union of Concerned Scientists warns that nuclear power plants are inherently hazardous. The report revealed that the Nuclear Regulatory Commission's inspectors were biased against enforcement, undermined by political considerations, weak, and ineffective.
>
> 1980: A *Columbia Journalism Review* survey finds few articles on the dangers of smoking over a seven year period. The *Review*'s managing editor concludes that there was a "striking and disturbing" pattern that revealed that "advertising revenues can indeed silence the editors of American magazines."
>
> 1982: David Burnham of the *New York Times* reports that, in the first twenty-one months in office, the Reagan administration increased the authority of the government to classify data, thereby reducing the information available to the public about the operation of the government, the economy, the environment, and public health.
>
> 1992: While the media provide the public with a continuous stream of stories about street crime and violence, environmental crimes of which corporations such as Exxon, International Paper, United Technologies, Weyerhauser, Pillsbury, Ashland Oil, Texaco, Nabisco, and Ralston-Purina have been convicted, go unreported.
>
> 1994: *Newsday* finds that the Pentagon is funneling public funds to giant military contractors to underwrite expenses connected with acquisitions and mergers. According to the General Accounting Office, no specific savings for taxpayers could be identified.

In his introduction to Jensen's catalog of twenty years of "censored news," media critic Michael Parenti contends that:

> True, the press has to be selective—but what principle of selectivity is involved? Media bias does not occur in a random fashion; rather it moves in the same overall direction again and again, favoring management over labor, corporations over corporate critics, affluent whites over inner-city poor, officials over protesters, the two-party monopoly over leftist third parties, privatization and free market "reforms" over public sector development, United States dominance of the Third World over revolutionary or populist social change, national-security policy over critics of that policy, and conservative commentators like Rush Limbaugh and George Will over progressive or populist ones like Jim Hightower and Ralph Nader (not to mention more radical ones).[100]

Ben Bagdikian points out that it is hardly surprising that media contents long have reflected commercial and political interests. What is relatively new is the possible consequences of the rapidly increasing concentration of media ownership. "It is normal for all large businesses to make serious efforts to influence the news, to avoid embarrassing publicity, and to maximize sympathetic public opinion and government policies. Now they own most of the news media that they wish to influence."[101]

Sources

The argument that media bias is largely a reflection of the ideology of routine news sources is discussed in some detail in Chapter 5. Here we will briefly characterize the liberal position that, to a considerable extent, news media bias is the result of American journalism's dependence on information provided by those in positions of political and corporate power and by selected "experts" who support their policy positions.[102] As a result of their dependence on this narrow range of information sources, news presentations by the various media organizations are remarkably uniform. Potential providers of socially, politically, and economically important information such as representatives of labor, minorities, consumers, the poor, women's organizations, and environmental groups are seldom consulted. Lack of coverage of the issues affecting their lives removes these topics from public debate and reduces pressure on government and corporations to respond to their needs.[103] Lack of coverage contributes to lack of policy.[104]

Journalists themselves express concern about their lack of real independence from government and corporate influence. An examination of almost a decade of reporting on public journalism published in the largest and most widely read United States journalism reviews—the *Columbia Journalism Review* and the *American Journalism Review*—reveal journalists' anxiety about the increasing profit orientation of news media and fear of corporate forces encroaching on their professional autonomy and increasingly undermining the quality of news coverage.[105]

Prominent broadcast journalists have acknowledged their dependence on official sources and its consequences:

> Occasional spicy dashes can disguise the conventional flavor of news reporting on television. ABC's Sam Donaldson has jousted with presidents, while adhering to limits that make the networks active participants in presidential media strategies. "I preach a good line, but I practice what most people in my

profession practice," Donaldson told a Southern California newspaper. "Once in a while, I like to think I get a little bit further down the road, but so do other reporters. As a rule, we are, if not handmaidens of the establishment, at least blood brothers of the establishment. . . . We end up the day usually having some version of what the White House . . . has suggested as the story." When reporters aren't listening to government officials they're usually consulting a few anointed authorities on political issues. In 1989, CBS anchor Dan Rather admitted that—like so many other journalists—he kept going back to "a shockingly small . . . circle of experts [who] . . . get called upon time after time after time."[106]

In the late 1980s, PBS's *McNeil Lehrer News Hour* and ABC's *Nightline* were two of television's most popular and critically acclaimed news programs. The former was presented as an early evening, one-hour comprehensive alternative to commercial network news. The latter offered "in depth" coverage of individual issues clearly on the public agenda. A study of the programs by David Croteau and William Hoynes supports the argument that news media, not only commercial but public as well, tend to present views on issues that are neither diverse nor inclusive but decidedly conservative.[107]

Croteau and Hoynes report that, during the six-month period covered by their study, government officials who appeared repeatedly on the programs were overwhelmingly conservative. Examples of frequent guests included Newt Gingrich, Richard Cheney, Orrin Hatch, and Henry Hyde. Those appearing as "experts," and who were identified as such tended to be drawn from conservative think tanks such as the American Enterprise Institute and the Center for Strategic and International Studies. Liberal think tanks such as the Institute for Policy Studies or the World Policy Institute were not represented. Those relatively few who did express views that were not decidedly conservative tended to come from mainstream news organizations such as the *New York Times* or the *Wall Street Journal* or from mainstream think tanks such as the Brookings Institution. Their commentary was more likely to be characterized as *partisan* rather than as *expert*. Insofar as "debates" over policy issues were presented, they tended to be between establishment insiders whose positions spanned the narrow range from centrist to conservative. This selection helped define the limits of legitimate views.

Croteau and Hoynes present a set of case studies to illustrate how both domestic and international issues discussed on the *McNeil Lehrer News Hour* and on *Nightline* reflected the interests of establishment elites. Stories on the environment often obscured the role of corporate polluters. Items on the economy equated the economy with corporate management and government and government officials to the exclusion of workers and consumers. Reports of student unrest in China in 1989 failed to offer in-depth analysis of its historical roots that included the consequences of China's free market experiments. Little attention was paid to China's human rights situation, but China was praised for its openness to Western investment. Coverage of the United States government's policies toward Central America failed to mention that these policies have been vigorously condemned by a significant part of the world community and by large sectors of the United States population.

Decontextualized News

As noted, the liberal argument claims that media organizations tend to produce news that is ideologically conservative by failing to report, or by underreporting on a wide range of topics. Such topics include popular opposition to government policies and corporate malfeasance. The argument also identifies media reliance on elite sources of information, such as government agencies or corporations, as a case of media conservative partiality. According to the argument, a third and paradoxical source of bias, is the apparent objectivity produced by the structure of news reporting. This can be seen in media coverage of political campaigns and social issues.

"Conservative bias," understood as serving commercial and established political interests as opposed to the needs and concerns of the public, has been a feature of news media products ever since the demise of the partisan press in the nineteenth century.[108] Purely factual or decontextualized reporting that lacks an explanatory framework offering a point of view

> fits the commercial interests of news organizations interest in reaching a diverse mass audience either within a metropolitan area or nationally. It is good business for news organizations to present information that appeals to the broad middle; impartial reporting militates against the publication or transmission of stories to which members of the audience or advertisers might take offense. It is stabilizing and more profitable for news organizations not to take sides and to avoid controversy, since advertisers want to avoid consumer boycotts and reach as many consumers as possible.[109]

In the case of political campaign coverage, news items tend to focus on the facts of the campaign itself, such as candidate strategies, itineraries, receipt of endorsements, and polls indicating which candidate seems to be winning the race.[110] Relatively little attention is given to candidate positions on social, political, and economic issues, though the issues may dramatically affect large segments of the population and the candidates may be anxious to discuss them.[111] In the case of social issue coverage, discussion tends to be limited to factual accounts of individual events, such as an oil spill or a case of gender discrimination. Causes of such events, other than the acts of particular individuals, are seldom considered. Little is reported that might reveal widespread problems inherent in the status quo and encourage popular participation in social movements.[112]

Reactions to/Evaluations of the Liberal Argument

At the heart of the liberal argument is the contention that the news media do not operate to provide citizens with the information they need to participate intelligently in democratic political life. Rather, they produce system-supporting propaganda by serving the commercial interests of their sponsors and the political interests of those in positions of power and authority. This result is produced through the selection and elimination of topics to be included in the news, reliance on elite sources of information, and presentation of the facts of politically relevant conditions and events as isolated bits of information generally devoid of explanation.

In their review of Herman and Chomsky's *Manufacturing Consent*, Kurt Lang and Gladys Engel Lang evaluate this set of claims, as well as the data commonly offered in their support. Their commentary acknowledges that the "filters" identified by Herman and Chomsky do exist and do work to limit the range of topics and perspectives presented as news. They agree that "media systems inevitably reflect, however imprecisely, the distribution of economic, political, and symbolic power in society. Those at the top, and especially the federal government with its huge public relations apparatus, hold a strategic advantage."[113]

That being said, Lang and Lang go on to offer criticisms of *Manufacturing Consent* that are applicable to much of the literature making the liberal argument. First, data consist largely of case studies. There is little information on sampling methods by which the news items were selected or details of the coding procedures used to analyze these items. While the absence of such information may not raise serious questions about the analysis of bias in an individual item, it casts serious doubt about the viability of claims about the bias of "the media" in general. Failure to recognize the limits of data leads to the assertion of unwarranted generalizations.

A second fundamental criticism concerns the mechanistic character of the liberal argument. The perspective offers a view of journalists as mere stenographers to power—lacking professional autonomy and serving as conduits for views that advance governing policies, goals of corporations, and the preservation of the capitalist system. This view is confirmed neither by the experience of journalists, nor by those for whom they work, nor by much of what they produce. Instead, Lang and Lang contend that information sources and those who report the news:

> do indeed cooperate but only to the extent that they need one another. When their interests diverge, the relationship becomes adversarial to the extent that neither the one nor the other is in full control of the product. Farther up the line, reporters may have to negotiate for approval from editors (or producers), editors from publishers (or executives), and publishers from their board. In the event of an open clash, the decision rests with the owners and their representatives, but even here the final outcome is by no means preordained. Some owners possessed of a social conscience are prepared to take on financial risks while other media personnel have sometimes been able to use the leeway, autonomy, prestige, and authority they enjoy to get their version of a major news event out to the public, thereby pressuring political leaders to confront a problem they prefer to ignore. There is a lot of interacting, much of it openly or tacitly collaborative but also with distinct elements of confrontation.[114]

The liberal argument is no more mechanistic than its conservative counterpart. Lang and Lang's criticism can be applied to that perspective as well. When there is conflict between "liberal" journalists and those who own and/or manage the media organizations for whom they work (a possibility seldom considered by "liberal media" theorists), it seems unlikely that the "liberal" journalists almost always prevail.

Mountains of "evidence" exist to substantiate accusations of media bias made by conservatives and by liberals alike. The limitations of the literature reviewed in this chapter indicate the need for a systematic and methodologically robust means for measuring such bias. Before discussing such a research tool, it is appropriate to consider some basic features of mainstream media and the ways in which the news they present appears to differ from the reporting offered by explicitly partisan journals.

NOTES

1. Ann Coulter, *Slander: Liberal Lies about the American Right* (New York: Crown Publishers, 2002); Bernard Goldberg, *Bias: A CBS Insider Exposes How the Media*

Distort the News (Washington, DC: Regnery Publishing, Inc., 2002); L. Brent Bozell III and Brent H. Baker, eds., *And That's the Way It Isn't: A Reference Guide to Media Bias* (Alexandria, VA: Media Research Center, 1990); L. Brent Bozell III, *Weapons of Mass Distortion: The Coming Meltdown of the Liberal Media* (New York: Three Rivers Press, 2005); William A. Rusher, *The Coming Battle for the Media: Curbing the Power of the Media Elite* (New York: William Morrow and Company, Inc., 1988).

2. S. Robert Lichter, Stanley Rothman, and Linda S. Lichter, *The Media Elite: America's New Power Brokers* (Bethesda, MD: Adler & Adler, 1986); John W. C. Johnstone, Edward J. Slawski, and William W. Bowman, *The News People: A Sociological Portrait of American Journalists and Their Work* (Urbana: University of Illinois Press, 1976); Christine L. Ogan, Charlene J. Brown, and David H. Weaver, "Characteristics of Managers of Selected Daily Newspapers," *Journalism Quarterly* 56, no. 3 (Winter 1979): 803–809; David H. Weaver and G. Cleveland Wilhoit, *The American Journalist* (Bloomington: Indiana University Press, 1986); David H. Weaver et al., *The American Journalist in the 21st Century: U.S. News People and the Dawn of a New Millennium* (Mahwah, NJ: Lawrence Erlbaum Associates, Inc., 2007).

3. Johnstone, Slawski, and Bowman, *The News People*; Ogan, Brown, and Weaver, "Characteristics of Managers," 803–809; Weaver and Wilhoit, *The American Journalist*; Weaver, et al., *The American Journalist in the 21st Century*.

4. Lichter, Rothman, and Lichter, *The Media Elite*, 22; Johnstone, Slawski, and Bowman, *The News People*, 20.

5. Lichter, Rothman, and Lichter, *The Media Elite*, 22.

6. Johnstone, Slawski, and Bowman, *The News People*, 195.

7. Weaver et al., *The American Journalist in the 21st Century*, 5.

8. Weaver et al., *The American Journalist in the 21st Century*, 8, 12.

9. Lichter, Rothman, and Lichter, *The Media Elite*, 294.

10. Bozell and Baker, *And That's the Way It Isn't*; Coulter, *Slander*.

11. Bozell and Baker, *And That's The Way It Isn't*, 54.

12. Bozell and Baker, *And That's the Way It Isn't*, 285–334; Coulter, *Slander*, 64–68.

13. Coulter, *Slander*, 66–67.

14. Bozell and Baker, *And That's the Way It Isn't*, 53.

15. Coulter, *Slander*, 65.

16. Lichter, Rothman, and Lichter, *The Media Elite*; Rusher, *The Coming Battle for the Media*, 47; Goldberg, *Bias*; Pat Buchanan, "The Media Have a Liberal Bias," in *Media Bias*, ed. Stuart A. Kallen (San Diego: Greenhaven Press, 2004), 10–13; Stanley Rothman and Amy E. Black, "Media and Business Elites: Still in Conflict?," *Public Interest* no. 143 (Spring 2001): 72–86.

17. Lichter, Rothman, and Lichter, *The Media Elite*, 28–30.

18. Leo Rosten, *The Washington Correspondents* (New York: Harcourt Brace, 1937).

19. Lichter, Rothman, and Lichter, *The Media Elite*, 28

20. Coulter, *Slander*, 57.

21. Bozell and Baker, *And That's the Way It Isn't*; Lichter, Rothman, and Lichter, *The Media Elite*; Weaver et al., *The American Journalist in the 21st Century*; Weaver and Wilhoit, *The American Journalist*; Coulter, *Slander*; Goldberg, *Bias*; Rothman and Black, "Media and Business Elites"; Pew Research Center for the People and the Press, "How Journalists See Journalists in 2004," http://people-press.org/reports/pdf/214.pdf (accessed May 18, 2007).

22. Weaver and Wilhoit, *The American Journalist*; Weaver et al., *The American Journalist in the 21st Century*.

23. Pew, "How Journalists See Journalists," 3, 24–26.

24. Pew Research Center for the People and the Press, "America's Place in the World 2005: An Investigation of the Attitudes of American Opinion Leaders and the American Public about International Affairs," http://people-press.org/reports/pdf/263.pdf, (accessed May 18, 2007), 21–22.

25. Weaver et al., *The American Journalist in the 21st Century*, 16; Bozell and Baker, *And That's the Way It Isn't*, 4; Lichter, Rothman, and Lichter, *The Media Elite*, 294.

26. Lichter, Rothman, and Lichter, *The Media Elite*, 31.

27. Weaver and Wilhoit, *The American Journalist*, 26.

28. Goldberg, *Bias*.

29. Goldberg, *Bias*, 60, emphasis in original

30. Bozell and Baker, *And That's the Way It Isn't*, 5.

31. Adam J. Schiffer, "Assessing Partisan Bias in Political News: The Case(s) of Local Senate Election Coverage," *Political Communication* 23, no. 1 (January–March 2006): 23–39; David W. Brady and Jonathan Ma, "Newspapers' Labeling of Politicians Reveals a Liberal Bias," in *Media Bias*, ed. Stuart Kallen (San Diego: Greenhaven Press, 2004, 13–16); Dennis T. Lowry and Jon A. Shidler, "The Sound Bites, the Biters, and the Bitten: An Analysis of Network TV News Bias in Campaign '92," *Journalism & Mass Communication Quarterly* 72, no. 1 (Spring 1995): 33–44; Guido H. Stempel III and John W. Windhauser, "Coverage by the Prestige Press of the 1988 Presidential Campaign," *Journalism Quarterly* 55, no. 4 (Winter 1989): 894–896, 919.

32. Bozell and Baker, *And That's the Way It Isn't*, 225–231, 246–248.

33. Bozell and Baker, *And That's the Way It Isn't*, 224–225.

34. Brady and Ma, "Newspapers' Labeling of Politicians," 13.

35. Rusher, *The Coming Battle*, 72.

36. Janet L. Murphy, "An Analysis of Political Bias in Evening Network News during the 1996 Presidential Campaigns" (PhD diss., The University of Oklahoma, 1998), Retrieved from Dissertation Abstracts 5–23–07; Lowry, "The Sound Bites."

37. Marvin Olasky, *The Press and Abortion, 1838–1988* (Hillsdale, NJ: Lawrence Erlbaum Associates, 1988); Marvin Olasky, *Prodigal Press: The Anti-Christian Bias of the American News Media* (Westchester, IL: Crossway, 1988): 7–38; Bozell, *Weapons*, 75–84; Bozell and Baker, *And That's the Way It Isn't*, 105–108.

38. Christopher Hewitt, "Estimating the Number of Homeless: Media Misrepresentation of an Urban Problem," *Journal of Urban Affairs* 18, no. 3 (1996): 431–477; Goldberg, *Bias*, 63–74.

39. John R. Lott Jr., *The Bias against Guns: Why Almost Everything You've Heard About Gun Control Is Wrong* (Washington, DC: Regnery Publishing, Inc., 2003); Bozell, *Weapons*, 127–135.

40. Bozell and Baker, *And That's the Way It Isn't*, 25; Bozell, *Weapons*, 116–126; Olasky, *Prodigal Press*, 40.

41. Goldberg, *Bias*.

42. Bozell, *Weapons*, 102–115; Olasky, *The Prodigal Press*.

43. Lichter, Rothman, and Lichter, *The Media Elite*, 166–219; Bozell, *Weapons*, 92–101.

44. Goldberg, *Bias*, 145–164; Lichter, Rothman, and Lichter, *The Media Elite*, 220–253.

45. Rich Noyes, "The Media Are Biased against Conservative Economic Policies" in *Media Bias*, ed. Stuart Kallen (San Diego: Greenhaven Press, 2004, 23–28); Lichter, Rothman, and Lichter, *The Media Elite*; Bozell, *Weapons*, 85–91; Bozell and Baker, *And That's the Way It Isn't*, 167–190.

46. Goldberg, *Bias*, 61.

47. Bozell and Baker, *And That's the Way It Isn't*, 99–114; Goldberg, *Bias*, 57–61.

48. Bozell and Baker, *And That's the Way It Isn't*, 101.

49. Goldberg, *Bias*, 169.

50. Goldberg, *Bias*, 73–74.

51. Hewitt, "Estimating," 440–441, 443.

52. Goldberg, *Bias*.

53. Goldberg, *Bias*, 75–96.

54. Goldberg, *Bias*, 169.

55. Olasky, *The Press and Abortion*, 150.

56. Bozell and Baker, *And That's the Way It Isn't*, 104.

57. Lott, *The Bias against Guns*, 16.

58. Lott, *The Bias against Guns*, 23.

59. Lott, *The Bias against Guns*, 24.

60. Lott, *The Bias against Guns*, 32.

61. Olasky, *Prodigal Press*, 31, 33.

62. Olasky, *Prodigal Press*, 31.

63. Lichter, Rothman, and Lichter, *The Media Elite*, 294.

64. Daniel Sutter, "An Indirect Test of the Liberal Media Thesis Using Newsmagazine Circulation," Unpublished Manuscript. University of Oklahoma.

65. Sutter, "An Indirect Test," 2.

66. Time Groseclose and Jeffrey Milyo, "A Measure of Media Bias," *The Quarterly Journal of Economics* 70, no. 4 (November 2005): 1192.

67. Groseclose and Milyo, "A Measure," 1192.

68. Groseclose and Milyo, "A Measure," 1221, emphasis in original.

69. Groseclose and Milyo, "A Measure," 1204.

70. Herbert Gans, "Are U.S. Journalists Dangerously Liberal?," *Columbia Journalism Review* 24, no. 4 (November/December 1985): 29–33.

71. David Croteau, "Challenging the 'Liberal Media' Claim," *Extra* July/August 1998, 4–5.

72. Lichter, Rothman, and Lichter, *The Media Elite*, 294.

73. Thomas E. Patterson and Wolfgang Donsbach, "News Decisions: Journalists as Partisan Actors," *Political Communication* 13, no. 4 (October–December 1996): 455–468.

74. Herbert Gans, "Are U.S. Journalists Dangerously Liberal?"; Herbert Gans, *Deciding What's News: A Study of CBS Evening News, NBC Nightly News, Newsweek and Time* (New York: Pantheon Books, 1979); Leo Sigal, *Reporters and Officials: The Organization and Politics of News Making* (Lexington, MA: Heath, 1973); Gaye Tuchman, *Making News: A Study in the Construction of Reality* (New York: Free Press, 1978).

75. Eric Alterman, *What Liberal Media? The Truth about Bias and the News* (New York: Basic Books, 2003); Ben H. Bagdikian, *The Media Monopoly* (Boston: Beacon Press, 2000); Philip J. Coffey, "A Quantitative Measure of Bias in Reporting of Political News," *Journalism Quarterly* 52, no. 3 (1975): 551–553. Robert L. Craig, "Business Advertising and the Social Control of News," *Journal of Communication Inquiry* 28, no. 3 (July 2004): 233–252; Lawrence Soley, "The Power of the Press has a Price," *Extra* (July/August 1997), http://www.fair.org/index/php?page-1387 (accessed May 24, 2007); Peter Hart and Julie Hollar, "Fear & Favor 2004—FAIR's Fifth Annual Report How Power Shapes the News" *Extra* (March/April 2005), http://www.fair.org/index/php?page-2486 (accessed May 24, 2007).

76. Robert Cirino, *Don't Blame the People: How the News Media Use Bias, Distortion, and Censorship to Manipulate Public Opinion* (Los Angeles: Diversity Press, 1971): 6–13; Martin A. Lee and Norman Solomon, *Unreliable Sources: A Guide to Detecting Bias in News Media* (New York: Lyle Stuart, 1990); Norman Solomon, *The Habits of Highly Deceptive Media: Decoding Spin and Lies in Mainstream News* (Monroe, ME: Common Courage Press, 1999); David Niven, "Bolstering an Illusory Majority: The Effects of the Media's Portrayal of Death Penalty Support," *Social Science Quarterly* 83, no. 2 (September 2002): 671–689; Laura Ashley and Beth Olson, "Constructing Reality: Print Media's Framing of the Women's Movement, 1966 to 1986," *Journalism & Mass Communications Quarterly* 75, no. 2 (Summer 1998): 263–277.

77. Niven, "Bolstering," 673.

78. Sandra Dickson, "Understanding Media Bias: The Press and the U.S. Invasion of Panama," *Journalism Quarterly* 71, no. 4 (Winter 1994): 809–809; John Zaller and Dennis Chiu, "Government's Little Helper: U.S. Press Coverage of Foreign Policy Crises, 1945–1991," *Political Communication* 13, no. 4 (October–December 1996): 385–405; Janet E. Steele, "Experts and the Operational Bias of Television News: The Case of the Persian Gulf War," *Journalism & Mass Communication Quarterly* 72, no. 4 (Winter

1995): 799–812; Michael Welch, Melissa Fenwick, and Meredith Roberts, "Primary Definitions of Crime and Moral Panic: A Content Analysis of Experts' Quotes in Feature Newspaper Articles on Crime," *Journal of Research in Crime and Delinquency* 34, no. 4 (November 1997): 474–494; Danny Schechter, "ABC News Was Biased against the U.S. War in Iraq," in *Media Bias*, ed. Stuart A. Kallen (San Diego: Greenhaven Press, 2004), 70–77.

79. Dave D'Alessio and Mike Allen, "Media Bias in Presidential Elections: A Meta-Analysis," *Journal of Communication* 50, no. 4 (Autumn 2000): 133–156; Philip J. Coffey, "A Quantitative Measure"; Thomas E. Patterson and Wolfgang Donsbach, "News Decisions: Journalists as Partisan Actors," *Political Communication* 13, no. 4 (October–December 1996): 455–468.

80. D'Alessio and Allen, "Media Bias in Reporting of Political News," 135.

81. David Niven, "A Fair Test of Media Bias: Party, Race, and Gender in Coverage of the 1992 House Banking Scandal," *Polity* 36, no. 4 (July 2004): 637–649; David Niven, "Objective Evidence on Media Bias: Newspaper Coverage of Congressional Party Switchers," *Journalism & Mass Communication Quarterly* 80, no. 2 (Summer 2003): 311–326; David Niven, "Partisan Bias in the Media? A New Test," *Social Science Quarterly* 80, no. 4 (December 1999): 847–857.

82. Niven, "Partisan Bias."

83. Albert C. Gunther, "Biased Press or Biased Public: Attitudes toward Media Coverage of Social Groups," *Public Opinion Quarterly* 56, no. 2 (Summer 1992): 147–167; Paul A. Beck, "Voters' Intermediation Environments in the 1988 Presidential Contest," *Public Opinion Quarterly* 55, no. 3 (Fall 1991): 371–394; Tien-Tsung Lee, "The Liberal Media Myth Revisited: An Examination of Factors Influencing Perceptions of Media Bias," *Journal of Broadcasting & Electronic Media* 49, no. 1 (March 2005): 543–564.

84. Albert C. Gunther and Stella Chih-Yun Chia, "Predicting Pluralistic Ignorance: The Hostile Media Perception and Its Consequences," *Journalism & Mass Communication Quarterly* 79, no. 4 (Winter 2001): 688–701; Stephen E. Bennett, Staci L. Rhine, and Richard S. Flickinger, "Assessing America's Opinions about the News Media's Fairness in 1996 and 1998," *Political Communication* 18, no. 2 (April–June 2001): 163–182; Laurie Mason and Clifford Nass, "How Partisan and Non-Partisan Readers Perceive Political Foes and Newspaper Bias," *Journalism Quarterly* 66, no. 3 (Autumn 1989): 564–570, 578; Robert P. Vallone, Lee Ross, and Mark R. Lepper, "The Hostile Media Phenomenon: Biased Perceptions and Perceptions of Media Bias in Coverage of the Beirut Massacre," *Journal of Personality and Social Psychology* 48, no. 3 (1985): 577–585; Russell Dalton, Paul A. Beck, and Robert Huckfeldt, "Partisan Cues and the Media: Information Flows in the 1992 Presidential Election," *The American Political Science Review* 92, no. 1 (March 1998): 111–126; Beck, "Voters' Intermediation."

85. Mark D. Watts et al., "Elite Cues and Media Bias in Presidential Campaigns: Explaining Public Perceptions of a Liberal Press," *Communication Research* 26, no. 2 (April 1999): 144–175.

86. Gerald Baldastry, *The Commercialization of News in the Nineteenth Century* (Madison: University of Wisconsin Press, 1992); Richard L. Kaplan, *Politics and the American Press: The Rise of Objectivity, 1865–1920* (New York: Cambridge University Press, 2002); Jeffrey Pasley, *The Tyranny of Printers: Newspaper Politics in the Early American Republic* (Charlottesville: University of Virginia Press, 2001).

87. David Croteau and William Hoynes, *The Business of the Media: Corporate Media and the Public Interest* (Thousand Oaks, CA: Pine Forge Press, 2001).

88. Terence H. Qualter, *Opinion Control in the Democracies* (New York: St. Martin's Press, 1985), ix.

89. Edward S. Herman and Noam Chomsky, *Manufacturing Consent: The Political Economy of the Mass Media* (New York: Pantheon Books, 1988), 302.

90. Bertram M. Gross, "Deeply Concerned about the Welfare of the Iraqi People: The Sanctions Regime against Iraq in the *New York Times* (1966–98)," *Journalism Studies* 3, no. 1 (Feb. 2002): 83–99.

91. Catherine Luther and Mark Miller, "Framing of the 2003 U.S.-Iraq War Demonstrations: An Analysis of News and Partisan Texts," *Journalism & Mass Communication Quarterly* 82, no. 1 (2005): 78–96.

92. John Zaller and Dennis Chiu, "Government's Little Helper."

93. Ben H. Bagdikian, *The Media Monopoly*, 3rd ed. (Boston: Beacon Press, 1992).

94. Croteau and Hoynes, *The Business of the Media: Corporate Media and the Public Interest*, 101.

95. Carolyn R. Lepre, Kim Walsh-Childer, and Jean C. Chance, "Newspaper Coverage Portrays Managed Care Negatively," *Newspaper Research Journal* 24, no. 2 (2003): 6–21.

96. Michelle Brophy-Baermann and Andrew J. Bloeser, "Stealthy Wealth: The Untold Story of Welfare Privatization," *Harvard International Journal of Press/Politics* 11, no. 3 (2006): 89–112.

97. Todd G. Shields, "Network News Construction of Homelessness: 1980–1993," *Communication Review* 4, no. 2 (2001): 193–218.

98. David L. Paletz, *The Media in American Politics: Contents and Consequences*, 2nd ed. (New York: Longman, 2002): 181–183.

99. Carl Jensen, *20 Years of Censored News* (New York: Seven Stories Press, 1997).

100. Jensen, *20 Years of Censored News*, 27–28.

101. Bagdikian, *The Media Monopoly*, 26.

102. Croteau and Hoynes, *The Business of the Media: Corporate Media and the Public Interest*; Mark Hartsgaard, *On Bended Knee: The Press and the Reagan Presidency* (New York: Schocken Books, 1998); Martin A. Lee and Norman Solomon, *Unreliable Sources: A Guide to Detecting Bias in News Media* (New York: Lyle Stuart, 1990); Michael Parenti, *Inventing Reality: The Politics of the Mass Media* (New York: St. Martin's Press, 1986).

103. Parenti, *Inventing Reality*, 74.

104. Virgil Hawkins, "The Other Side of the CNN Factor: The Media and Conflict," *Journalism Studies* 3, no. 2 (May, 2002): 225–240.

105. Tanni Haas and Linda Steiner, "Fear of Corporate Colonization in Journalism Reviewers' Critiques of Public Journalism," *Journalism Studies* 4, no. 3 (August, 2002): 325–341.

106. Lee and Solomon, *Unreliable Sources: A Guide to Detecting Bias in News Media*, 16–17.

107. Croteau and Hoynes, *The Business of Media: Corporate Media and the Public Interest*.

108. Baldastry, *The Commercialization of News in the Nineteenth Century*.

109. Bartholomew H. Sparrow, *Uncertain Guardians: The News Media as a Political Institution* (Baltimore: Johns Hopkins University Press, 1999), 121–122.

110. Bernard Berelson, Paul Lazarsfeld, and William McPhee, *Voting* (Chicago: University of Chicago Press, 1954); Thomas E. Patterson, *The Mass Media Elections: How Americans Choose Their President* (New York: Praeger, 1980); Doris A. Graber, *Mass Media and American Politics*, 6th ed. (Washington, DC: Congressional Quarterly Press, 2002).

111. Marion Just, Ann Crigler, and Tami Buhr, "Voice, Substance, and Cynicism in Presidential Campaign Media," *Political Communication* 16, no. 1 (1999): 25–43.

112. David A. Snow, E. Burke Rochford Jr., Steven K. Worden, and Robert D. Benford, "Frame Alignment Processes, Micro Mobilization and Movement Participation," *American Sociological Review* 51, no. 4 (August, 1986): 464–481.

113. Kurt Lang and Gladys Engel Lang, "Noam Chomsky and the Manufacture of Consent for American Foreign Policy," *Political Communication* 21, no. 1 (November, 2004): 94.

114. Lang and Lang, "Noam Chomsky and the Manufacture of Consent for American Foreign Policy," 96.

Chapter 2

Mainstream and Partisan Newsmagazines

Our reasons for selecting *Time* and *Newsweek* to represent mainstream news media for our study of media bias include the influence of their journalists, the social characteristics of their readers, their connections to other media organizations that widely disseminate their perspectives, the similarity of the material they present to that offered by other mainstream news media, and the breadth and depth of their issue coverage. We have chosen the *National Review* and *The Progressive* to represent conservative and liberal viewpoints respectively, on selected social issues for comparison to the coverage of these issues appearing in mainstream media. Each of these explicitly partisan publications has a long history of offering substantial, critical accounts of the social-political-economic status quo not found in mainstream media. Each has defined "conservative" and "liberal" positions on major social issues that have influenced and reflected the way in which elites and the politically informed public have conventionally understood and used the terms in their political discourse.

Mainstream Publications: *Time* and *Newsweek*

Ever since their introduction, *Time* (1923) and *Newsweek* (1933) have served as America's newsmagazines "of record."[1] "The newsmagazines arguably summarize the dominant news and editorial emphasis of the national media in the United States; their relatively leisurely deadlines usually allow them to canvass official sources (and other media) distilling the results in a narrative reflecting the principal themes in the news."[2] They observe the canons of the elite press represented by the *New York Times*, the *Los Angeles Times*, NPR's "All Things Considered," and "Morning Edition," and public television's "The News Hour with Jim Lehrer."[3] Such contents make *Time* and *Newsweek* appropriate representatives of major mainstream news media.

Journalists from *Time* and *Newsweek* who routinely cover the White House, Capitol Hill, the Pentagon, the State Department, and other federal agencies tend to develop close symbiotic relationships with political elites. This can enable them to get new "inside" information, decide on its importance, inform the public, and use the information to more fully contextualize their own accounts. Their analyses influence the work of journalists at other media organizations.[4]

While connections with elites enhance the influence of journalists at leading newsmagazines, they are not without difficulties. Because relationships are symbiotic, reporters are constantly at risk of being co-opted and, at least occasionally, serving as stenographers to power.[5] However "it is not always easy to determine where the line between 'elite' and 'journalist' should be drawn, or who influences whom. Arguably, a few top editors, correspondents, and editorialists exercise more sway over the spread of ideas than all but the most powerful public officials."[6]

An initial look at readership statistics suggests that on this basis alone, *Time* and *Newsweek* merit attention. Since their introduction, the publications have ranked one and two respectively in domestic sales of newsmagazines. In 2000, *Time* had approximately 4.1 million subscribers, an estimated weekly readership greater than twenty-five million, and ranked ninth in sales of all magazines in the United States. *Newsweek* had approximately 3.1 million subscribers, an estimated weekly readership greater than twenty million, and ranked fifteenth in sales of all magazines.[7]

While such numbers may be impressive, they are somewhat misleading. A 2004 survey conducted by the Pew Research Center found only 13 percent of the respondents reporting that they got news from magazines "such as *Time*, *Newsweek*, and *U.S. News and World Report*" regularly. The corresponding figures for daily newspapers were 54 percent, for television network news 34 percent, and for cable television news 38 percent. The newsmagazines' 13 percent was equaled by those who said they regularly went online to the news page of news aggregators such as AOL and Yahoo. Furthermore, online use is increasing while the proportion of newsmagazine readers has remained stagnant.[8]

Statistics indicating the absolute or relative size of their audiences are not as relevant to understanding the social and political importance of mainstream newsmagazines as are statistics revealing the social characteristics of their readers. Since the 1970s, researchers have noted that the readers of newsmagazines are distinguishable from the general public in two key ways: they are more educated and they are more affluent. Using data collected from the 1972 American

Leadership Study, Carol Weiss reported that elites engaged in "heavy reading" of newsmagazines.[9] More than two-thirds of elites from all sectors examined reported regularly reading both *Time* and *Newsweek*.[10] This trend has remained consistent for more than three decades. Journalism.org, in their annual "State of the News Media," report that "news magazine readers continue to represent something of an elite audience."[11] Newsmagazine readers are significantly wealthier than the average American, earning an average of $67,000 in 2005: this figure is nearly a third more than the average income for the general population ($51,466) in 2005.[12]

Additional market-based research also points to this continuing readership trend for the national news weeklies. Mendelsohn Media Research, Inc. (MRI) produces an annual "Affluent Head of Household Survey" which records the "media habits and lifestyles of the affluent population of the United States."[13] These data are widely used by media companies to attract advertisers and set advertising rates. In 2005, over thirteen thousand American households earning more than $85,000 were questioned regarding their media usage, including which publications they read regularly.[14] Based on data collected by the Mendelsohn survey, both *Time* and *Newsweek* continue to be among the preferred sources of news and information among the most affluent Americans, ranking fifth and sixth respectively in readership among both the overall sample of affluent heads of households and among those earning more than one million dollars.[15]

Both *Time* and *Newsweek* cite MRI data in their media kits that they make available to prospective advertisers. *Newsweek*'s media kit boasts that nearly half of their readers have "graduated college" and more than one quarter earn more than $50,000 per year, with strong readership among professional and managerial workers and top management.[16] *Time* reports similar numbers, citing MRI data.[17] Corporations recognize the economic importance of the newsmagazine audience. This is reflected in the fact that, although the number of newsmagazine readers has not increased in recent years, there has been an increase in the magazines' advertising revenue. For example, between 1988 and 2000, *Time* advertising dollars rose from $350 million to $661 million and *Newsweek* advertising dollars improved from $242 million to $440 million.[18]

The social characteristics of the newsmagazines' readers also give them political importance. In the United States, as well as in other Western democracies, those with relatively high income and more education are more likely to participate in political life. Such participation includes voting, discussing politics with friends, convincing friends to vote as self, working to solve community problems, attending political meetings, campaigning for candidates, and contacting officials or politicians.[19]

Both *Time* and *Newsweek* are parts of major media corporations. Today, the Time Warner Company owns, among many other businesses, book publishers (e.g. Little Brown & Co.), cable companies (e.g. CNN), film/distribution companies (e.g. Warner Brothers), as well as newsmagazines (including *Time*, *Time*

Asia, Time Atlantic, Time Canada, Time Latin America, Time South Pacific, and *Time for Kids*). The Washington Post Company, owner of *Newsweek* and *Newsweek International,* also owns, among other businesses, newspapers (e.g. *The Washington Post*), and television stations. Perspectives on social issues expressed in *Time* and *Newsweek* are likely to be transmitted as well by their associated companies, reaching wider and more varied audiences, both domestic and international. As noted below, this is seen as problematic by those making the liberal argument.

Perspectives on the news appearing in *Time* and *Newsweek* closely resemble those offered by other mainstream media. Doris Graber explains this correspondence:

> The heavy reliance by newspeople throughout the country on these eastern "elite" news sources [led by *Time, Newsweek, the New York Times, and* the *Wall Street Journal*] is one reason why patterns of American news coverage are broadly similar throughout the country. Regardless of regional and local differences that shape social and political views, Americans share most of their news. This provides a basis for nationwide public opinions that bear, to a marked degree, the imprint of the pacesetter media.[20]

Time and *Newsweek* have vast resources that include the large number and high prestige of their journalists, the dense network of ties those journalists have established to political, economic, military, social, and intellectual elites, the large number of their news bureaus, the space they have available to present reports on public affairs, and the time they have available to produce their reports. These resources, and the social characteristics of their audiences described earlier in this chapter, provide the publications with the possibility and the motivation to produce coverage that has greater breadth and depth than that offered by most other media organizations, with the possible exceptions of the *New York Times,* the *Washington Post*, and the *Wall Street Journal.* Their more elaborate coverage provides greater opportunities to analyze their products for the presence of bias. That is, their articles are apt to deal with the complexity of the costs, causes, and possible solutions for the political, economic, and social issues they discuss.

The comparatively thorough analysis of social issues of which mainstream newsmagazines are capable is illustrated by the June 30, 1975, *Time* report on street crime in America.[21] At that time, the problem was a major concern of the Ford administration. Just one week before the publication of *Time*'s article, President Ford had sent a special message to Congress characterizing previous government anti-crime efforts as being "far from successful."

The twelve-page *Time* report, "The Crime Wave," began with the presentation of several dramatic anecdotes and the introduction of extensive statistics in support of the claim that street crime had become "an enormous national problem." Crime rates in Houston, Chicago, Atlanta, and Detroit were cited and were accompanied by the "portrait of a gang leader" in Los Angeles. Citizen efforts to protect themselves were noted. These included purchasing firearms, creating community organizations, buying guard dogs, and forming vigilante groups.

Of particular interest to our study are the expert sources used by *Time* in the construction of its narrative, the complex set of causes of street crime that the article identified, and the array of possible solutions to the problem that the newsmagazine suggested. Sources consulted to explain the supposedly high level of street crime in America included some of the country's leading scholars: sociologists Robert Merton, Seymour Lipset, and Lloyd Ohlin; urbanologist Edward Banfield; criminologists Marvin Wolfgang, Han Mattick, and Walter Miller; political scientist James Q. Wilson; psychologists/psychiatrists Edward Stainbrook, Willard Gaylin, Bernard Yudowitz, and Frederick Hacker; legal theorist Norman Morris; and law professors John Heinz and James Vorenberg. Recognizing the presence of partisan perspectives on the issue, *Time* also conferred with former Attorney General William Saxbe (conservative: Nixon and Ford administrations), and former Attorney General Ramsey Clark (liberal: Johnson administration). Other non-academic sources included several judges, a district attorney, a former chief of California's Department of Corrections, a director of the Illinois Law Enforcement Commission, and, for a very different perspective, several convicts.

The numerous interrelated causes of street crime cited by the sources often reflected their disciplinary perspectives, their professional training, and experiences, or their present status in the criminal justice system. Conditions that were cited as "breeding" street crime included (in no particular order), the heterogeneity of American communities, racism, poverty amid affluence, poor schools, cultural emphasis on material success coupled with unequal access to the legitimate means for its achievement, job shortages, slums, an increasingly youthful population, and permissiveness and leniency in the courts. Psychological conditions discussed included parents' uncertainty concerning the standards to set for their children and themselves, faulty parent-child relationships, and widespread social disillusionment. As is often the case with mainstream newsmagazine discussions of a domestic social issue, "The Crime Wave" did not explicitly propose any remedial policy.

The resources of *Time* and *Newsweek* make it possible for the newsmagazines to produce, more frequently than other media outlets, what Gans described as "multiperspectival" news.[22] This involves articles that report comprehensively about national agencies and institutions, incorporate the reactions of high officials as well as those of citizens affected by public policies, indicate how national policies have worked out in practice, discuss the activities and opinions of ordinary Americans, and deal with a topic that is likely to be of personal concern to most citizens.[23] The report on street crime also met sociologist Charles Tilly's criteria for a "superior story."[24] It simplifies causal processes but, in general, draws on a wide range of specialized, technical knowledge as a basis for its assertions. Newsmagazine articles with such qualities are likely to influence the ways in which their elite audiences, including journalists from other mainstream

news media and political decision makers, understand the issues the publication
is addressing.

Partisan Publications: the *National Review* and *The Progressive*

The *National Review* has the largest circulation of the major conservative
newsmagazines in the United States, including the *American Conservative*, the
Weekly Standard, the *American Spectator*, and *Human Events*. The publication
bills itself as "America's premier magazine and website for reaching Republi-
can/Conservative opinion leaders who affect and shape policy on a wide range
of issues."[25] *The Progressive* has the largest circulation of the major liberal
magazines in America, including the *Nation*, the *American Prospect*, *In These
Times*, and *Mother Jones*. *The Progressive* defines its mission to be "a journalistic voice for peace and social justice at home and abroad. The magazine, its af-
filiates, and its staff steadfastly oppose militarism, the concentration of power in
corporate hands, the disenfranchisement of the citizenry, poverty, and prejudice
in all its guises. We champion peace, social and economic justice, civil rights,
civil liberties, human rights, a preserved environment, and a reinvigorated democracy."[26]

As in the case of *Time* and *Newsweek*, the importance of the readership of
the *National Review* and *The Progressive* is not so much its absolute size as its
social characteristics. The *National Review*'s website emphasizes that its subscribers tend to be affluent, well-educated, and influential as opinion leaders and
activists in their communities and nationally. Data compiled from a 2004 subscribers study showed that *National Review* readers had a median household
income of over $80,000; 74 percent had a college degree or beyond; 84 percent
were employed as professionals or managers, and 25 percent served on a corporate board. The survey also found that *National Review* subscribers did not sub-
scribe to either *Time* (92 percent) or to *Newsweek* (89 percent). This is consistent
with the finding, reported in our introduction, that those with strong political
beliefs tend to consider mainstream media biased.[27]

Like the *National Review*, *The Progressive* emphasizes that its subscribers
are politically engaged. Its website claims that, within a recent twelve-month
period, 77 percent had voted in the last election; 62 percent had written to an
elected official; 35 percent had participated in a rally, march, or boycott; 32 percent had written a letter to the editor; and 29 percent had participated in an environmental cause. The magazine describes its subscribers in cultural rather than
in occupational and economic terms, noting that "they are book buyers, magazine junkies, organic eaters, investors with a social conscience, and above all,
activists engaged in making the world a better place."[28]

Partisan magazines appear to be of particular interest for the critical perspectives they offer. During a conservative administration, liberal magazines flourish, and vice versa. For example, a study by the Project for Excellence in Journalism found that subscription rates to the *National Review* soared with the election of Bill Clinton in 1992 and peaked in 1994 during the administration's efforts at health care reform. Subscription rates to the liberal publication the *Nation* (the study did not report on *The Progressive*) were boosted in 2000 by the election of George W. Bush and have increased steadily to this date.[29]

The economy was the dominant factor in accounting for voter decisions in 1992.[30] Welfare reform was among several dimensions of the issue that received considerable public attention. The February 1992 article from *The Progressive*, described below, illustrates how a major partisan newsmagazine provides a critical analysis of an enduring social issue and defines an ideological perspective on that issue.[31]

"Cutting the Lifeline" drew on a wide variety of sources for its discussion of the transformation of America's welfare system. They included Janice Wallace, Patricia Davis, Katrina Mack, and Rose Ellis, all Aid to Families with Dependent Children (AFDC) recipients; Louis Sullivan, Secretary of Human Social Services; federal judges; mayors and other public officials; directors of state and local community service agencies; representatives of advocacy groups for the poor; and researchers working in numerous contexts, who investigate the sources of poverty and the consequences of social welfare policies.

The Progressive's sources included those expressing views contrary to the perspective of the publication. For example, in the article "Conservative Political Scientist," Lawrence Mead asserts that an "underclass" consisting of "street hustlers, welfare families, drug addicts, and former mental patients" was responsible for America's social and economic ills. We discuss our findings on the use of information sources in partisan publications in Chapter 5.

The Progressive focused on the problems surrounding recent changes in federal and state welfare policies. At the national level, the newly adopted Federal Support Act required, among other things, that people who rely on AFDC must take job-training programs. Several states imposed other requirements on AFDC recipients. For example, in Wisconsin, a "Learnfare" program cut government aid to families when their teenagers missed too many days of school. In Maryland, families could lose all of their AFDC benefits if they failed to see a doctor regularly, keep their children's school attendance up, or pay their rent on time. Michigan cut off support for "able-bodied" unemployed persons. A referendum in California called the "Taxpayer Protection Act" proposed that AFDC benefits would be cut as much as 25 percent to women who have more than one child.

Such proposals had widespread support from both Republicans and Democrats, including President George H. W. Bush, Louisiana's David Duke, Arkansas's Bill Clinton, and Wisconsin's Tommy Thompson. According to *The Progressive*, the legislation was driven by a faltering national economy that was forcing states to find new ways to save tax money. A politically expedient way of doing this was found in reducing welfare rolls. This approach was rationalized on the unsubstantiated ground that it was the cost of providing for a vast, freeloading poverty class that was largely responsible for the nation's economic underperformance. The rationale was fostered by widespread distain of the poverty class, commonly understood as composed primarily of black, able-bodied males who are unwilling to work, disinterested in job-training programs, and often engaged in anti-social behavior, and black women, usually without husbands, who have more children then they can support.

The Progressive pointed out that:

> The idea of a vast, free-loading "underclass" in America is pure myth. Two-thirds of the families that rely on welfare do so only for brief periods during times of intense economic distress. And AFDC payments are so low in most states that they no longer cover families' basic needs for food and shelter— hardly a free ride. Finally, despite the racial stereotype of large black families on welfare . . . the great majority of the poor in America are white.[32]

The publication offered this unambiguous evaluation of the new federal welfare policy:

> The programs mandated by the Federal Family Support Act have had some unbelievably stupid results: States are spending millions of dollars on job training programs in areas where there are no available jobs, and experiments that punish poor people for missing school or having babies are plunging thousands of families into economic ruin. . . . As the economic crisis worsens in the United States, contempt for the poor, particularly poor black women with children, is proving to have enormous political appeal. Welfare reform programs build on that contempt, while driving the neediest segment of our population deeper into despair.[33]

The Progressive identified several community programs that have been able to "turn welfare reform into something productive"—into efforts to break cycles of poverty, despair, and abuse. Madison, Wisconsin's Family Enrichment Center attempts to build better relationships between parents and children, teaching parents how to deal with stress, and preventing child abuse before it starts. The center teaches everything from cooking to high school equivalency classes. Its program "draws on participants' experience instead of trying to coerce poor people into changing their behavior without examining their needs." Portland, Oregon's Project Success provides counseling, educational testing, and academic or vocational training for teenage mothers who learn about parenting and finish high school.

"Cutting the Lifeline" concludes:

> Welfare "reform" policy has already failed. It does not save money, the number of welfare recipients around the country continues to rise, and the social costs

of current policies which throw away a generation of poor children will soon take an enormous toll. Welfare reform does not get people to work. Despite job-training programs, unemployment is still increasing. The only purpose welfare reform serves is to feed a mean-spirited desire to punish the poor—a sentiment which, in guiding policy, can only lead our country down the drain.[34]

The Progressive's critical discussion of welfare reform defines the "liberal" perspective on the issue in the sense in which, we believe, political elites, journalists, and the politically engaged public understand this position. The newsmagazine draws on a wide variety of sources, including poor people. The problem promoting welfare reform legislation is identified as the economic needs of the national and state governments and not the social and economic needs of the poor, toward whom there is considerable contempt. The costs of welfare reform are analyzed in terms of punitive consequences for the poor. Several community programs offering counseling, educational, and employment opportunities are cited as examples of "welfare reform" aimed at solving some of the problems of the poor themselves rather than at reducing stress on administrative budgets.

Brief Histories of *Time*, *Newsweek*, the *National Review*, and *The Progressive*

To provide some additional understanding of the "bias" of each of the publications under consideration, this section offers a brief description of some major events in its historical development.

Time

The inaugural issue of *Time*, America's first newsmagazine, was published on March 3, 1923. It was the creation of Briton Hadden and Henry Luce, who worked together at the *Yale Daily News* and later were reunited at the *Baltimore News*. Soon after their reunion, Hadden and Luce left for New York to develop a magazine that they believed would deliver news to the public more efficiently and effectively than any of the sources available at the time. Raising $86,000 from their Yale connections, the publication was launched with Luce as its business manager and Hadden as editor. Later, by agreement, they exchanged their jobs. Luce became permanent editor upon Hadden's sudden death in 1929.

At the time Luce and Hadden initiated their project, well-illustrated, well-edited general magazines providing upper-middle and upper-classes with conservative perspectives on political and literary matters had existed for decades. However, by the end of the nineteenth century, economic forces were transforming these publications into mass-market products, putting them in competition with newspapers. While once they had featured travel articles, historical pieces, and essays on literature and the arts, they now focused on political and social issues.[35]

Luce and Hadden proposed a newsmagazine that would present the whole of the world's news in a succinct, well-organized, and entertaining narrative style that would keep the busy public better informed than did its competitors such as *The Literary Digest* and *Forum*.[36]

> *The Digest* selected its subjects arbitrarily and treated them at length, quoting liberally from newspaper and other sources. *Time*, by way of contrast, would cover all the news, briefly and in its own organized way. There was another important difference. *The Digest* took pains to quote opinion on both sides of every public question. *Time* would do that too, but it would also "clearly indicate" which side it thought was right, or at least more correct. Both Luce and Hadden had definite opinions on the state of the nation and the world, and they did not intend to create an "on-the-other-hand" kind of publication in the manner of *Forum* or the *Digest*. . . . Without using an editorial page then, the newsmagazine would convey its proprietors' beliefs. And what were these beliefs? Fundamentally, a distrust of "interference" by government, a Republican viewpoint deriving from their backgrounds. This was coupled with an increasing distaste for the increasing cost of government, another sound Republican principle. They also expressed an interest in new ideas, but at the same time maintained an abiding respect for the old. They did not intend to argue these matters, just "to keep men well-informed." Only the news, they said; but when it came to talking about what the news meant, they could hardly avoid controversy.[37]

A forceful advocate of corporate capitalism, Luce used *Time* to project his view of the "American Century." The perspective proposed a politically, economically, and culturally dominant role for the United States in world affairs. Luce opposed Roosevelt and the New Deal, criticized Truman for being "soft on communism," but offered little by way of critical commentary on the Eisenhower administration and its foreign policy as carried forward by Secretary of State John Foster Dulles.

In 1964, more than forty years after *Time*'s introduction, Luce turned over his editorship to Hadley Donovan, who was the managing editor at *Fortune Magazine*. That year, the United States escalated its military involvement in the war in Vietnam. Donovan and *Time*, as well as virtually all other mainstream news organizations, supported the commitment, were optimistic about the outcome of the war, and were critical of the war's opponents.[38] "Day-to-day coverage was closely tied to official information and dominant assumptions about the war, and critical coverage didn't become widespread until consensus broke down among political elite and the wider society."[39]

Just before his death in 1967, Luce still affirmed the legitimacy of American military policy in Vietnam.[40] Four years later, Hadley Donovan wrote that:

> For my own part, I still happen to think that the U.S. was right to try in 1965 to prevent the forceful takeover that would have happened if we had not moved in as we did. I would say now, though I did not see it then, that we went on in 1966 and 1967 to expand the U.S. effort far out of proportion to our original

purposes, and that this enlarged commitment then began to take on a life of its own and even to work against our original purposes. It took me the better part of those two years to begin to see that. I wish I had been wiser sooner. . . . We first became involved in Viet Nam to contain China, and our contain-China policy first developed in the days when China and Russia seemed to be a monolithic Communist bloc. It is now safe for us to trade with China and safe to negotiate an ABM agreement with Russia, it should be safe, at last, to bring our soldiers home from Viet Nam.[41]

The 1973 Watergate scandal was the second major event that moved Donovan and *Time* away from Luce's staunch Republicanism and his commitment to "the American Century." Vietnam and Watergate began a general trend of the news media toward more critical reporting.[42] Patriotic deference of journalists to the president and unquestioning reliance on official sources of information no longer came automatically as it did in the past.[43]

Time's approach to domestic and social issues in the period after Luce is suggested by its coverage of the civil rights and anti-nuclear movements. On each of the topics, *Time* took a moderate stance. The magazine opposed racism as immoral and unreasonable, but argued that racial equality, while a desirable goal, could be achieved peacefully and without major institutional changes in American society.[44] It found merit in the anti-nuclear movement's concern over the dangers surrounding both military and peaceful applications of atomic energy, but opposed the movement's demands for a nuclear freeze.[45]

Over the years, *Time* had become increasingly involved in major economic ventures. By 2000, it was part of AOL Time Warner, whose holdings included online services (e.g. America Online), book companies (e.g. Little, Brown, and Company), cable television networks (e.g. HBO Home Video), film production distribution companies (e.g. Warner Bros. Studios), more than sixty other magazines (e.g. *Money Magazine*), recording labels (e.g. Elektra), theme parks (e.g. Warner Brothers Recreational Enterprises), sports teams (e.g. Atlanta Braves), and numerous joint undertakings with other companies (e.g. eBay).[46] *Time* had evolved from an independent newsmagazine whose editor-in-chief would use it as a vehicle for disseminating his ideological perspective, to operating as part of a profit-driven corporate empire.

On the occasion of *Time*'s seventy-fifth anniversary issue, Lance Morrow observed: "Born of the Wasp ascendancy in a self-confidently patriarchal age, the magazine . . . has passed, along with its parent company, through a series of self-transformations, from an age of industry and structural authority into a post-cold war era of free-flowing information and diversity."[47]

Newsweek

News-Week was founded by Thomas J. C. Martyn, a former foreign news editor at *Time*, and first appeared on February 17, 1933. The publication was supported by an investment of approximately 2.5 million dollars by members of several of the country's most socially and economically prominent families. In 1937, the new publication merged with *Today*, a popular magazine in part devoted to the news of the day, and was renamed *Newsweek*. Vincent Astor, venture capitalist and one of the owners of *Today*, provided *Newsweek* with an additional $600,000 and became the primary stockholder and chairman of its board until his death in 1959. Former *Today* editor Raymond Moley, who once served as a dissatisfied member of President Franklin Roosevelt's "Brain Trust" and subsequently had become increasingly conservative, took over the editorship of *Newsweek*.

Newsweek was launched as a commercial venture. Its investors believed the newsmagazine would compete successfully with *Time*, whose often flippant style (developed to compete with the verbose *Literary Digest*) was apparently alienating audiences interested in serious, less superficial presentation of the news. From the time of their forming until the early 1960s there were few, other than stylistic, differences between *Newsweek* and *Time*. "Politically there was no difference. *Time* reflected Luce's solid conservative Republicanism, and, as a disgruntled New Dealer, Moley had placed *Newsweek* on the same side. Both magazines, of course, would deny for some time that they were political at all."[48]

The Republican bias of the two newsmagazines did not go unnoticed by the more liberal segments of the country. For example, following the 1956 presidential election, *Ammunition*, the magazine of the United Auto Workers, reported the results of its findings concerning the magazines' election coverage: "Each was found to be loaded in favor of the GOP and against the Democrats. Loaded in every way: facts were sometimes suppressed, sometimes distorted, and Republicans almost always were given more space and friendlier treatment."[49]

Newsweek was purchased by the Washington Post Company in 1961. In 1963, Katherine Graham, whose father had acquired the *Washington Post* in 1933 and whose husband had succeeded him as publisher in 1946, became president of the Washington Post Company and publisher of *Newsweek* following her husband's suicide. Under her leadership, *Newsweek*'s coverage became increasingly distinct from that of *Time*. In the view of some, the magazine surpassed its longtime rival.

> Over the past few years, *Newsweek* has often been superior to *Time* in . . . recognizing many of the major trends of the 1960's, such as the awakening of black aspirations, change in the mood of the younger generation, the decline of the validity of and belief in the Cold War rhetoric of anti-communism and containment. . . . *Newsweek*, uncommitted to any formal ideological position, was more receptive to deviations from traditional thinking and as a result usually covered these events with more perspective and accuracy.[50]

Under Graham's leadership, in 1963 *Newsweek* published "The Negro in America," two years before the riots of African Americans in the Watts district of Los Angeles. Subsequently, *Newsweek*'s response to the July 1967, riots of African Americans living in economically depressed areas of Newark and Detroit further illustrated the newsmagazine's willingness to report on a rapidly changing society in progressive ways. In a statement introducing *Newsweek*'s report, then-editor Osborn Elliot noted:

> In the 22 page section that follows, there is analysis aplenty—but this time there is advocacy as well. The reason for this marked change of approach is that the editors have come to believe that at this particular time, on this particular subject, they could not fulfill their journalistic responsibility, or their responsibility as citizens, by simply reporting what X thinks of Y, and why Z disagrees.[51]

The proposals offered by the editors of *Newsweek* were based on several explicit premises: America has failed to achieve the equality for many of its citizens that lies at the heart of its national ideology; America has the resources to bring about that equality; the nation can (and should) generate the will to bring it about. Concrete proposals advanced in the report included several that are decidedly liberal as that label is conventionally understood. These include:

- The government should expand adult job-training as fast as possible, tripling current dollar allocations.
- To provide maximum housing at minimum cost, Congress should raise the appropriation for rent supplements.
- The federal government should subsidize reading programs and expand programs to pay college expenses for borderline high school graduates.
- Federal money should be made available to reduce interest rates and guarantee payment of loans to ghetto businesses.

Newsweek's 1981 retrospective on the Vietnam War also illustrates the newsmagazine's willingness to present highly critical views of the nation's recent past and what might be learned from it. Its report "What Vietnam Did to Us" focuses on interviews with combat survivors of Charlie Company. Two quotations suggest the tone of the feature:

> The fall of Saigon in 1975, two years after the last U.S. soldiers left, only reinforced their belief that the war had been a waste of American life, youth and fortune. . . . What we lost in Vietnam was something more than a war. . . . It was pride, self-esteem and belief that we really are a great country.[52]

The citation of the two articles above is not intended to suggest that, under Katharine Graham's leadership *Newsweek* adopted a consistently liberal ideological perspective. Rather, they are presented to illustrate how far the newsmagazine had come from the days when *Newsweek*'s viewpoint was indistinguishable from that of Luce's *Time*.

Newsweek routinely reports detailed expressions of partisan opinion. However, the publication is explicitly committed to "balanced" coverage. This is carried out in the manner described by Gans:

Political balance is usually achieved by identifying the dominant, most wide-spread, or most vocal positions, then presenting "both sides." Producers and editors see to it that both Republican and Democratic politicians are filmed or quoted; that ecology stories quote both environmentalists and businessmen or women. . . . *Newsweek*'s columnists are chosen to balance "liberals" and "conservatives"; contributors to the magazine's "My Turn" column are selected in the same way.[53]

The *National Review*

Unlike *Time* and *Newsweek*, the *National Review* has never presented itself as an attempt to provide the American public with "unbiased" or "balanced" political-ly relevant information, nor has it ever been a commercial venture. Since its introduction in November, 1955, the publication has pursued three related politi-cal/ideological objectives: forging a conservative movement in America by bringing together those committed to different varieties of conservative thought; offering pro-capitalist, pro-traditionalist, anti-communism/liberal understandings of contemporary social-political-economic issues; promoting conservative poli-cies, elites, and organizations. "If any single publication mirrored or even domi-nated the development of the Right after the mid-50s, *National Review* was it."[54]

The *National Review* was edited by its founder, William F. Buckley Jr., from its very beginning until his retirement in 2004. Drawing on his substantial inherited wealth and $290,000 raised from twenty-five investors, Buckley, only twenty-nine at the time, intended to produce a newsmagazine targeted at elite decision makers rather than a mass audience. The publication was to be ideolog-ically acceptable to most, if not all, varieties of American conservatives. Buck-ley already had achieved national recognition with his books *God and Man at Yale* (1951),[55] and *McCarthy and His Enemies* (1954).[56] In the former, Buckley criticized his alma mater for the socialism and atheism he found dominant in its campus culture. In the latter, he attempted to legitimate the highly controversial, aggressive, anti-communist campaign of Wisconsin Senator Joseph McCarthy (while anti-socialist, anti-atheist themes resonated well with the views of most conservatives, the McCarthy book was not well received by conservatives, whose perspective was more libertarian).

In its early years, the *National Review* continued the conservative polemic against Franklin Roosevelt's New Deal. In 1964, the publication supported the candidacy of Barry Goldwater. Major contributors to the *National Review* such as conservative theorist Russell Kirk and economist Milton Friedman advised Goldwater, while Brent Bozell, with whom Buckley had co-authored *McCarthy and His Enemies*, is rumored to have ghost-written Goldwater's *Conscience of a Conservative*. When Goldwater was overwhelmed by Lyndon Johnson in the 1964 election (Goldwater received only fifty-two of the 538 electoral votes) Buckley attributed the outcome to a "vile campaign" waged against Goldwater by the mainstream media. Thereafter, complaints of the "liberal bias" of the media became a prominent component of American conservative rhetoric. Subsequently:

> The magazine's analysis of . . . the riots and unrest of the late '60s and early '70s, Watergate, the Carter presidency, the Reagan presidency—have not broken with the framework of conservative principles established during the first decade of *National Review*. The themes of the moral and intellectual bankruptcy of liberalism, the liberal bias of the media, the traditional American quality of the principle of limited government, liberty under the law, and Christian revelation have been consistently reformulated and applied.[57]

At a June 2004 award ceremony, a current contributor to the *National Review* said of Buckley (in Buckley's own inimitable style), "thus did he waken their minds to the possibility that liberalism is not the *philosophia ultima*, but just another item in the baleful catalog of modern ideologies."[58]

The Progressive

Founded by Senator Robert LaFollette of Wisconsin on January 9, 1901, *LaFollette's Weekly* (which was renamed *The Progressive* in 1929) had as its goal "winning back for the people the complete power over government—national, state, and municipal—which had been lost to them."[59]

Subsequently, LaFollette ran for president on the Progressive Party ticket in 1924 advocating "government takeover of the railroads, elimination of private utilities, easier credit for farmers, the outlawing of child labor, the right of workers to organize unions, increased protection of civil liberties, an end to United States imperialism in Latin America, and a plebiscite before any President could launch the nation into war."[60]

The Progressive has consistently supported individuals, organizations, and causes of the American Left. For example, in 1931, the journal took the unpopular position of defending communists who were being attacked and imprisoned. It backed FDR in the early '30s, encouraged development of the Progressive Party in the '40s. In the '50s, it vehemently opposed McCarthyism, warned of the dangers of involvement in Vietnam as early as 1963, and in the late '70s vigorously attacked the development of nuclear weaponry.[61]

Special issues of *The Progressive* on McCarthy and on the hydrogen bomb received public attention far beyond the usual readership of the publication. Coverage of both of these subjects illustrates the willingness of *The Progressive* to take on powerful political adversaries and defend the freedom of expression embodied in partisan publications and critical to the operation of a political democracy.

The Progressive published a special report in April 1954 titled "McCarthy: A Documental Record." Articles provided evidence challenging the veracity of many of McCarthy's claims. These included McCarthy's assertion that he knew the number of known communists working and shaping policy in the State Department; that he had evidence that Defense Secretary General George Marshall had advanced the interest of Soviet Russia since 1942, and that President Harry Truman had concealed from the F.B.I. a list of Soviet spy suspects. Another article noted how McCarthy had acted irresponsibly and had attempted to undermine the freedom of the press by denouncing as being practically indistinguishable from the communist *Daily Worker* such leading American publications as the *Washington Post*, the *St. Louis Post-Dispatch*, the *Denver Post*, the *Christian Science Monitor*, and *Time*.

Possibly the most controversial issue of *The Progressive* ever published appeared in November 1979. Written by anti-nuclear freelance author Howard Morland, and fully supported by *The Progressive*'s editor Edwin Knoll, "The H-Bomb Secret—How We Got It: Why We're Telling It" demonstrated that, using publicly available information, an investigative reporter could explain, in ordinary language, how the hydrogen bomb worked and why the public should have this information so that they might assess the dangers of the nuclear weapons infrastructure.

An early draft of the report came to the attention of the federal government. A few days before its scheduled publication, a federal court in Milwaukee issued a prior restraint order. Government concern appeared to be based on the incorrect belief that the article presented a blueprint for building an H bomb. The injunction rested on a unique legal theory that certain information is "born classified" and, as such, meets the definition of "Restricted Data" as set forth in the Atomic Energy Act.[62] However, the case was abandoned by the government six months later and the article was published. In its ninetieth anniversary issue, *The Progressive* offered this assessment of the affair: "The H-Bomb case captured the attention of the nation. It showed that a doughty little magazine far from the citadels of influence, acting in a righteous cause, could take on the most powerful government and win."[63]

Many of Robert LaFollette's views continued to be advanced generations later by Edwin Knoll, who edited *The Progressive* from 1973 to 1994. These included distrust of governmental and corporate power and distress over what he saw as American imperialism. Knoll also expressed concern over the operation of mainstream news media, pointing out that they tended to ignore matters of public interest such as environmental and health issues, consumer news, tax policy, regulatory agencies, and corporate subsidies.[64] As Knoll succinctly characterized the magazine in its seventy-fifth anniversary edition: "For many years, a New York restaurant had advertised, 'Where does the Russian Tea Room stand? Just to the left of Carnegie Hall.' And where does *Progressive* stand? Just to the left period."[65]

Features of *Time* and *Newsweek* That Concern Either Conservatives or Liberals

Features That Concern Conservatives

Conservatives cite readership studies as evidence of a liberal bias in *Time* and *Newsweek* contents. Carol Weiss found that regular readership of *The Washington Post* (parent company of *Newsweek*) was positively associated with liberal attitudes among the elite she studied.[66] Similarly, Daniel Sutter determined that both *Time* and *Newsweek* had higher readership levels in "liberal" markets across the United States (based on voter patterns during the 1996 presidential elections).[67]

In addition to examining readership patterns and reader characteristics, Conservative critics also point to the editorial staff and owners of *Time* and *Newsweek*. *Newsweek* is owned by the "strenuously liberal" Myer-Graham family, which also owns *The Washington Post*, widely seen by both supporters and critics as left-leaning.[68] *Time*'s editorial staff and leadership have also been criticized as having a liberal slant. A change in leadership following the death of *Time*'s founder Henry Luce resulted in a shift to the left for the magazine.[69] Even during Luce's tenure, the magazine's practice of adopting a "dramatic 'theory' for each story" resulted in coverage that was "simplified for the sake of explication and (all too often) adorned with a moral for the education of the innocent."[70] William Rusher argues that *Newsweek* followed this journalistic model when it was created ten years after *Time*. For Rusher, this technique represented a form of "advocacy journalism," which developed between the first and second World Wars and was expanded in the 1960s and 1970s by liberal journalists during the Johnson and Nixon administrations.[71]

Features That Concern Liberals

Liberal criticisms of *Time* and *Newsweek* center on the newsmagazine's location within a profit-driven system of corporate media which produces news that fails to serve the public good. Eric Alterman points to the increasing pressure for profit placed on news media as an area for concern. Market share means potential customer base for advertisers, and news divisions must produce market share. The role of media to produce news "that citizens require to carry out their duties as intelligent, informed members of a political democracy" is abandoned as mainstream news organizations view news "as profit centers, which must carry the weight of the shareholder demands."[72] According to a 2004 study by the Pew Research Center for People and the Press, more than half of journalists believed that bottom-line pressures were "seriously hurting" the quality of news coverage.[73] Fifty-six percent of those who felt that journalism was harmed stated that the press was too timid in their coverage.[74] Alterman concludes that it is naïve to "ignore the power of the money at stake to determine the content of news in the decisions of corporate executives."[75] Sparrow points out that economic pressures from institutional investors (pension funds, insurance companies, banks, foundations, and endowments) are "always there." "These pressures in the production of political news almost necessarily predispose news organizations to give favorable coverage to their own interests and those of corporate America and less favorable coverage to redistributive policies, pro-labor issues, and most political and economic reforms."[76]

For Ben Bagdikian "the threat does not lie in the commercial operation of the mass media but rather in the narrowing of choice that comes from the increasing monopolization of ownership by fewer and fewer corporate entities."[77] Vertical and horizontal integration of media companies under a shrinking number of media mega-corporations, while benefiting profits for owners and stockholders, can have negative outcomes for citizens and democracy itself. Both mainstream newsmagazines examined in this book have corporate histories which exemplify Bagdikian's argument about media monopolization. *Newsweek* was purchased by The Washington Post Company in 1961. Time, Inc., which began publishing *Time Magazine*, merged with Warner Communications in 1989 and was purchased by America Online in 2000. The newly formed company, Time Warner, Inc., became the world's largest media conglomerate, with business properties in broadcast and cable television, motion pictures, book and magazine publishing, and internet services.

As an example of the way in which a corporate conglomerate can operate, Bagdikian refers to the occasion when *Time Magazine* ran a cover story and excerpts from Henry Kissinger's memoirs published by Little Brown, one of Time, Inc., companies. It was also included as a selection for the Book-of-the-Month-Club, also owned by Time, Inc. Such cross-promotion that can result from ownership across a variety of media properties within a single corporation is known as "synergy."[78] Alterman argues that the synergy created by increasing monopolization of media corporations and the ownership of media and other types of companies within a single corporate entity (such as Time Warner), have a strong impact on how news outlets cover their corporate "family members."[79]

> There is a potential conflict of interest for a journalist who seeks to tell the truth, according to the old *New York Times* slogan "without fear or favor," about not only one of the companies its parent corporation may own, but also those with whom one of the companies may compete, or perhaps a public official or regulatory body that one of them may lobby, or even an employee at one of them with whom one of his superiors may be sleeping, or divorcing, or re-marrying, or one of their competitors, or competitor's lover, ex-lovers, and so on.[80]

Censorship, whether imposed externally by editors or advertisers, or internally by journalists themselves who fail to pursue leads which may reveal damaging information about a corporate entity or advertiser, undermines the intention of a free press.[81]

The content of news is not the only potential consequence of a corporate-controlled profit-driven media system. "Large media corporations have their own political action committees to give money to favored candidates or, in the governing fashion, to defeat unfavored ones. Some media corporations also own other industries that will benefit from the right candidates."[82]

Their histories, journalists, ties to elite individuals and organizations, corporate structures, and roles as profit-making organizations in a capitalist economy have all, at one time or another, convinced some of the public, particularly the politically engaged, that *Time* and *Newsweek* offer "biased" accounts of the political world. However, whether or not this conclusion had any merit with respect to coverage of a particular issue or set of issues over a specified period of time can only be determined by looking at the contents of the newsmagazines themselves. Chapter 3 suggests how such an assessment can be carried out.

Notes

1. Herbert J. Gans, *Deciding What's News: A Study of CBS Evening News, NBC Nighly News, Newsweek and Time* (New York: Random House, 1979).

2. Robert M. Entman, *Projections of Power: Framing News, Public Opinion and U.S. Foreign Policy* (Chicago: University of Chicago Press, 2004).

3. David L. Paletz, *The Media in American Politics: Contents & Consequences*, 2nd ed. (New York: Longman, 2002), 72.

4. G. Cleveland Wilhoit and David H. Weaver, *The American Journalists: A Portrait of U.S. News People and Their Work*, 2nd ed. (Bloomington: Indiana University Press, 1991).

5. Gans, *Deciding What's News*, 133.

6. Entman, *Projecting Power*, 11.

7. http://www.journalism.org/Node/1187 (accessed August 12, 2007).

8. http://www.journalism.org/Node/1459 (accessed August 12, 2007).

9. Carol H. Weiss, "What America's Leaders Read," *Public Opinion Quarterly* 38, no. 1 (Spring 1974): 1–22.

10. Weiss, "America's Leaders," 7.

11. Project for Excellence in Journalism, "The State of the News Media 2007: An Annual report on American Journalism," Project for Excellence in Journalism, 2007, http://www.stateofthemedia.org/2007/narrative_magazines_audience.asp?cat=2&media=8 (accessed May 29, 2007).

12. Project for Excellence in Journalism, "State of the News Media."

13. Monroe Mendelsohn Research, Inc., "The Mendelsohn Affluent Survey," http://www.mmrsurveys.com/MendelsohnAffluentSurvey.htm (accessed May 29, 2007).

14. Monroe Mendelsohn Research, Inc., "The Summary Report of Selected Findings for 2006," http://www.mmrsurveys.com/data/Survey_2006.pdf (accessed May 29, 2007).

15. Monroe Mendelsohn Research, Inc., 28.

16. "*Newsweek* U.S. Mendelsohn Affluent Profile," *Newsweek* Media Kit online, http://www.newsweekmediakit.com/newsite/pdf/us_mmr.pdf (accessed May 29, 2007)

17. *Time*, Inc., "2006 MRI: Time U.S. Audience Profile," http://www.time.com/time/mediakit/1/us/timemagazine/audience/mri/index.html (accessed May 29, 2007).

18. http://www.journalism.org/Node/139 (accessed August 12, 2007).

19. Samuel H. Barnes and Max Kaase, *Political Action: Mass Participation in Five Western Democracies* (Beverly Hills, CA: Sage, 1979).

20. Doris A. Graber, *Mass Media and American Politics*, 4th ed. (Washington D.C.: CQ Press, 1993).

21. *Time Magazine*, "The Crime Wave," (June 30, 1975), 10–24.

22. Gans, *Deciding What's News*.

23. Gans, *Deciding What's News*, 313–314.

24. Charles Tilly, *Why? What Happens When People Give Reasons . . . Why* (Princeton, NJ: Princeton University Press, 2006).

25. http://wwww.nationalreview.com (accessed September 5, 2007).

26. http://www.progressive.org/ads (accessed September 25, 2007).

27. http://wwww.nationalreview.com (accessed September 5, 2007).

28. http://www.progressive.org/ads (accessed September 25, 2007).

29. http://www.journalism.org/Node/1119 (accessed August 12, 2007).

30. R. Michael Alvarez and Jonathon Nagler, "Economics, Issues and the Perot Candidacy: Voter Choice in the 1992 Presidential Election," *American Journal of Political Science* 39, no. 3 (August 1995): 714–744.

31. Ruth Conniff, "Cutting the Lifeline, Real Welfare Fraud," *The Progressive* (February 1992), 25–31.

32. Conniff, "Cutting the Lifeline, Real Welfare Fraud," 26.

33. Conniff, "Cutting the Lifeline, Real Welfare Fraud," 26.

34. Conniff, "Cutting the Lifeline, Real Welfare Fraud," 31.

35. John Tebbel and Mary Ellen Zuckerman, *The Magazine of America* (New York: Oxford University Press, 1991).

36. Theodore Peterson, *Magazines in the Twentieth Century* (Urbana: University of Illinois Press, 1964).

37. Tebbel and Zuckerman, *The Magazine in America*, 161.

38. Todd Gitlin, *The Whole World Is Watching: The Media in the Making and Unmaking of the New Left* (Berkeley: University of California Press, 1980).

39. Daniel C. Hallin, *The Uncensored War* (Berkeley: University of California Press, 1986), x.

40. Robert Edwin Herzstein, *Henry R. Luce, Time, and the American Crusade in Asia* (New York: Cambridge University Press, 2005).

41. Hedley Donovan, "Coming to Terms with Viet Nam," *Time Magazine* (June 14, 1971), 30.

42. Bob Woodward, *Five Presidents and the Legacy of Watergate* (New York: Simon & Schuster, 1999); Thomas Patterson, *Out of Order* (New York: Knopf, 1993).

43. Entman, *Projections of Power*.

44. Richard Lenz, *Symbols, the News Magazines, and Martin Luther King* (Baton Rouge: Louisiana State University Press, 1990).

45. Robert M. Entman and Andrew Rojecki, "Freezing Out the Public," *Political Communication* 10, no. 2 (April–June, 1993).

46. *Columbia Journalism Review*, "Who Owns What?" http://www.cjr/resources/ (accessed October 9, 2006).

47. Lance Morrow, "The Time of Our Lives," *Time* (March 9, 1998), 84–91.

48. Tebbel and Zuckerman, *The Magazine in America*, 174.

49. Quoted in Peterson, *Magazines in the Twentieth Century*, 334.

50. Chris Wells, "*Newsweek* (a Fact) Is the New Hot Book (an Opinion)," *Esquire* (November, 1969), 155, quoted in Alan Nourie and Barbara Nourie, *American Mass Market Magazines* (Westport, CT: Greenwood Press, 1990), 314.

51. Osborn Elliot, "A Time for Advocacy," *Newsweek* (Nov. 20, 1967), 32.

52. Peter Goodman, "What Vietnam Did to Us," *Newsweek* (Dec. 14, 1981), 49.

53. Gans, *Deciding What's News*, 175.

54. George H. Nash, *The Conservative Intellectual Movement in America since 1945* (New York: Basic Books, 1976), 441.

55. William H. Buckley Jr., *God and Man at Yale* (Chicago: Regnery, 1951).

56. William H. Buckley Jr. and Brent Bozell, *McCarthy and His Enemies* (Chicago: Regnery, 1954).

57. Nourie and Nourie, *American Mass Market Magazines*, 296.

58. Daniel D. Kirkpatrick, "National Review Founder to Leave Stage," *The New York Times*, June 29, 2004, Section A, 18.

59. http://www.progressive.org/aboutus (accessed September 25, 2007).

60. John Nichols, "Portrait of the Founder, Fighting Bob LaFollette," *The Progressive* (January 1999), 10–14.

61. Mathew Rothschild, "Ninety Years of Stubborn Sound," *The Progressive* (January 1999), 4.

62. James C. Goodale, "Born Classified—*The Progressive Magazine* Case," *New York Law Journal* (March 23, 1979), 1–7.

63. Samuel H. Day Jr., "Edwin Knoll and the H-Bomb Case," *The Progressive* (January 1999), 25.

64. Samuel H. Day Jr. and William Stief, "On the 'Objective Press'," *The Progressive* (January 1999), 23–25.

65. Edwin Knoll, "Just to the Left: Seventy-Five Years But Who's Counting," *The Progressive* (July 4, 1984), 4.

66. Weiss, "What America's Leaders Read," 13.

67. Daniel Sutter, "An Indirect Test of the Liberal Media Thesis Using Newsmagazine Circulation," Unpublished Manuscript. University of Oklahoma, 19.

68. William Rusher, *The Coming Battle for the Media: Curbing the Power of the Media Elite* (New York: Morrow, 1988), 92.

69. Rusher, *The Coming Battle*, 91.

70. Rusher, *The Coming Battle*, 139.

71. Rusher, *The Coming Battle*, 140–141.

72. Eric Alterman, *What Liberal Media? The Truth about Bias and the News* (New York: Basic Books, 2003), 24.

73. Pew Research Center for the People and the Press, "How Journalists See Journalists in 2004," http://people-press.org/reports/pdf214.pdf (accessed May 18, 2007), 1.

74. Pew, "How Journalists See Journalists," 2.

75. Alterman, *What Liberal Media?*, 27.

76. Bartholomew H. Sparrow, *Uncertain Guardians: The News Media as a Political Institution* (Baltimore: The Johns Hopkins University Press, 1999), 76.

77. Bagdikian, *The Media Monopoly*, 6th ed. (Boston: Beacon Press, 2000), 223.

78. David Croteau and William Hoynes, *The Business of Media: Corporate Media and the Public Interest* (Thousand Oaks, CA: Pine Forge, 2001), 74.

79. Alterman, *What Liberal Media?*, 22–23.

80. Alterman, *What Liberal Media?*, 23.

81. Croteau and Hoynes, *The Business of Media*, 170–176.

82. Bagdikian, *Media Monopoly*, 94.

Chapter 3

Measuring Media Bias

Defining media bias has become a favorite pastime of scholars, politicians, pundits, and the American people. We previously considered the prevailing methods for defining or identifying bias. The discussions of existing models for studying bias (See Introduction and Chapter 1) and the popular liberal and conservative positions (Chapter 1) regarding media bias illustrate the complexity of the issue of bias and the difficulty in finding a definition methodologically sufficient to be tested which retains relevance for inclusion in popular debate.

Identifying the Bias of a News Story

The bias or partisanship of a publication can be understood as a consistent tendency to provide more support to one of the contending parties, policies, or points of view in a sustained conflict over a social issue. For any given media outlet, the stronger the tendency to provide support in this way, the greater the bias. This conceptualization is consistent with both ordinary language use and with definitions of media fairness employed in public opinion research.[1] For example, a newspaper would be said to be politically biased in its reporting on election campaigns if it consistently tended to provide more support to Republican than to Democratic candidates. Similarly, charges of bias would be made about a newspaper's reporting on the debate over abortion rights if it consistently tended to provide more support to a "pro-choice" than to a "pro-life" position. More generally, a newspaper would be said to be biased if its reporting on each of a variety of enduring salient social issues consistently tended to support what is commonly understood as a liberal or conservative point of view.

In concrete terms, a sustained conflict might refer to a political contest of a rather limited period of time, such as the length of a mayoral campaign, or to an indefinite period stretching over decades, such as the debate over abortion rights. For present purposes, a sustained political conflict will be understood as a political conflict that has lasted over a period of at least twenty-five years.

There are several advantages to using this definition. First, the length of time suggests that analysis will concern media accounts of issues that are of substantial importance in American social life. Second, data drawn from the specific twenty-five year period to be considered here, 1975–2000, enables investigation of the ways in which a news organization's pattern of issue coverage might reflect the political context in which it appears (the period 1975–2000 includes five administrations: three Republican and two Democratic). Third, it suggests that each of the news sources selected for study will be one having some influence; it has remained commercially viable over decades because it has remained of interest to at least some segment or segments of the American public and/or business.

Identifying Widely Discussed Social Issues

The research reported in this book focuses on *Time, Newsweek, National Review*, and *Progressive* coverage of several issues that remained prominent in the United States between 1975 and 2000. To identify social issues that have persisted over the twenty-five year period, ten social problems textbooks available in the Purdue University library were consulted. Two texts were selected for each of the five five-year periods. Once two texts were found for a five-year period, the selection process stopped for that period and moved on to consider the next five-year period. For two of the five periods, these were the only two textbooks available. Fourteen issue areas were discussed in all ten texts (see Table 3.1). From among these, four were selected as the issues whose coverage will be considered here. These are issue areas in which differing partisan perspectives were described on at least one full page in the texts. They are: crime (includes drugs, violent personal crime, property crime, and public order crimes, but not white collar crime, corporate crime, or organized crime); the environment (includes natural resources, pollution, and environmentalism/the environmental movement); gender (includes public policies concerning women, media representations of women, and feminism/the women's movement, but not gay/lesbian issues); and poverty.

Table 3.1 Domestic Issues Discussed in Selected Social Problems Textbooks: 1975–2000

Chapter Topics
Aging, ageism
Crime/violence/deviant behavior/law enforcement/criminal justice
Education
Environment/nuclear power
Family
Gender, sexism
Healthcare
Mental disorders
National security
Population and immigration
Poverty/welfare
Race/racism/ethnic relations
Religious conflict
Sexuality

Textbooks (chronological order): Perry and Perry 1976; Horton and Leslie 1978; Sullivan et al. 1980; Reasons and Perdue 1981; Eitzen and Zinn 1986; Farley 1987; Feagin and Feagin 1990; Coleman and Cressey 1990; Kornblum and Julian 1995; Eitzen and Baca Zinn 1997.[2]

Six of the ten social problems textbooks we examined also contained chapters on international issues. Those discussed in more than one book were: warfare and international conflict, global ecological problems, and economic inequality among nations. Chapters did not present what might be construed as contrasting conservative and liberal positions on subtopics within any of these issue areas. Much of the material was descriptive. Solutions offered to the problems generally were vague. For example, one text suggested that a step toward solving global ecological problems involved forging international economic and political cooperation that allowed regional and national diversity.

Pursuing analysis of media bias in the coverage of international social problems using the methodology described on the following pages would confront an additional problem. Between 1985 and 1995, international news coverage declined in *Time* from 24 percent to 14 percent and in *Newsweek* from 22 percent to 12 percent.[3] Locating an adequate number of articles for analysis in the three international issue areas would be unlikely.

Applying a Social Problems Model to Media Bias

Basing the method for measuring bias on the definition developed above requires explicating the nature of support by a media outlet. In the United States, there has been sustained conflict surrounding a number of damaging conditions that are generally understood as social problems or issues, such as those identified in Table 3.1. However, as Edelman points out, a social problem is not a verifiable entity but a construction that furthers ideological interests.[4] There is a:

> diversity of meanings inherent in every social problem, stemming from the range of concerns of different groups, each eager to pursue courses of action and call them solutions. National security is a different problem for each of the parties concerned with it such as the various branches of the armed services, the General Dynamics Corporation, that firm's workers, the Women's International League for Peace and Freedom, and potential draftees. The problem becomes what it is for each group precisely because their rivals define it differently. In this sense a problem is constituted by the differences among its definitions.[5]

As noted earlier, the definition of a social issue involves specification of its cost (who or what is wronged and what is the nature and extent of the grievance?), its cause (who or what is responsible for the wrong?), and a solution (what can be done to solve the problem?).

The definition of a social issue through the specification of cost, cause, and solution tends to evoke in an audience a distinctive pattern of judgments and opinions.[6] Hall notes that:

> the more one accepts the principle that how people act will depend in part on how the situations in which they act are defined, and the less one can assume either a natural meaning to everything or a universal consensus on what things mean—then the more important, socially and politically becomes the process by means of which certain events get recurrently signified in particular ways. This is particularly the case when events in the world are problematic . . . where powerful interests are involved or when there are starkly opposing interests at play. The power involved here is an ideological power; the power to signify events in a particular way.[7]

The power of a publication, then, consists in its ability to signify issues in particular ways. It provides support to the extent that it relies on sources favorable to one of the sides involved in a social conflict over an issue and defines that issue in terms of the same costs, causes, and solutions as those identified by that side.

Sources

The way in which a newspaper or newsmagazine defines an issue is influenced significantly by the sources on which it relies for information concerning that issue. Journalists generally treat "official sources" such as government officials and leaders of major political groups, conservative foundations, and business organizations as the most "objective," qualified, and credible sources and cite those most frequently.[8] Such elites tend to be the "primary definers" of social issues, identifying their costs, causes, and solutions. Their interpretation of a problem "then commands the field in all subsequent treatment and sets the terms of reference within which all further coverage and debate takes place."[9] However, in the absence of elite consensus, it becomes unclear who will serve as an issue's "primary definer."[10] Furthermore, journalists are not mere reproducers of official sources' "primary definitions." Their professional values and practices are of crucial importance in shaping news products.[11] Additionally, even social movement activists and other non-official sources concerned with an issue sometimes are able to influence media representations, although they may be disadvantaged in the struggle over signification.[12]

We view a source as providing support for one of the parties or sides involved in conflict over an issue when that source defines the issue in terms of the same costs, causes, and solutions as does that party. Provision of such support by a source can be illustrated by brief reference to media discussions of the issue of abortion.

Abortion was a major topic of social controversy in many states during the 1960s and became a major national political issue in 1973, when the United States Supreme Court legalized it throughout the country with its *Roe v. Wade* ruling. The Court affirmed the legal right of all women to obtain abortions early in pregnancy and declared most existing state abortion laws unconstitutional. The decision ruled out any legislative interference in the first trimester of pregnancy and put limits on what restrictions could be passed on abortions in later stages of pregnancy.

In the case of the issue of abortion, it is non-official sources, particularly organization activists, who are among those at the forefront of the struggle to influence media representations. Leading organizations opposing the imposition of limitations on access to abortion include the National Organization for Women (NOW), the National Abortion and Reproduction Rights Action League (NARAL), Planned Parenthood, and the Center for Reproductive Law and Policy. Major organizations opposing the right to abortion include National Right to Life, the Eagle Forum, the Pro-Life Action League, and the American Life League. Chapter 5 contains a detailed discussion of how sources were utilized by the two explicitly partisan publications analyzed for this study, the *National Review* and *The Progressive*, and raises questions about the extent to which information sources actually influence the partisanship of media content.

Costs

Social conflict over an issue can involve dispute concerning who or what is actually or potentially wronged, and the nature and extent of the grievance. Different understandings of costs serve the ideological interests of different groups.[13] The two examples below illustrate how costs are differently identified by conflicting groups.

Groups supporting woman's unrestricted right of access to abortion define the costs of restricting access as denying the right of a woman to control her own body through "freedom of choice," increasing rates of illegal and dangerous abortions, and most generally, government intrusion into the private lives of citizens. Those arguing for limitation of access to abortion or to specific medical practices, define the costs of unrestricted access as threatening the sanctity of the traditional American family and undermining our society's support of the fundamental value of human life. The unborn child, they contend, has a "right to life."

The costs of poverty and policies implemented to alleviate poverty can be understood as either individual or societal in nature. Poverty has an enormous psychological impact and is associated with depression, alcohol and drug abuse, divorce, and domestic violence. Poverty policies, or "welfare" as it is often termed, have their own consequences as well. Proponents of welfare or aid to the poor argue that financial assistance provides a needed safety net for those who cannot obtain adequate employment. Opponents assert that aid (in particular aid provided without a work requirement) serves as a disincentive for recipients to seek employment. Opponents also argue that the structure of aid contributes to a disintegration of the nuclear family unit as it "rewards" women for rearing children outside of marriage.

Causes

Conflict over costs is central to the definition of some issues such as abortion. In this case, opposing sides compete for media acceptance of their basic understanding of what the issue is all about. For other issues, such as poverty or the environment, there is extensive debate not only over the identification of costs, but also over the specification of a cause or causes. Politics is largely a competition between alternative causal stories proposed to explain a given phenomenon.[14] The placement of "blame" in these causal stories also frames discussion about possible solutions since responsibility for action is often linked to those individuals, groups, or processes identified as responsible for its development.

There are two broad approaches to poverty taken by the media. The first focuses on the suffering of the poor and discusses topics such as hunger, homelessness, low quality housing, and victimization of violent crime. The second concerns problems associated with poverty that threaten the non-poor such as crime, drugs, gangs, and costs such as increased taxes to deal with these and related troubles.[15] Despite this difference, a common question remains: What causes poverty? Here the fundamental conflict is found between those who argue that poverty is the product of the structure and activities of corporations, markets, and the state, and those who maintain that poverty is caused by government intervention in the labor market, welfare programs, and the culture of the poor that fails them by promoting character traits that impede their progress in society.

Media coverage of the environment is similar to coverage of poverty. Two prevailing causal stories are told by the media about the environment. Environmental problems are explained as the result of lax government policies which allow large corporations to legally produce excessive amounts of waste and pollutants, as well as a failure of government agencies to properly enforce existing laws by holding corporations accountable for violations. Alternatively, environmental issues such as pollution or overflowing landfills are framed as caused by individual citizens' failure to recycle or properly dispose of potentially toxic products.[16]

Solutions

An additional indicator of a publication's support of one of the opposing sides of an issue is its identification of the same authorities and strategies for dealing with the issue.

> The language that constructs a problem and provides an origin for it is also a rationale for vesting authority in people who claim some kind of competence. Willingness to suspend one's own critical judgment in favor of someone regarded as able to cope creates authority. If poverty stems from individual inadequacies, then psychologists, social workers, and educators have a claim to authority in dealing with it; but, if an economy that fails to provide enough jobs paying an adequate wage is the source of poverty, then economists have a claim to authority. Military threats, crime, mental illness, and every other problem yields claims to authority, though the claim is disputed in each case because diverse reasons for the problem compete for acceptance.[17]

There are occasions when actors want to avoid assignment of responsibility for dealing with an issue. For example, industries avoid political, economic, and public relations costs by deflecting criticism of the role they play in causing pollution. They attempt this by promoting public understanding of pollution as the responsibility of individuals to be dealt with apolitically. "The fight against pollution is equated with antilitter efforts rather than with auto emission controls, smokestack filters, or prohibitions on non-returnable containers."[18]

Proposing solutions almost invariably results in assigning responsibility for action. For example, identifying an extension of government provided healthcare benefits (Medicaid) to recipients who are able to obtain employment until private, employer-provided insurance is available (often after ninety days of employment) places the responsibility on government and government policies to alleviate the problem of poverty. Researchers examining media coverage of social issues have found that the media rarely discuss solutions.[19] Instead, emphasis is placed on blaming either individuals or public policies for the growth or continuation of social problems such as poverty or crime. Kensicki links public apathy with the absence of news articles on social problems which include a call to action or discussion of potential solutions.[20] In his research on coverage of pollution, poverty, and incarceration, articles overwhelmingly failed to mention possible solutions. In fact, a portion of the articles "reported a solution as either unlikely or extremely unlikely."[21] Fewer than two percent of the six hundred articles Kensicki examined contained a "call to action."

Additionally, Dreier found that media coverage of urban problems failed to discuss grassroots organizations working to alleviate their impacts on communities.[22] Activist groups enter the news only when their actions "involve drama or conflict" such as strikes or large-scale protests.[23] Instead, there is a focus on blaming government agencies for a failure to protect citizens (e.g. against crime, pollution) or exacerbating the problem (e.g. creating a dependency on welfare among the poor). Public policies which are successful are rarely discussed.

By not posing possible solutions, declaring social problems too difficult to solve, and failing to cover activists working for change, Gamson et al. argue, the media contributes to social and political apathy among the general public.[24] As Dreier concludes "the media give their audience of readers and viewers little reason for optimism that ordinary people working together effectively can make a difference, that solutions are within reach, and that public policies can make a significant difference."[25]

Specifying the Measurement Model

Classifying Sources

Articles generally cite several sources of information. Those sources which explicitly identify themselves as advocates of a perspective on an issue were coded as either conservative or liberal as that position is defined in Tables 3.3, 3.4, 3.5, and 3.6 to come in this chapter. On many issues, partisan sources are likely to include: advocacy groups, books, business organizations, experts, foundations, think tanks, government agencies, newsmagazines, newspapers, non-governmental organizations, officials, ordinary citizens, polls, and research reports.

Unlike much, if not most, of the popular as well as scholarly writing on media bias produced over the past several decades, this study makes no assumptions about the inherently conservative nature of government agencies and officials as sources of information. Similarly, unlike much previous work, experts, newsmagazines, newspapers, television news, polls, and research reports (other than those produced by business organizations, foundations, or think tanks) will be treated as neutral sources. These methodological decisions will result in some coding that politically conservative readers might find objectionable (e.g., classifying *The New York Times* as a neutral source) and some that liberal readers might find troublesome (e.g., classifying a government agency report as a neutral source). Such reactions are the inevitable fate of any effort to put the study of media bias on a more empirical foundation. Table 3.2 below specifies our source categories and criteria of partisanship.

Table 3.2 Source Categories and Criteria of Partisanship

Sources	Criteria
Advocacy group	Explicit support of partisan position
Book	Explicit support of partisan position
Business organization	Except for circumstances in which a business organization has adopted a liberal policy on an issue being discussed, business organizations are considered conservative actors oriented toward maximizing private profit
Expert	Except for circumstances in which an individual identified as having a special skill or knowledge derived from training or experience advocates a partisan position on an issue being discussed, all experts are considered non-partisan
Foundation, think tank	Self-identification on its website as generally supporting conservative or liberal policies and/or advocacy of a partisan position on an issue being discussed
Government agency	Except for circumstances in which an agency adopts a partisan position on an issue being discussed, government agencies are considered non-partisan
Newsmagazine	All mainstream, putatively non-partisan newsmagazines are considered non-partisan
Newspaper	All mainstream, putatively non-partisan newspapers are considered non-partisan

Continued on next page

Table 3.2—Continued

Sources	Criteria
Non-governmental organization	All non-governmental organizations that do not operate as advocacy groups are considered non-partisan
Official	Public officeholder explicitly advocates a partisan position on an issue being discussed
Ordinary citizen	Individual advocates a partisan position on an issue being discussed
Poll, research report	All polls and research reports produced by independent agencies are considered non-partisan
Other	A public person advocates a partisan position on an issue being discussed

Classifying Positions

Under the assumptions noted earlier, operational definitions were developed for "liberal" and "conservative" positions on each of the four enduring issues. Tables 3.3, 3.4, 3.5, and 3.6 provide an overview of the operational definitions used to code the articles analyzed for each issue area.

Table 3.3 Conservative and Liberal Positions for the Issue of Crime

Conservative	
Sources (exx.):	Sen. Robert Dole (R, KS); Major Frank Rizzo (D, Philadelphia); Official in the Texas Department of Corrections
Drugs	
Costs:	connection to other serious crimes; threat to the moral order; lost productivity; public expense of control; treatment and ineffective attempts at rehabilitation
Causes:	narco-traffickers/dealers; leniency of criminal justice system; belief that casual drug use is a victimless crime
Solutions:	stricter law enforcement and the imposition of heavier penalties for violation of drug laws for both suppliers and users
Street Crimes (includes violent personal crimes and property crimes)	
Costs:	public safety
Causes:	sub-cultural factors; lack of social integration and social control

Continued on next page

Table 3.3—Continued

Solutions:	stricter law enforcement; incapacitation of criminals; elimination of most gun control laws

Public order crimes (includes gambling, prostitution, and pornography)
Costs:	failure to sustain the moral order
Causes:	failure of criminal justice system
Solutions:	stricter law enforcement

Liberal
Sources (exx.):	The National Organization for the Reform of Marijuana Laws; Jessica Mitford, author; The American Civil Liberties Union

Drugs
Costs:	suffering of the addicted, their families, and associates; concern for civil rights of the accused; war on drugs is a war on minorities
Causes:	treating drug use as a criminal rather than a public health problem
Solutions:	development of treatment programs and selective decriminalization; improving social conditions associated with high rates of drug use

Street crime (includes violent personal crimes and property crimes)
Costs:	public safety; some argue that these crimes do less harm to society than do many of the crimes committed by white collar individuals and corporations; concern for civil rights of the accused
Causes:	racial, ethnic, and economic inequality
Solutions:	eradication of unemployment, sub-employment and racial discrimination; gun control

Public order crimes (includes gambling, prostitution, and pornography)
Costs:	victimless crimes
Causes:	criminalization of victimless crimes
Solutions:	decriminalization

Table 3.4 Conservative and Liberal Positions for the Issue of Environment

---

Conservative

Sources (exx.):   The Environmental Protection Agency during the Reagan administration; Pacific Gas and Electric; Engineer for General Electric Nuclear Division

Depleting Natural Resources

Costs: increasing economic costs; increasing dependence on foreign sources

Causes: continuing and increasing needs of business, industry, government, and the public; population pressure

Solutions: additional exploration and extraction; greater use of nuclear power and coal; development of new energy technologies

Pollution

Costs: threat to public health; degradation of environment, but threats exaggerated

Causes: most of what does exist is the unavoidable by-product of maintaining the American standard of living and sustaining economic growth through competitiveness in world markets; some is the result of the carelessness of citizens; population growth

Solutions: acknowledged problems responsibilities of individual companies and citizen efforts

Environmentalism/Environmental Movement

Costs: creating unwarranted levels of environmental concerns among public; supporting expensive and ineffective environmental policies that are detrimental to economic growth and sometimes to the environment itself

Causes: exaggerated environmental fears based largely on faulty science; support of legislation without application of cost-benefit analysis; lack of appropriate concern with jobs and the economy

Solutions: better public understanding that environmental problems have been exaggerated and that environmental groups are interest groups and not philanthropic enterprises

Liberal

Sources (exx.):   The Environmental Policy Institute; Member of Sullivan Co., IA Board of Supervisors Task Force on Uranium Mining; The Health and Energy Learning Project

---

Continued on next page

Table 3.4—Continued

Depleting Natural Resources

Costs:	degradation of environment and loss of biodiversity due to additional exploration and extraction
Causes:	wasteful patterns of resource use; corporate takeover of public land
Solutions:	greater government regulation; conservation

Pollution

Costs:	threat to public health; degradation of environment; loss of biodiversity
Causes:	wasteful patterns of resource use; resistance of industry to employ effective pollution-reducing devices; hazardous technologies (e.g. nuclear power) and products (e.g. pesticides)
Solutions:	responsibility of entire industries; increased governmental regulation; conservation

Environmentalism/Environmental Movement

Costs:	support movement but some concern about rift in liberal community between environmentalists and labor
Causes:	a genuine concern for public health and nature
Solutions:	a government with serious environmental concerns and effective regulatory policies

Table 3.5 Conservative and Liberal Positions for the Issue of Gender

Conservative

Sources (exx.):	*Man and Marriage* by George Gildner; Eagle Forum; The Christian Action Council

Public policies concerning women (includes abortion rights, sex-discrimination laws, and no-fault divorce)

Costs:	unrestricted right of access to abortion undermines our society's support of the fundamental value of human life; each of these policies threatens the sanctity of the traditional (two-parent, heterosexual, clearly defined gender roles) American family; some laws routinely are applied in ways that unfairly discriminate against men
Causes:	feminism, women's movement
Solutions:	a government with serious commitment to the preservation of the traditional American family and to the unborn's "right to life."

Continued on next page

Table 3.5—Continued

Media representations of women
Costs: images often demeaning and exploitative
Causes: commercial interests
Solutions: return to traditional gender representations

Feminism/feminist movement
Costs: attempt to impose an inappropriate equality in men and women that conflicts with their innate differences; lack of recognition of the value of men in the lives of women
Causes: decline in commitments to the traditional family and to traditional moral values; liberalism; humanism
Solutions: better public understanding of the costs women have incurred as a result of the movement's successes such as no-fault divorce laws (devastating economic consequences for women and children) and encouraging pursuit of careers (delaying child-bearing too long because of career demands)

Liberal
Sources (exx.):   The Equal Employment Opportunity Commission during the Clinton administration; University "feminist sociologist"; Gloria Steinem, women's movement leader

Public policies concerning women (includes abortion rights, sex-discrimination laws, and no-fault divorce)
Costs: none (support these policies)
Causes: gender inequality
Solutions: a government seriously concerned with gender equality and policies to bring it about

Media representations of women
Costs: images often demeaning and exploitative
Causes: commercial interests; gender inequality
Solutions: representation in full range of occupational, professional, and social roles

Feminism/feminist movement
Costs: none; support movement
Causes: gender inequality
Solutions: a government with serious concern for gender inequality and policies to bring it about

---

Table 3.6 Conservative and Liberal Positions for the Issue of Poverty

Conservative	
Sources (exx.):	Chuck Hobbs, former Reagan advisor; a Cleveland landlord; the Hudson Institute
Costs:	problems associated with poverty that threaten the non-poor such as crime, drugs, gangs, and paying for means to deal with these and other troubles such as welfare dependency
Causes:	government intervention in the labor market; welfare programs themselves; the culture and associated behaviors of the poor
Solutions:	a genuine free-market economy; replacing welfare with work programs
Liberal	
Sources (exx.):	Barbara Ehrenreich, author; *The Undeserving Poor* by Michael Katz; the Economic Policy Institute
Costs:	substandard housing and homelessness; hunger; inferior education; inadequate health care; victimization of violent crime; likelihood of pathologies such as alcoholism, child abuse, suicide; extent of costs underestimated; conditions worsening
Causes:	the structure and activities of corporations, markets, and the state
Solutions:	affordable housing; better schools; tax reforms producing more equal distribution of wealth; greater government assistance for the poor; more jobs and better pay

Sample and Measure

For each of the four magazines, all articles dealing with the selected topics that were published between 1975 and 2000 and were at least one full page in length were included in the study. However, articles containing fewer than three of the four indicators subsequently were excluded from analysis to ensure that discussion of the issue was extensive enough to warrant consideration. In all, 873 articles were coded by the authors.

Articles received a score for each of the four indicators discussed above (sources, costs, causes, solutions). In the case of sources, the scores represented the sum of the proportion of the total number of sources cited in an article that are coded as conservative (0 to +1.0) and the proportion of the total number of sources cited in an article that are coded as liberal (0 to -1.0). There are pitfalls to any analysis which relies on a simple "counting" of sources which should be considered. Numerous quotations from liberal sources can appear in an article supporting a conservative position, and vice versa. This practice can be employed both to clarify and support the position being advocated by constructing the perspective it opposes. This practice would result in a lowering of an overall positive score of the conservative article or a decrease in the overall negative score of the liberal article.

In order to move beyond the limitations of existing research which has been based upon assumptions about the inherently conservative or liberal nature of particular business or government agencies and officeholders, determinations regarding partisanship were based on the content and context of the source's comment. Sources were coded as conservative or liberal *only* if their cited statements or their affiliated organization's official position explicitly reflected a partisan stance as defined in the tables above. In instances where a source could not be identified, as in the case of an individual named without further reference, or an organization or publication that could not be found through a routine web search, it was dropped from the analysis and was not counted in the total number of sources cited in an article. Articles in which there were no entries in a category, such as one in which no sources were cited, had no score assigned to that category. Additional details about coding for sources can be found in Chapter 5.

At its limit, an article could have a conservative score for sources of +1.0 or a liberal score of -1.0. The same procedure was followed for assigning cost, cause, and solution scores. From this it follows that, at its limit, an article could have a total score ranging from +4.0 (all sources that classify as conservative, and discussion of costs, causes, and solutions all of which uniformly classify as conservative) to -4.0 (all sources that classify as liberal, and discussion of costs, causes, and solutions all of which uniformly classify as liberal). Finally, to determine the overall bias score for an article, the total score was divided by the number of indicators present in the article. This resulted in a final range of +1.0 (totally conservative) to -1.0 (totally liberal), normalizing the scores for comparison.

To illustrate the application of the measure, one article was selected from the *National Review* (Example 3.1), and another from *The Progressive* (Example 3.2). Each of the items, written in the early 1990s, deals with abortion. If the measure of article bias operates as intended, a *National Review* article will have an overall positive score and a *Progressive* article will have an overall negative score. Because each of the journals is explicitly partisan, the scores should be much closer to +1.0 or -1.0 than might be expected from comparable articles in newsmagazines that purport to offer unbiased accounts of social issues.

Example 3.1 Bias Score Coding for the *National Review* article

"The Abortion War" by Mark Cunningham. *National Review* (Nov. 2, 1992) 42–46.
Sources: n=18; score = +0.22
Conservative = +0.39
Aborted Women: Silent No More by David Reardon
Abortion Rites: A Social History of Abortion by Marvin Olasky
De Moss Foundation, The

Continued on next page

Example 3.1—Continued

First Things
National Review, The
Nurturing Network, The
Women Exploited by Abortion
Liberal = -0.17
Alan Guttmacher Institute, The
Hentoff, Nat
National Abortion Federation, The
Neutral
Abortion and the Politics of Motherhood by Kristen Luker
Boston Globe, The
Gallup Survey
Los Angeles Times, The
Readers Digest, The
60 Minutes
USA Today
Washington Post, The

Costs: n=3; score = +1.0
Conservative = +1.0
The practice of abortion itself
The existence of "abortion mills"
Loosing a cultural war in which society will abandon the traditional understanding of motherhood and human life as sacred (in a secular as well as a religious sense)
Liberal = 0
None
Neutral
None

Causes: n=1; score = +1.0
Conservative = +1.0
Feminist ideologies and committed career women who want gender equivalence and the approval of society for their lifestyle and philosophy
Liberal = 0
None
Neutral
None

Solutions: n=2; score = +1.0
Conservative = +1.0
Increasing public understanding that women are not as happy as the feminists promised. Many are poorer and more lonely.
Increasing public understanding of why and how most abortions are actually performed

Continued on next page

Example 3.1—Continued

Liberal = 0
None
Neutral
None
Raw Bias Score +3.22
Adjusted Bias Score +3.22/4 = +0.83

Example 3.2 Bias Score Coding for the *Progressive* article

"The Right to Life Rampage" by Laura L. Sydell. *The Progressive* (August, 1993) 24–27.
Sources: n=19; score = -0.37

Conservative = +0.26
- American Family Association Law Center
- Babington, Kim (OC) (identified as anti-abortion activist)
- Feminists for Life
- Operation Rescue National
- Raney, Meredith (OC) (identified as anti-abortion activist)

Liberal = -0.63
- American Civil Liberties Union
- Alan Guttmacher Institute, The
- Center for Reproductive Law and Policy
- Finkle, Dr. Brian (OC) (gynecologist attacked by anti-abortion activists)
- Lowrey, Nita (Rep. D. NY)
- National Abortion Federation
- National Coalition of Abortion Providers
- Planned Parenthood Federation of America
- Pollard, Kim (OC) (worker at Aware Woman Center for Choice)
- Rasmussen, Jeri (OC) (owner of a women's health clinic)
- Windel, Patricia (OC) (owner of Aware Woman Center for Choice)

Neutral
- American Nurses Association
- Reno, Janet (United States Attorney General)

Costs: n=3; score = -0.40

Conservative = +0.3
- Some federal legislation proposed to protect abortion providers and their patients violates First Amendment right of anti-abortion activists

Liberal = -0.7
- Serious harassment of abortion providers, patients, and their families, friends, and neighbors
- Reduction in the number of abortion providers nationally

Neutral
- None

Continued on next page

Example 3.2—Continued

Causes: n=1; score = -1.0
Conservative = 0
    None

Liberal = -1.0
    Anti-abortion fanatics
Neutral
    None

Solutions: n=2; score=-1.0
Conservative = 0
Liberal = -1.0
    Legislation to protect abortion providers and their patients from harassment
    Increasing the number of abortion providers
Neutral
    None

Raw Bias Score -2.77
Adjusted Bias Score -2.77/4 = -0.69

Scale Evaluation

Each component (sources, causes, costs, solutions) was equally weighted for the creation of an indexed bias score for each article coded. Internal consistency (using Cronbach's alpha) was high for the four item index, measuring at 0.79. Item to total correlation coefficients indicate that three of the four components (causes, costs, and solutions) correlated highly with the indexed bias score (see Table 3.7). Reliability analysis also shows that alpha levels would be reduced if causes, costs, or solutions were removed from the bias scale, but would be increased (from .79 to .81) if sources were removed. This final component, sources, was significantly, but less strongly correlated ($r=.55$) with the bias score. In addition, covariance levels for each component against sources were lower than for other pairs.

These lower scores should not be interpreted to indicate a weakness resulting from the inclusion of sources in the measurement model. The inclusion of sources remains essential for assessing media bias. The lower correlation values generally reflect the common practice of including "opposing" sources in articles to establish "journalistic balance." In the case of partisan publications such as the *National Review* and *The Progressive*, an opposing viewpoint may be offered followed by criticism and counterpoints. These journalistic practices may result in a sources score that seem "misaligned" with the remaining components of the measurement model.

Table 3.7 Inter-Item Correlation and Scale Reliability

| | Inter-Item Correlation | | | | Scale Reliability | |
| | | | | | Item to | Alpha if |
	Sources	Causes	Costs	Solutions	Total	Deleted
Sources	1.00	.34*	.33*	.40*	.55*	.81
Causes		1.00	.67*	.65*	.89*	.67
Costs			1.00	.54*	.85*	.72
Solutions				1.00	.85*	.70

* $p<.01$(2-tailed).

Intercoder Reliability

Each article for each publication was assigned to its issue area and then catego-rized by publication date. Each author coded approximately half of the articles. Assignment of an author to an issue area or publication was random. Reliability was assessed during the initial measurement testing phase by randomly selecting three articles for each topic from each magazine to be independently coded by the author who did not initially code it. A subset of articles representing 12 per-cent (N=48) of the articles was coded during the initial stage of the research project (N=399). Reliability analysis comparing the adjusted bias scores for each of the forty-eight items resulted in an alpha of 0.97. (Computation of reliability for raw bias scores produced an alpha of 0.92. Scale compression had little ef-fect on reliability.) Findings demonstrate a high level of consistency in coding decisions. Because of the high alpha coefficients obtained from reliability analy-sis, no attempt was made to resolve discrepancies in their coding. The initial coder's score was used in all further analysis.

Discussion

The research reported in this book attempts to move beyond the limitations of existing studies which attempt to quantify media bias by focusing on a single element, such as counting sources cited, comparing lines of coverage given to opposing perspectives, or the location of coverage of opposing perspectives. Methodologically, these approaches are flawed in that they typically rely on a single measure/indicator for media bias, equate frequency of coverage with sup-port for a particular side/perspective, and generally fail to consider the content of source comments or the context in which these citations are located. Our measure, which equally weights four separate indicators, provides a quantitative model that can be applied to print coverage of a variety of issues areas to reeva-luate the media bias question.

Chapters 4, 5, and 6 present the major findings of our research, comparing bias across publications and across issue areas over the period of analysis (Chapter 4), the nature and role of source selection in understanding media bias (Chapter 5), and the impact of historical conditions on coverage of the crime, environment, gender, and poverty from 1975 to 2000 (Chapter 6).

Notes

1. Stephen E. Bennett, Staci L. Rhine, and Richard S. Flickinger, "Assessing American's Opinions about the News Media's Fairness in 1996 and 1998," *Political Communication* 18, no. 2 (April–June 2001):163–182.

2. John Perry and Erna Perry, *Face to Face: The Individual and Social Problems* (Boston: Little Brown, 1976); Paul B. Horton and Gerald R. Leslie, *The Sociology of Social Problems*, 6th ed. (Englewood Cliffs, NJ: Prentice Hall, 1978); Thomas Sullivan, Kenrick Thompson, Richard Wright, George Gross, and Dale Spady, *Social Problems, Divergent Perspectives* (New York: John Wiley & Sons, 1980); Charles E. Reasons and William D. Perdue, *The Ideology of Social Problems* (Sherman Oaks, CA: Alfred Publishing, 1981); D. Stanley Eitzen with Maxine Baca Zinn, *Social Problems*, 3rd ed. (Boston: Allyn & Bacon, 1986); John E. Farley, *American Social Problems: An Institutional Analysis* (Englewood Cliffs, NJ: Prentice Hall, 1987); Joe R. Feagin and Clairece Booher Feagin, *Social Problems: A Critical Power-Conflict Perspective*, 3rd ed. (Englewood Cliffs, NJ: Prentice Hall, 1990); James W. Coleman and Donald R Cressey, *Social Problems*, 3rd ed. (New York: Harper & Row, 1990); William Kornblum and Joseph Julian, *Social Problems*, 8th ed. (Englewood Cliffs, NJ: Prentice Hall 1995); D. Stanley Eitzen with Maxine Baca Zinn, *Social Problems*, 7th ed. (Boston: Allyn & Bacon, 1997).

3. Neil Hickey, "Money Lust: How Pressure for Profit Is Perverting Journalism," *Columbia Journalism Review* 18, no. 2 (July/August 1998): 32.

4. Murray Edelman, *Constructing the Political Spectacle* (Chicago: University of Chicago Press, 1988).

5. Edelman, *Constructing the Political Spectacle*, 15.

6. Katherine Beckett, "Media Depictions of Drug Abuse: The Impact of Official Sources," *Research in Political Sociology* 7 (1995): 161–182; William A. Gamson and Katherine E. Lasch, "The Political Culture of Social Welfare Policy," in *Evaluating the Welfare State: Social and Political Perspectives*, ed. Shimon E. Spiro and Ephraim Yuchtman-Yaar (New York: Academic Press, 1983), 397–415; William A. Gamson and Andre Modigliani, "The Changing Culture of Affirmative Action," *Research in Political Sociology* 3 (1989): 137–177; Shanto Iyengar, "Television News and Citizen Explanation of National Affairs," *American Political Science Review* 80, no. 3 (September 1988): 815–831.

7. Stuart Hall, "The Rediscovery of 'Ideology:' Return of the Repressed in Media Studies," in *Culture, Society, and the Media*, ed. Michael Gurevitch, Janet Woollacott, Tony Bennett, and James Curran (New York: Routledge, 1982), 56–90.

8. Mark Fishman, "Crime Waves as Ideology," *Social Problems* 25, no. 5 (June 1978): 631–543; Herbert J. Gans, *Deciding What's News: A Study of CBS Evening News, NBC Nightly News, Newsweek and Time* (New York: Random House, 1979); Trudy Lieberman, *Slanting the Story: The Forces That Shape the News* (New York: New Press, 2000); David Morgan, *The Flacks of Washington: Government Information and the Pub-*

lic Agenda (New York: Greenwood Press, 1986); Dan D. Nimmo, *Newsgathering in Washington: A Study in Political Communication* (New York: Atherton Press, 1964); Leo Sigal, *Reporters and Officials: The Organization and Politics of News Making* (Lexington, MA: Heath, 1973); D. Charles Whitney, Marilyn Fritzler, Steven Jones, Sharon Mazzarella, and Lana Rakow, "Geographic and Source Bias in Network Television News 1982–1984," *Journal of Broadcasting and Electronic Media* 33, no. 2 (1989): 159–174

9. Stuart Hall, Charles Critcher, Tony Jefferson, John Clarke, and Brian Roberts, *Policing the Crisis: Mugging, the State and Law and Order* (New York: Holmes and Meier 1978), 58.

10. Philip Schlesinger, "Rethinking the Sociology of Journalism: Source Strategies and the Limits of Media Centrism," in *Public Communication: The New Imperatives*, ed. Marjorie Ferguson (Thousand Oaks, CA: Sage, 1990), 61–83.

11. Steven Chibnall, *Law and Order News* (London: Tavistock, 1974); Richard V. Erickson, Patricia Baranek, and Janet B. L. Chan, *Representing Order: Crime, Law, and Justice in the News Media* (Toronto: University of Toronto Press, 1989); Schlesinger, "Rethinking the Sociology of Journalism."

12. William A. Gamson and Gadi Wolfsfeld, "Movements and Media as Interacting Systems" *The Annals of the American Academy of Political and Social Science*, no. 528 (1993): 114–125; Todd Gitlin, *The Whole World Is Watching: The Mass Media in the Making and Unmaking of the New Left* (Berkeley: University of California Press, 1980); Douglas McAdam, *Political Process and the Development of Black Insurgency, 1930–1970* (Chicago: University of Chicago Press, 1982).

13. Edelman, *Constructing the Political Spectacle*.

14. Deborah Stone, "Causal Stories and the Formation of Policy Agendas," *Political Science Quarterly* 104, no. 2 (Summer 1989): 281–300.

15. Robert M. Entman, "Television, Democratic Theory and the Visual Construction of Poverty," *Research in Political Sociology* 7 (1995): 139–159.

16. David L. Paletz, *The Media in American Politics: Contents & Consequences* (New York: Longman, 2002).

17. Edelman, *Constructing the Political Spectacle*, 20.

18. Paletz, *The Media in American Politics*, 182.

19. Linda J. Kensicki, "No Cure for What Ails Us: The Media-Constructed Disconnect between Social Problems and Possible Solutions," *Journalism and Mass Communication Quarterly* 81, no. 2 (2004): 53–73; Peter Dreier, "How the Media Compound Urban Problems," *Journal of Urban Affairs* 27, no. 2 (2005):193–201.

20. Kensicki, "No Cure."

21. Kensicki, "No Cure," 61.

22. Dreier "How the Media."

23. Dreier, "How the Media," 198.

24. William A. Gamson, David Croteau, William Hoynes, and Theodore Sasson, "Media Images and the Social Construction of Reality," *Annual Review of Sociology* 18 (1992): 373–393.

25. Dreier, "How the Media," 199.

Chapter 4

Comparing *Time*, *Newsweek*, the *National Review*, and *The Progressive* Coverage of Selected Social Issues, 1975–2000

In this chapter, we analyze 873 articles on crime, the environment, gender, and poverty that appeared in *Time*, *Newsweek*, the *National Review*, and *The Progressive* from 1975 to 2000. Each of the articles contains at least three of the four components (sources, costs, causes, and solutions) outlined in Chapter 3. Coverage of the four issue areas in the *National Review* and *The Progressive* were initially studied in order to test the bias measure. Results from these partisan publications are included in the discussion below for comparison to *Time* and *Newsweek*, our two putatively non-partisan publications.

Comparing Issue Focus across Publications

The amount of attention given to the four issue areas included in the study varied significantly among the four magazines (see Table 4.1). Overall, poverty received the least coverage by the magazines, while gender and the environment received the most coverage. Coverage in the two partisan publications (the *National Review* and *The Progressive*) was more issue concentrated than coverage of the issues areas in *Time* and *Newsweek*. More than half (53.3 percent) of all articles in *The Progressive* and nearly one-third (31.2 percent) of the analyzed *Newsweek* articles dealt with a single issue area, the environment. Gender issues were discussed more frequently than the other issues areas for the two remaining publications, accounting for more than 40 percent of the articles in the *National Review*, and over 35 percent of the articles in *Time*.

Table 4.1 Issue Area Coverage by Publication

	Time	*Newsweek*	*National Review*	*The Progressive*	Total
Crime	58	61	35	20	174
	23.9%	26.4%	17.2%	10.3%	19.9%
Environment	79	72	43	104	298
	32.5%	31.2%	21.1%	53.3%	34.1%
Gender	87	67	84	44	282
	35.8%	29.0%	41.2%	22.6%	32.3%
Poverty	19	31	42	27	119
	7.8%	13.4%	20.6%	13.8%	13.6%
Total	243	231	204	195	873
	100.0%	100.0%	100.0%	100.0%	100.0%

Notes: Chi-Square (*Time* and *Newsweek* compared) =5.577, *n.s.*
Chi-Square (all four magazines compared) =74.399, $p<.001$, Cramer's V=.169, Lambda=.09, $p<.01$

When comparing both partisan and non-partisan publications, significant Chi-Square values indicate that issues discussed are significantly associated with magazine name (i.e. publications emphasize different issue areas). Cramer's V values indicate a moderate association between publication and issue area coverage. *Time* and *Newsweek* devoted the smallest percentage of its articles (7.8 percent and 13.4 percent respectively) to the issue of poverty, while crime received the least coverage for the *National Review* (17.2 percent) and *The Progressive* (10.3 percent). Differences in issue concentration for coverage of the four selected issue areas between *Time* and *Newsweek* were not significant, however.

Comparing Bias across Publications

Table 4.2 provides an overview of bias scores obtained by each publication for each issue area. Predictably, partisan publications (the *National Review* and *The*

Table 4.2 Articles by Levels of Bias by Topic Area for Each Publication (Percentage)

Publication	Crime	Environment	Gender	Poverty	Total
Conservative (+.21 to +1.00)					
Time	8.6	6.3	2.3	10.5	5.8
Newsweek	45.9	19.4	26.9	38.7	31.2
National Review	77.1	95.4	95.2	100.0	93.1
The Progressive	0.0	0.0	2.3	0.0	0.5
Liberal (-.21 to -1.00)					
Time	25.9	53.2	64.4	42.1	49.8
Newsweek	21.3	58.3	52.2	45.2	45.0
National Review	14.3	0.0	0.0	0.0	2.5
The Progressive	90.0	92.3	93.2	96.3	92.8
Balanced (-.20 to +.20)					
Time	65.5	40.5	33.3	47.4	44.4
Newsweek	32.8	22.2	20.9	16.1	23.4
National Review	8.6	4.7	4.8	0.0	4.4
The Progressive	10.0	7.7	4.6	3.7	6.7

Progressive) were highly consistent in their coverage of the four issue areas. More than nine in ten articles in *The Progressive* received adjusted bias scores less than -.20 (defined as liberal). Similarly, over 90 percent of the *National Review* articles received adjusted bias scores greater than +.20 (defined as conservative). By comparison, fewer than half of the articles coded for *Newsweek* and *Time* received a score within these ranges. In contrast, 23 percent and 44 percent of articles in *Newsweek* and *Time* respectively received scores that were defined as "balanced" by our measure. In fact, eighteen percent of *Time* articles received 0.0 adjusted bias scores. The number of "balanced" articles in the two mainstream newsmagazines was significantly larger than the number of articles scored as "balanced" in the *National Review* and *The Progressive*. Only about 5 percent of *National Review* and *Progressive* articles received a "balanced" adjusted bias score.

"Balanced" coverage should not be equated with neutral or positionless coverage. The measure takes into account how each element weighs against the others. For example, while equal numbers of explicitly liberal and conservative sources may "cancel out" or "nullify" source bias, the incorporation of only liberal perspectives on whom to blame (causes), and how to alleviate the problem (solutions) would result in an overall negative (liberal) adjusted bias score. (The role of sources in bias is discussed more fully in Chapter 5.) There were cases, however, when "balanced" truly meant that the opposing views were given "equal" voice. For example, *Time* magazine published an article entitled "Who Should Still Be on Welfare" in August 1999. The article cites thirteen sources— five neutral, four conservative, and four liberal, resulting in a 0.0 score for sources. These sources range from former Republican Congressman Fred Grandy, who argues that "Tough love has its place in welfare reform," to a National Governor's Association report which criticizes pressuring welfare recipients to work when few jobs are available which earn enough to lift them out of poverty.[1] The article also alternates between liberal and conservative assessments of the cause of welfare and possible solutions:

> At the heart of the fight over hard-to-serve people is a dispute over character. Are they, as liberals say, workers held back by lack of skills, child-care problems, and other facts beyond their control? Or are they, as conservatives insist, underachievers at best and shirkers at worst?[2]

Comparing Bias across Issue Areas

Mean adjusted bias scores also illustrate the stark differences between *Time* and *Newsweek* and the *National Review* and *The Progressive*. For all issue areas combined, the *National Review* and *The Progressive* received mean adjusted bias scores of +0.610 and -0.605 respectively (see Table 4.3). The mean adjusted bias scores for *Time* and *Newsweek* were -0.228 and -0.086 respectively. Bias levels in coverage varied significantly across issue areas for three of the four publications examined for this study. Mean adjusted bias scores in *The Progressive*'s coverage of crime, environment, gender, and poverty did not vary significantly from each other. For the *National Review*, this difference was due in large part to the coverage of crime (Mean=+0.393, sd=.43). The *National Review* coverage of the three remaining issue areas received remarkably similar overall mean bias scores. The large standard deviation obtained for this issue area reflects the divergent conservative perspectives on one type of crime: drug use. Coverage of drug use, the drug war, and drug crime in the *National Review* included both libertarian (legalization, decriminalization) and more traditional conservative (mandatory sentencing, greater law enforcement) viewpoints on the issue. Based on our measurement model, the libertarian perspective on drugs was coded as a "liberal" viewpoint, resulting in a less "conservative" mean adjusted bias score and higher standard deviation for crime coverage in this publication.

Table 4.3 Mean Adjusted Bias by Issue Area

	Time[a]	*Newsweek*[b]	*National Review*[c]	*The Progressive*[d]
Crime	-.051	.150	.391	-.543
	(.21)	(.44)	(.43)	(.28)
Environment	-.222	-.213	.610	-.617
	(.29)	(.45)	(.22)	(.22)
Gender	-.367	-.190	.672	-.602
	(.35)	(.48)	(.24)	(.28)
Poverty	-.163	-.035	.671	-.605
	(.27)	(.50)	(.22)	(.24)
Total	-.228	-.086	.610	-.605
	(.32)	(.48)	(.29)	(.24)

Note: Standard deviation in parentheses.
[a] *Time* $F=13.765$, $df=3,239$, $p<.01$
[b] *Newsweek* $F=8.409$, $df=3,227$, $p<.01$
[c] *National Review* $F=9.250$ $df=3,200$ $p<.01$
[d] *The Progressive* $F=0.178$, $df=3,191$, n.s.

While there were substantial variations in bias levels across the four publications examined, emphasis should be placed on how *Time* and *Newsweek* vary generally from coverage in partisan publications and how the two publications differ from each other in their coverage of the four issue areas we examined. It means little to say that *Time* and *Newsweek*, two putatively non-partisan publications, are less biased than the *National Review* and *The Progressive*, two publications widely recognized for their partisanship. However, two conclusions are suggested by the comparison. First, *Time* and *Newsweek* are significantly more "balanced" than their partisan counterparts. Second, like their partisan counterparts, the newsmagazines' coverage of the selected issue areas has been remarkably consistent over the twenty-five year period of study. "Balanced" coverage here should not be interpreted as "unbiased" but rather reflects the clustering of mean bias scores within the balanced region for articles appearing in *Time* and *Newsweek*. Individual articles examined in *Time* and *Newsweek* included both very liberal and very conservative adjusted bias scores. Balanced coverage, then, means that taken together, mean bias scores for these articles resulted in overall coverage was close to 0.0 (and therefore "balanced").

Partisan Publications and Bias Consistency

The overwhelming majority (98.5 percent) of the articles published in the two partisan publications analyzed contained some level of bias. 95.1 percent of *National Review* articles were coded as "conservatively" biased and 97.4 percent of *Progressive* articles contained a "liberal" bias. Fewer than two percent (four *Progressive* and two *National Review* articles) received a 0.0 overall bias score, meaning the article was "balanced" or contained no evident bias in the combination of sources cited or the causes, costs or solutions discussed.

Nine articles received "crossover" bias scores. *The Progressive* contained only one article receiving a positive (conservative) bias score and the *National Review* published eight articles (14.3 percent) receiving negative (liberal) bias scores. Seven of the eight negatively scored *National Review* articles focused on drug use, drug policy, and criminal enforcement of drug laws. Throughout much of the twenty-five years of study, the *National Review* provided two opposing viewpoints on drug use and drug laws: a libertarian view advocating decriminalization of drugs, and more traditional conservative arguments emphasizing mandatory sentencing and stiffer penalties for drug offenses. Legalization arguments focused on support for medical marijuana statutes, critiques of the war on drugs, and attacks on drug laws as restrictions on personal liberties.

On February 12, 1996, the *National Review* published "The War on Drugs Is Lost." The article is prefaced with an editorial statement regarding the history of the journal's coverage of this issue and the process leading to its shift in position:

> It is our judgment that the war on drugs has failed, that it is diverting intelligent energy away from how to deal with the problem of addiction, that it is wasting our resources, and that it is encouraging civil, judicial, and penal procedures associated with police states. We all agree on movement toward legalization, even though we may differ on just how far.[3]

Coverage of drugs and drug-related issues published after this date consistently take the libertarian view. The average bias score for articles covering crime prior to this date was +0.44; after this article, the average bias score was +0.19. As subtopics (drugs, street crime, gun control) were not recorded as part of this analysis, it was not possible to measure the full effect of this shift (based on t-tests, these differences were not significant at the .05 level). However, as discussed above, coverage of drugs resulted in seven of the eight negatively (liberal) scored articles found in the *National Review*, suggesting that coverage of drugs influenced the journal's bias score for this issue area.

Findings suggest a high level of consistency in media bias across topics and over time for these two partisan publications. The *National Review* and *The Progressive* have, with only minor exceptions, covered crime, the environment, gender issues, and poverty in much the same way from 1975 to 2000. The greatest variation was found in coverage of crime by the *National Review*, scores due largely to its bifurcated coverage of drugs and the drug war. A more detailed discussion of the impact of historical, political, and social events on coverage in the four publications is provided in Chapter 6.

Not only did the *National Review* and *The Progressive* maintain a consistent bias in their coverage over time, but their levels of bias were nearly identical over the four issue areas examined. Once again, coverage of crime provides an exception given the increasing dominance of libertarian views toward drug use in the *National Review*.

Comparing Coverage of Issues in *Time* and *Newsweek*

Coverage of the four issue areas in *Time* and *Newsweek* reveal variation between the levels of bias present in coverage for the two newsmagazines (see Table 4.4). *Time* was significantly more liberal than *Newsweek* in its overall coverage of the four issue areas (based on total mean adjusted bias scores). In addition, for each of the four issue areas examined, *Newsweek*'s coverage was less biased (closer to 0.0). Coverage in *Newsweek* for all four issue areas had greater variability in bias, with larger standard deviations in mean bias scores than *Time* (sd=0.48 for *Newsweek* overall compared to sd=0.32 for *Time* overall). This finding suggests that *Newsweek*'s coverage provided more diversity in perspectives than did *Time*'s.

Crime
The coverage of crime in *Time* and *Newsweek* differed significantly over the period of study. It should be pointed out, however, that the mean bias scores for coverage of crime for both publications were among the least biased (i.e. average scores closest to 0.0) for the four issue areas examined. *Newsweek*'s coverage of crime was more conservative and represents the only instance where the mean average bias score is greater than 0.0. Nearly half (45.9 percent) of *News-*

week's articles on crime received adjusted bias scores greater than +0.20, or conservative as defined by the parameters of our measure (See Table 4.2). As is true of all of the issue areas examined, *Newsweek*'s coverage was more varied (based on standard deviation scores) than *Time*'s. Coverage of crime in *Time* magazine was more balanced. Nearly two-thirds of all crime-related articles in *Time* received adjusted bias scores in the "balanced" range, compared to approximately one-third of *Newsweek* articles scoring in this range. Two articles can be used to illustrate crime coverage in *Time* and *Newsweek*.

Table 4.4 Mean Adjusted Bias by Issue Area for *Time* and *Newsweek*

	Time	*Newsweek*
Crime [a]	-.051	.150
	(.21)	(.44)
Environment [b]	-.222	-.213
	(.29)	(.45)
Gender [c]	-.367	-.190
	(.35)	(.48)
Poverty [d]	-.163	-.035
	(.27)	(.50)
Total [e]	-.228	-.086
	(.32)	(.48)

Note: Standard deviation in parentheses.
[a] $t = -3.17$, $df = 117$, $p<.01$
[b] $t = -1.51$, $df = 149$, n.s.
[c] $t = -2.66$, $df = 152$, $p<.01$
[d] $t = -1.01$, $df = 48$, n.s.
[e] $t = -3.79$, $df = 472$, $p<.01$

A *Newsweek* article titled "New Federal War on Drugs" (abs= +0.67) argues that more money is needed to fund the current program. [4] The article criticizes Reagan's budget proposal to cut monies for the DEA and Customs offices and flat-line allocation to the Justice Department and implies that President Reagan's plan to "link up the resources of the Drug Enforcement Administration, the Internal Revenue Service, the FBI and the Treasury Department" may make the drug investigation and prosecution processes less rather than more effective. [5]

The character of *Time*'s coverage of crime issues is illustrated by its June 15, 1996, cover story, "Law and Order" (abs=-0.01) by senior writer Richard Lacayo. The article responds to data indicating that, while still distressingly high, after decades of increases, rates of violent crimes were falling across the entire country. Thirteen sources were cited in the article. Using the criteria specified in Table 3.2, one of these was classified as conservative, two as liberal, and the remaining ten as ideologically neutral. The article does not mention that the costs of violent crime in America are borne disproportionately by minorities and by the poor. While some might find ideological meaning in this omission, our measure of bias analyzes media contents, not exclusions, however the latter might be assessed. Consequently, the article's adjusted bias score was calculated on the basis of three, rather than four factors.

The story cites the "usual suspects" to account, in part, for the reduction of violent crime. These include: a decline in the proportion of young males in the general population, the leveling off of crack cocaine use, a moderate unemployment rate, and tougher sentencing that get more felons off the street and keeps them off longer. Taken as a whole, this set of causes is neither conservative nor liberal as we believe politicians, journalists, and the politically interested public understand these labels in discussions of crime rates.

Proactive community policing and creating local task forces focused on deterring specific problems are offered as promising new approaches to crime. "For decades, (experts) held that crime was too deeply connected to underlying social causes, meaning everything from the state of the economy to the breakdown of the family. Such things are still assumed to play their part in producing crime. What has changed is the view that police are useful only to chase down bad guys after they strike."[6] The argument is that public policy can make a difference and that police can make a difference. Such a view is not readily understood as conservative or as liberal.

Environment

Coverage of the environment and environmental issues was similar in *Time* and *Newsweek*. Mean adjusted bias scores for the two publications were not significantly different. Once again, however, *Newsweek*'s coverage was more varied (sd=0.45) than coverage in *Time* (sd=0.29). Reporting in *Time* was more moderate overall, receiving few extremely conservative or extremely liberal scores.

Newsweek's coverage included articles scoring at both ends of the bias spectrum over the period of study. Strongly conservative articles blame environmentalists for lost jobs and slowing economic progress. An article from 1976 asserted that recent court cases favoring environmental groups had strengthened the movement, which increasingly was looking to the courts for satisfaction (abs = +0.78). The article discussed a decision that effectively blocked the construction of a coal powered power plant in Utah, which "would have provided 3,500 jobs and increased payrolls by up to $100 million"[7] and the designation of a section of the New River in North Carolina as a national scenic river, barring the construction of a proposed dam. "Hundreds of cases now await litigation, and in many of them, the environmentalists have a good chance of accomplishing precisely what Utah's Rampton said killed Kaiparowits (proposed coal powered plant): delaying and starving their opposition to death in endless legal wrangles."[8] In contrast, a 1999 article (abs = -1.00) cites weak regulations for limiting emissions and "urban sprawl" as causes of a warming trend in Great Lakes waters.[9] "Even if everyone plays by the rules, megatons of greenhouse gases will continue to waft into the stratosphere for decades to come."[10]

Gender

Mean adjusted bias scores for gender coverage was significantly different for the two newsmagazines. *Time*'s coverage of gender was significantly more liberal than that found in *Newsweek*. In fact, *Time* magazine's coverage of gender represents the only instance where the average bias scores lies far outside of the "balanced" range of -0.20 to +0.20 (see Table 4.1).

Newsweek coverage of gender ranged widely (*sd*=0.48). This variation is due, in part, to the inclusion of columnists in *Newsweek* who provide partisan commentary on a variety of social and political issues. George Will, an opinion writer for the *Washington Post* and a regular columnist for *Newsweek*, offers a consistently conservative viewpoint for the newsmagazine. One of Will's articles, "A Cold War among Women" (abs= +0.73), examines the increased expectations of women brought by feminism and women's liberation.[11] Blaming academic psychology and sociology for making women uncomfortable in their roles as mother and housewife, Will argues that "women were especially susceptible to the postwar feeling of expansiveness and possibility" which led many outside of their homes and into employment.[12] A second example (abs= +0.79) from 1996 comes from columnist Kenneth L. Woodward, who lambasts United Church of Christ's revision of their hymnals to remove what church officials deemed sexist references.[13] Woodward laments that the "hymn doctors," in changing "Son of God" in the Hymn "Silent Night" to "Child of God," have "neutered Jesus."[14] In addition to avoiding "male pronouns for God," Woodward adds that some of these changes offer "new and frankly feminist creations" not previously included in earlier hymnal editions.[15]

Other *Newsweek* articles addressing gender issues scored as strongly liberal in their bias. "The Battle over Abortion" published in 1989 is one example.[16] The article (abs= -0.64) cites several representatives and executives from the Planned Parenthood Federation and NARAL and points to the efforts of pro-life groups to overturn the existing regulations. The article also makes clear that most Americans support abortion, quoting a clinic director who points out that "Americans favor abortion in the case of rape, incest, and their own personal circumstance."[17]

Time's coverage of gender issues was more consistent over the period of study (based on a smaller standard deviation). Nearly two-thirds of *Time*'s articles on gender scored as "liberal" and only 2.3 percent (10 articles) received adjusted bias scores within the "conservative" range (compared to 26.9 percent of *Newsweek* articles on gender). *Time*'s coverage of gender was the most liberally biased of all four issue areas. This is illustrated by a cover story on women's equality (abs= -0.77) in which journalist Jay Cocks dismisses what he terms "shoofly Schlaflyisms" that "men and women will be less distinctive, or less sexual, if they work at the same jobs or compete at the same sports."[18] He counters:

> Equality does not eradicate differences in gender, it exalts them, which should be some comfort to cowering sexists still clinging to every advantage they have ever wrangled or wrung out of women. Equality is only a threat if reality is. In the rubble of busted pedestals and shredded stereotypes are the pieces of a new perception: of the real, working, workable way of equality, of self-awareness, of mutual respect.[19]

Poverty

Poverty received the least coverage of the four issue areas examined (see Table 4.2). *Newsweek* devoted thirty-one articles and *Time* devoted only nineteen articles to the topic which met the criteria for inclusion in our study. As noted above, *Newsweek*'s coverage was more varied (sd=0.50) than *Time*'s (sd=0.27). This variation reflected presentation of both strongly liberal and strongly conservative positions on the issue of poverty.

Newsweek was more likely to publish articles scored as "conservative" than *Time*, but the differences between mean adjusted bias scores were not significant. More than one-third of *Newsweek* articles received "conservative" adjusted bias scores, compared to only 10.5 percent of *Time* articles. Both newsmagazines were critical of the proposed welfare reform of the 1990s. For example, Joe Klein, a *Newsweek* contributor, was skeptical of the proposed legislation to improve the situation of those in poverty. In a 1996 article (abs = -0.78) that was published following the passage of the Personal Responsibility and Work Reconciliation Act, he deemed the "current welfare system . . . an abomination. It is inflexible, bureaucratic, heartless."[20] Likewise, *Time* contributors Nancy Gibbs and Cathy Booth wrote that existing welfare programs excluded many of the working poor who struggle to make ends meet who are ineligible for many traditional welfare programs because they earn incomes at or just above the poverty line (abs= -0.53). "When Capitol Hill revolutionaries vow to lift millions of Americans off the dole and into the work force, this is where they would land first, among the more than ten million Americans who hover one rung above welfare on the nation's 'ladder of opportunity.'"[21]

Consistency in Coverage of Issues over Time

The four publications maintained high levels of consistency in their coverage of each of the four issue areas over the twenty-five years of coverage examined. Regression lines show very little change in levels of bias over time (see Figures 4.1–4.4). The largest changes can be seen in the *National Review*'s coverage of the environment (r^2=0.13, p<.05; Durbin-Watson=1.59, p<.05), which became more conservative over time. Additionally, *Newsweek*'s coverage of gender

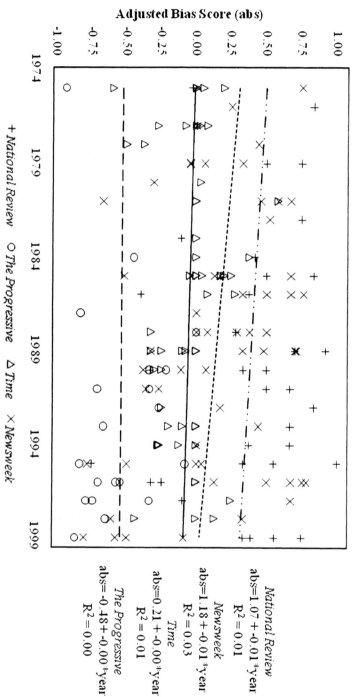

Figure 4.1 Articles on Crime

+ National Review   ○ The Progressive   △ Time   × Newsweek

National Review
abs=1.07 + -0.01*year
R² = 0.01

Newsweek
abs=1.18 + -0.01*year
R² = 0.03

Time
abs=0.21 + -0.00*year
R² = 0.01

The Progressive
abs=-0.48 + -0.00*year
R² = 0.00

Figure 4.2 Articles on Environment

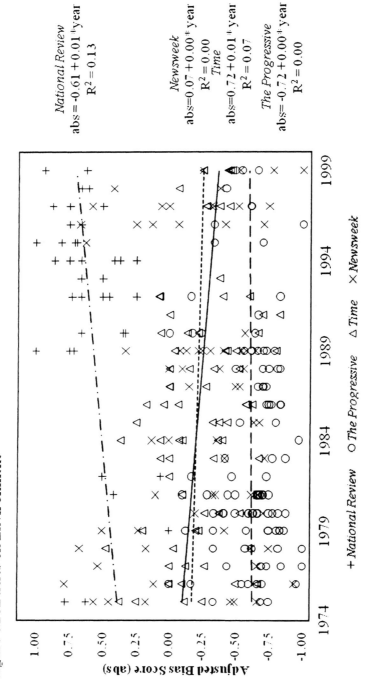

National Review
abs = -0.61 + 0.01*year
$R^2 = 0.13$

Newsweek
abs = 0.07 + 0.00*year
$R^2 = 0.00$
Time
abs = 0.72 + 0.01*year
$R^2 = 0.07$

The Progressive
abs = -0.72 + 0.00*year
$R^2 = 0.00$

+ *National Review*   O *The Progressive*   △ *Time*   × *Newsweek*

Figure 4.3 Articles on Gender

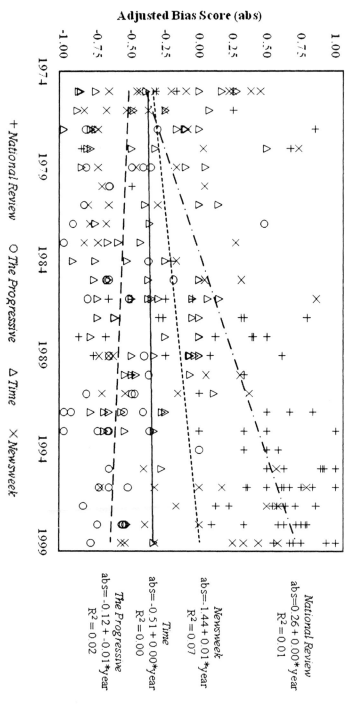

Adjusted Bias Score (abs)

+ *National Review*   O *The Progressive*   △ *Time*   ✕ *Newsweek*

National Review
abs=0.26+0.00*year
R²=0.01

Newsweek
abs=-1.44+0.01*year
R²=0.07

Time
abs=-0.51+0.00*year
R²=0.00

The Progressive
abs=-0.12+-0.01*year
R²=0.02

Figure 4.4 Articles on Poverty

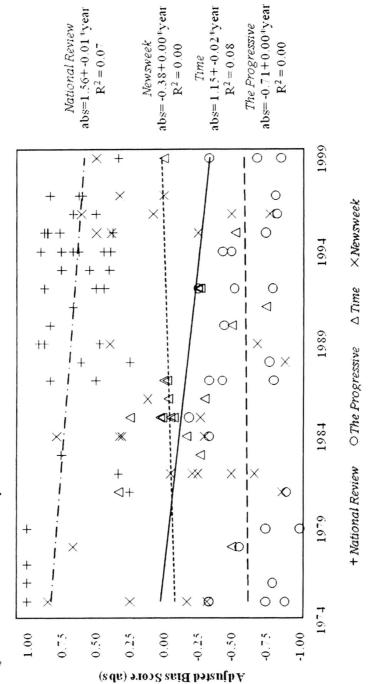

National Review
abs=1.56+-0.01*year
$R^2 = 0.07$

Newsweek
abs=-0.38+0.00*year
$R^2 = 0.00$

Time
abs=1.15+-0.02*year
$R^2 = 0.08$

The Progressive
abs=-0.71+0.00*year
$R^2 = 0.00$

Adjusted Bias Score (abs)

+ National Review   ○ The Progressive   △ Time   × Newsweek shifted significantly closer (r^2=0.08, p<.05; Durbin-Watson=1.73, p<.05) to "balanced" or 0.0 from 1975 to 1999 and *Time*'s coverage of the environment became more "liberal" (r^2=0.07, p<.05; Durbin-Watson=1.96, p<.05) during the same period. The Durbin-Watson values indicate that none of these differences appear to be due to time trend effects. However, it is important to note that, in the cases of *Time* and *Newsweek*, overall bias scores for both issue areas lie near or within the "balanced" category (see Table 4.3). While significant, these shifts in coverage reflect neither a turn to the right by *Newsweek* in its coverage of gender nor a turn to the left by *Time* in its coverage of the environment.

Newsweek had a larger standard deviation in overall adjusted bias scores and for adjusted bias scores for each issue area than *Time* (and the other two publications). Its overall bias scores, however (with the exception of crime) were closer to 0.0 (balanced). Individual articles may be more "biased" but overall coverage appears to be "balanced" (based on overall adjusted mean scores). This may be due, in part, to *Newsweek*'s regular columns such as "My Turn," "Judgment Calls," and "Public Lives" which feature partisan commentators such as Milton Freedman, Meg Greenfield, Joe Klein, and Robert Samuelson. Because we believe that discussion of any bias of a media outlet should include consideration not only of its news reports but its editorial contents as well, this study did not distinguish between news items and commentaries in the content analysis. It is not clear that any ideological bias found in the one will be replicated in the other. For example, Entman[22] reports disjunctions between newspaper coverage supporting United States military interventions in Granada, Libya, the Balkans, and Somalia and their editorials demonizing administrations for these very actions. Future research might further investigate the relationship between the ideological bias appearing in the news reports of various newspapers, newsmagazines, and television news organizations and that expressed in their editorials.

Proposing Solutions

As discussed in Chapter 3, media coverage of social issues often does not propose potential solutions. This failure contributes to a sense that social problems cannot be alleviated, or that solutions are beyond the reach of individuals or society at large. Of the nearly nine hundred articles examined, more than one-third (39.2 percent) failed to discuss potential solutions to the issues presented. *The Progressive* was the least likely of the four publications examined to propose solutions to their readers, with less than half (47.2 percent) of its articles posing solutions (see Table 4.5).

The inclusion of solutions differed significantly among the newsmagazines examined for three of the issue areas: crime, environment, and poverty. Cramer's *V* values indicate a moderate association between publication and the inclusion of solutions for crime and the environment. This association was strong (Cramer's V=0.34) for articles on poverty. Articles published in the four news-magazines on gender issues did not differ in their likelihood of including a discussion of solutions. In addition, there were no significant differences in the inclusion of solutions between *Time* and *Newsweek* for any of the issue areas.

Table 4.5 Percentage of Articles Not Addressing Solutions

	Crime[c]	Environment[d]	Gender[e]	Poverty[f]	Total[a]
Time[g]	24.1	30.4	42.5	21.1	32.5
	(14)	(24)	(37)	(4)	(79)
Newsweek	26.2	44.4	46.3	41.9	39.8
	(16)	(32)	(31)	(13)	(92)
National	14.3	41.9	46.4	14.3	33.3
Review[h]	(5)	(18)	(39)	(6)	(68)
The	60.0	57.7	38.6	51.9	52.8
Progressive	(12)	(60)	(17)	(14)	(103)
Total[b]	27.0	45.0	44.0	31.1	39.2
	(47)	(134)	(124)	(37)	(342)

Note: Frequency in parentheses
[a] Chi-Square (between magazines overall) =22.76, df=3, p<.01, Cramer's V=0.16.
[b] Chi-Square (between topics overall) = 20.98, df=3, p<.01, Cramer's V=0.16.
[c] Chi-Square (between magazines) = 10.44, df=3, p<.05, Cramer's V=0.24.
[d] Chi-Square (between magazines) = 13.77, df=3, p<.01, Cramer's V=0.22.
[e] Chi-Square (between magazines) = 0.93, df=3, *n.s.*, Cramer's V=0.06.
[f] Chi-Square (between magazines) = 13.56, df=3, p<.01, Cramer's V=0.34.
[g] Chi-Square (between *Time* and *Newsweek*) = 2.74, df=1, *n.s.*, Cramer's V=0.02.
[h] Chi-Square (the *National Review* and *The Progressive*) = 15.46, df=1, *n.s.*, Cramer's V=0.07.

Topically, solutions were most likely to be posed within articles dealing with crime and poverty. Articles on environmental problems and gender issues were less likely to include a discussion of possible solutions. This is not surprising since both crime and poverty are closely connected to well-defined public policy and legislative positions. For crime, mandatory sentencing regulations, additional monies for rehabilitation, gun control legislation, decriminalization (for drugs), and enforcing three-strike laws are law-and criminal justice–based solutions. An increase or decrease in benefits, more job training, and employment requirements for beneficiaries are policy based solutions to the problem of poverty. A wide variety of issues were included as "gender" related, many of which do not have well-defined policy solutions. While abortion can be associated with a repeal (for those who are pro-life) or protection (for those who are pro-choice) of *Roe v. Wade*, this type of clear solution is not available for other gender issues such as divorce, sexual harassment, or feminism. The relative absence of solutions for the environment is more difficult to explain, however. It may be related to the findings of Dreier[23] and Gamson et al.,[24] which focus on blaming government agencies for their failure to protect citizens (or the environment) or declaring a problem (such as pollution) too great to be solved.

Table 4.6 Adjusted Bias Scores Based on Inclusion of Solutions

Issue Area	Solutions Present	Solutions Absent
Time		
Crime	-0.059	-0.023
Environment	-0.232	-0.200
Gender	-0.405	-0.316
Poverty	-0.141	-0.242
Overall	-0.233	-0.225
Newsweek		
Crime[a]	+0.070	+0.375
Environment	-0.156	-0.259
Gender[b]	-0.032	-0.326
Poverty[c]	+0.115	-0.243
Overall	-0.121	-0.034
National Review		
Crime	+0.365	+0.511
Environment	+0.604	+0.618
Gender[d]	+0.722	+0.614
Poverty	+0.697	+0.517
Overall	+0.615	+0.599
The Progressive		
Crime	-0.602	-0.503
Environment	-0.663	-0.584
Gender	-0.591	-0.619
Poverty	-0.674	-0.544
Overall	-0.639	-0.575

[a] $t = +2.501$, $df=59$, $p<.05$
[b] $t = +2.615$, $df=65$, $p<.05$
[c] $t = -2.052$, $df=29$, $p<.05$
[d] $t = -2.084$, $df=82$, $p<.05$

In general, bias was not related to the inclusion or exclusion of solutions. There were no significant differences in mean bias scores for articles including or not including a discussion of solutions overall for any of the four publications examined. In addition, there were only four issue areas for any of the publications where there was a significant difference between articles containing solution discussions and those which did not contain a discussion of solutions (see Table 4.6). Three of these instances were found in *Newsweek* magazines, where discussions of crime, gender, and poverty were significantly more balanced (closer to 0.0) when solutions were present in the article. The final instance of this is found in the *National Review*, where coverage of gender was significantly more conservative when solutions were discussed. The tendency for *Newsweek* coverage to be more balanced (less biased) when solutions were discussed may speak to the importance of moving beyond the "blaming" of opponents that may contribute to biased coverage of issues in mainstream media.

Discussion

One of the most important findings of this research is the overall "centrist" nature of *Time* and *Newsweek*'s coverage of the four issue areas between 1975 and 2000. The only significant difference found between the mean adjusted bias scores for *Time* and *Newsweek* was for coverage of crime (*Newsweek* mean=+0.150, *Time* mean= -0.051). Even with this difference in coverage, both means lie within our "centrist" or "balanced" category (-0.20 to +0.20). These findings provide little support for the claims about substantial liberal or conservative media bias in elite "mainstream" media. At most, what can be said is that, during this twenty-five year period, with respect to crime, environment, gender, and poverty, coverage in *Time* and *Newsweek* tended center-left. The one possible exception to this is *Time*'s coverage of gender, which lay outside the "centrist" or "balanced" score category (mean= -0.367). However, this value is still starkly more balanced than the bias levels found in both the *National Review* (mean abs= +0.672) and *The Progressive* (mean abs= -0.602) in their coverage of gender.

In addition, the impressive consistency in coverage over the twenty-five year period of study should be emphasized. Claims that media "adjust" their coverage to changes in political climate are not supported by this finding. The period of study covers five presidential administrations (three Republican, two Democratic) and numerous "significant" political, social, and legislative events for each issue area (Three Mile Island disaster, debate over "partial birth abortion," welfare reform, mandatory sentencing laws for drug crimes, etc.). It is important to point out, however, that regression lines cannot fully take into account short-term shifts in coverage within a long time period. Chapter 6 will deal more fully with the impact of historical context on coverage.

Several caveats must be reiterated. This research does not definitively conclude that there is no or little bias in "mainstream" newsmagazines across the entire spectrum of political, social, and economic issues. Nor does it imply that there is no variation in coverage of an issue within a single publication. Figures 4.1 through 4.4 illustrate the variation in coverage for each of the four issues areas across the publications examined. Just over one-quarter (28.7 percent) of *Newsweek* articles and nearly 14.4 percent of articles analyzed in *Time* magazine received bias scores greater than +0.60 or less than -0.60 which could be defined as strongly biased. We have repeatedly noted the high levels of variation in adjusted bias scores for *Time* and *Newsweek* in their coverage of the four issue areas selected. The lack of significant bias found overall, however, indicates that while conservatively or liberally biased articles were present in both publications, a single biased perspective did not dominate the discussion of an issue but were countered or mitigated with articles offering opposing opinions and articles which were "balanced" in their coverage.

This research does provide suggestive evidence that for the coverage of crime, environment, gender, and poverty in *Time* and *Newsweek* during the twenty-five years examined, claims of bias by both the left and the right may be exaggerated. Our failure to find significant bias in coverage of this set of social issues is consistent with the failure of other studies to find partisan bias in news reporting on presidential campaigns, about which liberals and conservatives also have expressed objections.[25]

Although, given our methodology, it seems to us unlikely, researchers applying the measurement instrument used in this study, who select different publications, and examine different time periods, may find results that vary from those reported here. As noted earlier, bias in international issues may vary from bias in domestic issues. Likewise, bias in coverage of domestic issues not examined in this research (such as education, race, capital punishment, gun control) may differ from those examined in this analysis. What is clear from these findings, however, is a critical need for additional research which applies clear, methodologically sound models (whether quantitative or qualitative) to examine the issue of ideological bias in mainstream media.

Notes

1. Adam Cohen and Hilary Hylton, "Who Should Still Be on Welfare?" *Time* (August 16, 1999), 22–28.

2. "Who Should Still Be on Welfare?" 26–27.

3. "The War on Drugs is Lost," *National Review* (February 1996), 34.

4. "New Federal War on Drugs," *Newsweek* (May 11, 1981), 27.

5. "New Federal War on Drugs," 27, 28.

6. Richard Lacayo, "Law and Order," *Time* (June 15, 1996), 51.

7. Susan Fraker and Evert Clark, "Environment: Double Header," *Newsweek* (April 26, 1976), 32.

8. "Environment: Double Header," 32.

9. Peter Annin and Sharon Begly, "Great Lake Effect," *Newsweek* (July 5, 1999), 52–54.

10. "Great Lake Effect," 54.

11. George F. Will, "The Cold War among Women," *Newsweek* (June 26, 1978), 100.

12. "The Cold War," 100.

13. Kenneth L. Woodward, "Hymns, Hers, and Theirs," *Newsweek* (February 12, 1996), 75.

14. "Hymns, Hers, and Theirs," 75.

15. "Hymns, Hers, and Theirs," 75.

16. Eloise Salholz, Ann McDaniel, Patrick King, Nadine Joseph, Gregory Cerio, and Ginny Carroll, "The Battle over Abortion," *Newsweek* (May 1, 1989), 28–32.

17. "The Battle over Abortion," 29.

18. Jay Cocks, "How Long Till Equality?" *Time* (July 12, 1982), 29.

19. "How Long Till Equality?" 29.

20. Joe Klein, "Monumental Callousness," *Newsweek* (August 12, 1996), 45.

21. Nancy Gibbs and Cathy Booth, "Working Harder, Getting Nowhere" *Time*, July 3, 1995, 17–18.

22. Robert M. Entman, *Projections of Power: Framing News, Public Opinion, and U.S. Foreign Policy* (Chicago: University of Chicago Press, 2004).

23. Peter Dreier, "How the Media Compound Urban Problems," *Journal of Urban Affairs* 27, no. 2 (2005): 193–201.

24. William A. Gamson, David Croteau, William Hoynes, and Theodore Sasson, "Media Images and the Social Construction of Reality" *Annual Review of Sociology* 18 (1992): 373–393.

25. Dave D'Alessio and Mike Allen, "Media Bias in Presidential Elections: A Meta-Analysis," *Journal of Communication* 50, no. 4 (2000): 133–157; C. Richard Hofstetter, *Bias in the News: Network Television Coverage of the 1972 Election Campaign* (Columbus: Ohio State University Press, 1976); Marion R. Just, Ann N. Crigler, Dean E. Alger, and Timothy E. Cook, *Crosstalk: Citizens, Candidates, and the Media in a Presidential Campaign* (Chicago: University of Chicago Press, 1996); Thomas E. Patterson, *The Mass Media Election: How Americans Choose Their President* (New York: Praeger, 1980); Thomas E. Patterson and Robert D. McClure, *The Unseeing Eye: The Myth of Television Power in National Elections* (New York: G. P. Putnam's Sons, 1976).

Chapter 5

The Use of Information Sources in Partisan Publications

As noted in previous chapters, considerable responsibility has been assigned to information sources for the bias supposedly found in mainstream news media. Here we examine source use by the *National Review* and *The Progressive* to determine their role in producing the viewpoints that characterize these explicitly partisan publications. Our findings call into question the assumption that reliance on certain categories of sources, such as public officials or government agencies, by either mainstream or partisan media, necessarily produces accounts that express a particular ideological bias.

The Role of Sources

In the introduction to his pioneering study of news production, Leon Sigal critiques two views of the relationships among the press, the government, and the public in a democracy.[1] The first, which he terms "classical democratic theory," maintains that the press provides the electorate with politically relevant information and that, on the basis of this information and a consideration of their own interests, citizens vote to elect officials who they believe will maintain and/or initiate policies they support. This can be diagrammed:

press → electorate → officials → policy. The model addresses neither the question of the sources used by the press in making the news nor the nature of news itself.

A second model, which Sigal identifies as a variant of classical democratic theory, portrays the press as a "surrogate for public opinion" that directly affects policymakers. While details of the relationship between the press and public opinion are not fully specified in Sigal's statement of this view, the model can be diagrammed: press ↔ public opinion → officials → policy. Here, news sources are not discussed and apparently are not problematic. What appears to matter most is that the public, presumably informed by the press, reacts in ways subsequently reported to the public and to policymakers. It is press accounts of public opinion to which officials respond in determining policy. The active role played by officials and the press in the construction of public opinion is not considered.

Sigal's own research, focusing on the interactions of reporters and officials in the news rooms of the *New York Times*, the *Washington Post*, and the Washington bureau of the *Times*, found that officials were the sources of more than half of all news items, and that more than 70 percent of news items were drawn from situations, such as interviews, press conferences, press releases, and official proceedings, over which newsmakers had either complete or substantial control. Such findings led Sigal to view press-government relations in a way that ignores the public. His model can be diagrammed: press ↔ officials → policy.

Consistent with this model, subsequent studies have also found that, although there is an enormous array of information sources potentially available, media tend to rely heavily on key spokespersons from particular bureaucratic organizations that serve as routine, predictable providers of material.[2] News gathering has come to be understood largely as "a matter of the representative of one bureaucracy (the news organization) picking up prefabricated news items from representatives of another bureaucracy."[3]

Media analysts have claimed that official sources are used to cite the "facts of the case" without further investigation.[4] Reliance on officials as "primary definers" has been seen widely as producing news that reflects dominant social values and narrow boundaries established by institutional elites. Media generally fail to examine the claims and perspectives of state agents in an independent, critical manner and report events in ways supporting established policies. Reliance on elite sources produces media accounts that are ideologically conservative in terms of the surrounding political culture.[5]

Researchers investigating media coverage of a wide range of both international and domestic issues have emphasized this conclusion. For example, studies of reporting of the Vietnam War called attention to the central role played by the White House, the Pentagon and the State Department in supplying information.[6] "Media coverage and interpretation of the war took for granted that the United States intervened in the service of generous ideals, with the goal of defending South Vietnam from aggression and terrorism."[7] Opposition to the war was ridiculed.[8] "The media emphasized the government's position until respected sources widely voiced their dissent."[9] Subsequent studies of the first Gulf War,[10] terrorism,[11] and the war in Iraq[12] produced comparable findings.

In a like manner, studies of media representation of domestic issues emphasized the role of official sources as primary definers of social issues producing accounts that are centrist/conservative in terms of the politics of the period. For example, research on crime reporting called attention to media reliance on White House spokespersons and law enforcement officials at all levels of political organization as information sources. Media tend to politicize crime-related issues through their use of "law and order" rhetoric emphasizing social control rather than social reform.[13] Studies of media reporting on the environment,[14] affirmative action,[15] welfare policy,[16] and the "war of terrorism"[17] also have highlighted the media's institutionalized information gathering practices that tend to produce accounts of issues supporting established authorities and policies.

Officials such as public officeholders and spokespersons for government agencies and business organizations represent legitimated institutions and are referred to as "conventional sources" by journalists.[18] Reporting based on such sources perpetuates the status quo because it does not criticize the existing social order. Alternative viewpoints are less likely to be voiced.[19]

Although studies do give prominence to primary definers as shapers of news content, few have concluded that journalists are mere stenographers to power. Analysts have pointed out that media have the ability to negotiate and struggle with sources over the production of meaning that can mitigate sources' capacity to determine news content.[20] Nevertheless, the prevailing view of media researchers appears to be that although journalists "may be critical of what they are told and of the sources themselves, the sources usually have the first say, thereby putting the critics in a reactive and as such inferior position."[21] Furthermore, there seems to be agreement that in the future "hard news content is likely to remain dominated by the organizational gate keeping model with its symbiotic press-government relations at the core."[22] "Symbiotic press-government relations" are the core of Sigal's model.

Explicitly Partisan and Mainstream Media

John Dewey[23] argued that the grist of democracy is not what the various media tell us; instead, it is the conversation that ensues. This argument had some merit at a time when various independent media provided citizens with a range of perspectives on social and political affairs that informed and animated public discussion and debate. While the number of media in America has grown beyond anything the Dewey was likely to have imagined almost eight decades ago, they are far from independent.[24] Today, the dominant media tend to present a remarkably homogeneous, centrist/conservative, and often cynical view of political life.[25] "No 'extreme' views are considered legitimate, though the characterization of 'extreme' is often applied to politics considered normal in other democracies."[26] Our media system is vastly different from what it was in the eighteenth, nineteenth, and early twentieth centuries, when an ardent partisan press dominated American journalism and served the nation well.[27]

In this present context, it is important to understand the processes by which leading, explicitly partisan media construct accounts of public affairs that express their ideological positions. These accounts offer citizens alternatives to the dominant perspective present in the vast majority of mainstream media. They can inform, enliven, and encourage the political discussion that supposedly is at the heart of political democracy. Although their audience is considerably smaller than that of mainstream outlets, partisan media also can have a more direct impact on participation through the provision of "mobilizing" information such as specific calls to action and the identification of specific opportunities to act.[28] How large a role explicitly partisan media play today in American democracy remains an empirical question. However, it seems likely that the further development of the Internet and other communication technologies will continue to increase their importance.[29]

Sigal found that officials (public officeholders, leaders of large political groups and large bureaucratic organizations) were the sources of more than half of all news items, and that more than 70 percent of news items were drawn from situations, such as interviews, press conferences, press releases, and official proceedings, over which newsmakers had either complete or substantial control.[30] Most researchers concur that journalists do rely heavily on state officials.[31]

The research reviewed above concluded that such heavy reliance on official sources by the mainstream press has resulted in issue coverage the studies characterized as centrist/conservative. This finding, together with the work of Sigal and others, suggests two hypotheses:

Hypothesis 1:   Explicitly conservative publications will employ official sources at least as frequently (for at least 70 percent of their news items) as do mainstream publications.

Hypothesis 2:   Explicitly liberal publications will employ official sources less frequently than do mainstream media.

The following content analysis investigates these hypotheses. Failure to find these patterns would indicate a need to reevaluate previous discussion of the impact of sources on mainstream coverage of social issues. It would also indicate the need for a model of the relations among explicitly partisan publications, the government, and the public in a democracy different from all three of the models of the mainstream press outlined by Sigal.[32]

Sources and Issues

Data presented in Chapter 4 showed that, over the twenty-five-year period, the *National Review* and *The Progressive* published a similar number of total articles on the four issues. Coverage of gender dominated the *National Review*'s coverage of these issues, accounting for more than forty percent of the articles analyzed. Environmental issues were central to *The Progressive* coverage, accounting for more than half of all articles on the four issues selected for analysis. *Progressive* articles on average contained more citations (M=8.39) than *National Review* articles (M=5.01).

For both newsmagazines, frequency of various sources differed significantly by issue (the *National Review* x^2=181.550, df=36, $p<.001$; *The Progressive* x^2=199.37, df=36, p<.001). Cramer's *V* values for both indicate a moderate association between issue area and source type for each publication (see Tables 5.1 and 5.2). For example, experts comprised 24.18 percent of *National Review* citations in articles on crime, but only 4.79 percent of all sources cited in the *National Review* articles on poverty. Officials comprised 27.46 percent of sources in *Progressive* articles on crime, but only 8.48 percent of *The Progressive*'s sources in articles on gender.

If "substantial reliance" on a source type is defined as its use accounting for more than 20 percent of all sources providing information for discussing a particular issue, the following patterns occur: Both the *National Review* and *The Progressive* made considerable use of official sources (public officeholders and government agencies) in their articles on crime and poverty. (As will be noted, this is far less extensive than previous studies have claimed.)

Additional differences between the use of sources by these two partisan newsmagazines should be noted. In no issue area did the *National Review* make considerable use of material provided by advocacy groups or by ordinary

Table 5.1 Source Use in the *National Review* by Issue

Source Type	Crime n	%	Environment n	%	Gender n	%	Poverty n	%	Total n	%
Advocacy Groups/ Spokespersons	4	2.61%	9	4.19%	72	14.15%	2	1.37%	87	8.51%
Books	19	12.42%	10	4.65%	44	8.64%	18	12.33%	91	8.89%
Business Organizations	0	0.00%	5	2.33%	6	1.18%	1	0.68%	12	1.17%
Experts	37	24.18%	49	22.79%	72	14.15%	7	4.79%	165	16.13%
Foundations/ Think Tanks	5	3.27%	12	5.58%	12	2.36%	17	11.64%	46	4.50%
Government Agencies	18	11.76%	30	13.95%	40	7.86%	13	8.90%	101	9.87%
Newsmagazines	1	0.65%	3	1.40%	8	1.57%	2	1.37%	14	1.37%
Newspapers	14	9.15%	15	6.98%	38	7.47%	17	11.64%	84	8.21%
Non-governmental Organizations	0	0.00%	8	3.72%	16	3.14%	5	3.42%	29	2.83%
Officials	35	22.88%	15	6.98%	78	15.32%	32	21.92%	160	15.64%
Ordinary Citizens	1	0.65%	5	2.33%	17	3.34%	16	10.96%	39	3.81%
Polls and Research	13	8.50%	38	17.67%	53	10.41%	7	4.79%	111	10.85%
Other	6	3.92%	16	7.44%	53	10.41%	9	6.16%	84	8.21%
Total	153	99.99%	215	100.00%	509	100.00%	146	100.00%	1023	100.00%
#articles	*35*		*43*		*84*		*42*		*204*	
Mean Number of Sources	*4.37*		*5.00*		*6.06*		*3.48*		*5.01*	

$x^2=181.550, df=36, p<.001$; Cramer's $V=.24$

Table 5.2 Source Use in *The Progressive* by Issue

Source Type	Crime		Environment		Gender		Poverty		Total	Percent
	n	%	*n*	%	*n*	%	*n*	%	*n*	%
Advocacy Groups/ Spokespersons	21	10.88%	125	13.41%	100	29.24%	43	20.48%	289	17.23%
Books	10	5.18%	19	2.04%	17	4.97%	3	1.43%	49	2.92%
Business Organizations	5	2.59%	68	7.30%	17	4.97%	9	4.29%	99	5.90%
Experts	15	7.77%	119	12.77%	35	10.23%	16	7.62%	185	11.03%
Foundations/ Think Tanks	5	2.59%	10	1.07%	5	1.46%	8	3.81%	28	1.67%
Government Agencies	4	2.07%	53	5.69%	7	2.05%	2	0.95%	66	3.94%
Newsmagazines	3	1.55%	11	1.18%	11	3.22%	1	0.48%	26	1.55%
Newspapers	13	6.74%	30	3.22%	14	4.09%	8	3.81%	65	3.88%
Non-governmental Organizations	5	2.59%	22	2.36%	7	2.05%	11	5.24%	45	2.68%
Officials	53	27.46%	215	23.07%	29	8.48%	45	21.43%	342	20.39%
Ordinary Citizens	17	8.81%	160	17.17%	42	12.28%	43	20.48%	262	15.62%
Polls and Research	10	5.18%	42	4.51%	7	2.05%	3	1.43%	62	3.70%
Other	32	16.58%	58	6.22%	51	14.91%	18	8.57%	159	9.48%
Total	193	100.00%	932	100.00%	342	100.00%	210	100.00%	1677	100.00%
#articles	*21*		*104*		*48*		*27*		*200*	
Mean Number of Sources	*9.19*		*8.96*		*7.13*		*7.78*		*8.39*	

x^2=199.317, *df*=36, *p*<.001; Cramer's *V*=.19

citizens. In no issue area did *The Progressive* rely heavily on experts. In addition, neither newsmagazine made extensive use of other media outlets/publications as sources of information in their coverage of these four issue areas. Finally, the *National Review* cited polls and research more frequently than *The Progressive*.

Official Sources

Official sources accounted for approximately one-quarter of all sources cited by the *National Review* (25.51 percent) and by *The Progressive* (24.33 percent). This number represents the sum of two source categories: public officeholders and government agencies (see Table 5.3, Model 1). Defined more broadly to include public officeholders, government agencies, business organizations, and non-governmental organizations, official sources accounted for approximately thirty percent of all sources cited by the *National Review* and just under one-third of all sources cited by *The Progressive* (see Table 5.3, Model 2). Further, there was no significant association between use of official sources and newsmagazine for Model 1 and Model 2 (described above). Using an even more inclusive definition of official sources to include public officeholders, government agencies, business organizations, non-governmental organizations, advocacy groups, and foundations and think tanks, the percentages approach only half of all sources used by the two publications (see Table 5.3, Model 3). For Model 3, *The Progressive* was significantly associated with the use of official sources in their overall coverage.

Table 5.3 Official Sources Used by Each Newsmagazine

	Model 1	Model 2	Model 3[a]
National Review	25.51%	29.52%	44.01%
The Progressive	24.33%	32.92%	51.82%

[a] x^2=21.99, df=1, p<.001; Cramer's V=.090

Model 1 includes public office holders and government agencies.

Model 2 includes public office holders, government agencies, business organizations, and non-governmental organizations.

Model 3 includes public office holders, government agencies, business organizations, non-governmental organizations, advocacy groups, foundations and think tanks.

Even within the broad definition allowed for Model 3, this portion of sources defined as "official" still falls far short of the 70 percent figure for mainstream publications cited by Sigal.[33] In addition, more inclusive definitions of official sources tip greater reliance on official sources from the *National*

Review to *The Progressive*. This finding calls into question another of the most common claims appearing in the literature on news media and politics. At least in the case of explicitly partisan media discussions of domestic social issues, substantial use of official sources does not seem to be associated with conservative analysis. Neither of our hypotheses (that conservative media outlets would rely as heavily on official sources as mainstream media outlets and that liberal media outlets would rely less on official sources) regarding source use was supported.

Official Sources by Issue Area

Issue area was significantly associated with the use of official sources overall for Model 1 and Model 2 definitions of official sources (see Table 5.4).

Table 5.4 Reliance on Official Sources by Issue Area for Three Source Models

	Crime	Environment	Gender	Poverty	Total
Model 1[a]					
Official sources	110	313	154	92	669
	31.8%	27.3%	18.1%	25.8%	24.8%
Non-official sources	236	834	697	264	2031
	68.2%	72.7%	81.9%	74.2%	75.2%
Model 2[b]					
Official sources	120	416	200	118	854
	34.7%	36.6%	23.5%	32.2%	31.6%
Non-official sources	226	721	651	248	1846
	65.3%	63.4%	76.5%	67.8%	68.4%
Model 3					
Official sources	155	572	389	188	1304
	44.8%	45.9%	45.7%	52.8%	48.4%
Non-official sources	191	675	462	168	1496
	55.2%	54.1%	54.3%	47.2%	51.6%

[a] x^2=33.61, df=3, $p<.001$; Cramer's V=.112
[b] x^2=40.47, df=3, $p<.001$; Cramer's V=.122

Articles about crime and the environment used official sources most heavily, supporting earlier findings by researchers regarding the reliance on official sources for these issue areas.[34] Coverage of gender was the least likely to include official sources. This may be due to the topics included within the issue area of gender, which may not lend themselves to the use of official sources. For example, government officials may be less likely to be cited than experts, polls and research, and ordinary citizens when discussing sexual harassment, abortion, or the women's movement. The use of advocacy groups and their spokespersons for discussion of gender-related issues is illustrated in the higher proportion of "official sources" under Model 3, which includes these types of sources.

As stated above, both newsmagazines relied more heavily on official sources in their coverage of crime and the environment. Table 5.5 contains an overview of official source use for both partisan newsmagazines for each issue area. This reliance was similar for both publications for the issue area of crime. There was a significant association between publication and the use of official sources for the environment, however. *The Progressive* relied much more heavily on official sources in their coverage of the environment within each of the three official source models. In comparison, the *National Review* used official sources less frequently in their coverage of the environment than in any of the four issue areas examined for this book. The *National Review* was more likely to rely on official sources in their coverage of gender issues within Model 1 and Model 2. No significant association was found for the most inclusive definition (Model 3) of official sources for articles on gender and gender issues.

Table 5.5 Frequencies and Percentages of Official Sources by Issue Area for the *National Review* and *The Progressive*

	Crime	Environment	Gender	Poverty	Total
National Review					
Model 1	53	45[a]	118[d]	45	261
	34.6%	20.9%	23.2%	30.8%	25.5%
Model 2	53	58[b]	140[e]	51	302
	34.6%	27.0%	27.5%	34.9%	29.5%
Model 3	62	79[c]	224	70	435
	40.5%	36.7%	44.0%	47.9%	42.5%
The Progressive					
Model 1	57	268	36	47	408
	29.5%	28.8%	10.5%	22.4%	24.3%
Model 2	67	358	60	67	552
	34.7%	38.4%	17.5%	31.9%	32.9%
Model 3	93	493	165	118	869
	48.2%	52.9%	48.2%	56.2%	51.8%

[a] x^2=5.39, df=1, p<.05; Cramer's V=.068
[b] x^2=9.88, df=1, p<.01; Cramer's V=.093
[c] x^2=18.23, df=1, p<.001; Cramer's V=.126
[d] x^2=22.11, df=1, p<.001; Cramer's V=.161
[e] x^2=11.29, df=1, p<.001; Cramer's V=.115

There is a caveat to add to these conclusions. The full extent to which media content incorporates material from official sources may never be known. Unless the reports are clearly labeled, federal government produced, pre-packaged items "prepared for purposes of publicity or propaganda" have been banned since 1951. However, at least since the early 1990s, twenty different federal agencies have spent billions of dollars on public relations materials that are offered to the media and subsequently disseminated by them across the country as information produced by private sector news organizations.[35]

Ordinary Citizens as Sources

While official sources were dominant for both newsmagazines, the inclusion of "ordinary citizens" was more common in *The Progressive* (15.62 percent of all sources) than the *National Review* (3.81 percent of all sources). The inclusion of ordinary citizens was most common in articles on issues relating to poverty and welfare. Often, these articles center on the story of one individual or community affected by a larger political or economic issue. In *The Progressive*, ordinary citizens made up over one-fifth of the sources cited in poverty and welfare-related articles. Detrick Thomas, a homeless man who was arrested for "being an unauthorized person in a parking lot" in Atlanta in 1993 was presented in a *Progressive* article as a victim of a nationwide trend to make homelessness illegal.[36] The article incorporated perspectives from liberals and conservatives on the issue. Deputy Mayor Bill Lynch (coded as a conservative official), argued that "This is not what the park was created for . . . it impedes the use of the park for all the community" following his decision to demolish homeless encampments in New York City parks.[37] A liberal attorney, who fought cases for homeless individuals affected by these regulations, is also cited in the article alleging that arrests of the homeless and the seizure of their personal property were not based in the law and should be stopped.

Comparing Levels of Partisanship

Partisanship was significantly associated with issue area for both newsmagazines. Neutral sources made up approximately half of all sources in *Progressive* and more than two-thirds of all sources in *National Review* articles. The frequency of neutral sources was significantly associated with topic for both newsmagazines. In its coverage of gender issues, nearly half of the sources found in the *National Review* were partisan sources (both liberal and conservative combined). Nearly two-thirds of sources cited in gender related articles in *The Progressive* were partisan sources (see Table 5.6).

Source Alignment

Source alignment refers to the use of sources that coincide with the overall ideological perspective of the newsmagazine. For example, a liberal source such as The Center on Policy Initiatives was considered an aligned or consistent source for *The Progressive* while a conservative source such as The Enterprise Institute was considered an aligned source for the *National Review*. Twenty-five percent of all sources in *The Progressive* were liberal sources, while twenty-one percent of the sources cited in the *National Review* were conservative sources. Table 5.6 contains information regarding source alignment for each issue area for both newsmagazines.

Table 5.6 Source Alignment for Each Issue Area by Newsmagazine

	National Review		*The Progressive*		Total	
	n	*%*	*n*	*%*	*n*	*%*
Gender[a]						
Consistent Sources	115	22.6%	165	48.3%	280	32.9%
Oppositional Sources	94	18.5%	56	16.4%	150	17.6%
Neutral Sources	300	58.9%	121	35.3%	421	49.5%
Total	509	100.0%	342	100.0%	851	100.0%
Environment[b]						
Consistent Sources	31	14.4%	338	36.3%	369	32.2%
Oppositional Sources	18	8.4%	145	15.6%	163	14.2%
Neutral Sources	166	77.2%	449	48.2%	615	53.6%
Total	215	100.0%	932	100.1%	1147	100.0%
Crime						
Consistent Sources	25	16.3%	47	24.4%	72	21.8%
Oppositional Sources	14	9.2%	17	8.8%	31	9.0%
Neutral Sources	114	74.5%	129	66.8%	243	70.2%
Total	153	100.0%	193	100.0%	346	100.0%
Poverty						
Consistent Sources	45	30.8%	60	28.6%	105	29.5%
Oppositional Sources	9	6.2%	25	11.9%	34	9.6%
Neutral Sources	92	63.0%	125	59.5%	217	61.0%
Total	146	100.0%	210	100.0%	356	100.1%

[a]$x^2=64.369$, $df=2$, $p<.001$; Cramer's $V=.28$, Tau=.07
[b]$x^2=59.732$, $df=2$, $p<.001$; Cramer's $V=.23$; Tau=.05

For coverage of gender and the environment, source alignment was significantly different for the newsmagazines: gender x^2= 64.369, df=2, $p<.001$; environment x^2 = 59.732, df=2, $p<.001$). Cramer's V values for both indicate a moderate association between newsmagazine and source type for these two issue areas (see Table 5.4). The lack of source alignment for poverty and crime was largely due to the considerable frequency of neutral sources (such as experts, newspapers, newsmagazines, and polls and research) in articles by both newsmagazines. Once neutral sources were removed, only gender articles maintained a statistically significant Chi-Square value for association between newsmagazine and source alignment (x^2= 18.235, df=1, $p<.001$). The highest levels of source alignment were found in coverage of poverty in the *National Review* (30.82 percent of sources were conservative) and coverage of gender in *The Progressive* (48.25 percent of sources were liberal). *The Progressive*'s coverage of gender represents the only case in either newsmagazine where aligned sources outnumber neutral sources on an issue.

Oppositional Sources

Thirteen percent of *National Review* and fourteen percent of *Progressive* sources presented positions in ideological opposition to the newsmagazine's explicit ideology. The use of oppositional sources was greatest in coverage of gender for both newsmagazines. Of the sources cited in *The Progressive*, 16.37 percent were conservative sources; 18.47 percent of sources in *National Review* articles on gender were liberal sources. There was a significant association between consistent and oppositional sources by newsmagazine for all of the issue areas except the environment when neutral sources were removed from the analysis. *The Progressive* included more oppositional sources (as percentage of all sources) in its coverage of the environment and poverty, while the *National Review* included a larger percentage of oppositional sources in its coverage of crime and gender.

The inclusion of a larger percentage of oppositional sources in crime coverage in the *National Review* in part reflects the coding of libertarian views on drug use (decriminalization) as liberal. Throughout much of the twenty-five years of study, the *National Review* provided two opposing viewpoints on drug use and drug laws: a libertarian view advocating decriminalization of drugs, and more traditional arguments emphasizing mandatory sentencing and stiffer penalties for drug offenses. In early 1996, the newsmagazine published an article regarding an official shift in position from stiffer drug laws and sentencing for drug offenses toward legalization. Because subtopics (drugs, street crime, and gun control) were not recorded as part of this analysis, it was not possible to measure the full effect of this shift. However, it appears that coverage of drugs influenced the partisanship of sources for this issue area.

The high numbers of oppositional sources may be due, in part, to the inclusion of arguments to be deconstructed or countered within an article. For example, in his *National Review* article defending Charles Murray's book *Losing Ground*, Tom Bethell cites several liberal reformists and scholars, including Mario Cuomo, Senator Patrick Moynihan, and history professor Michael Katz.[38] While the article contained numerous "liberal" sources, the content and tone of the article was decidedly conservative. This calls into question the common practice of counting sources as an indicator of bias or balance in coverage.

Discussion

Explicitly partisan publications provide an important, albeit limited, set of voices within a media system often criticized for a lack of diversity in political and ideological perspectives. As such they merit consideration in their own right. Data presented in this chapter indicate that none of the models discussed by Sigal, including his own, depicts the set of relationships that exist among explicitly partisan publications, the government, and the public in a democracy.[39] This is to be expected since partisan publications can play several roles in a political democracy not usually considered appropriate for the mainstream press. These include framing events in explicitly normative terms and calling for partisan political action. A model, consistent with the data presented above, can be diagrammed:

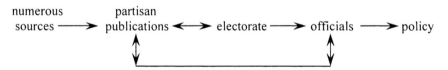

Unlike Sigal's "classical democratic theory" model and its variant, our partisan press model attends to information sources. Unlike Sigal's own model, it does not emphasize the symbiotic relationship between reporters and officials in the process of constructing the news. In the model, "numerous sources" includes both officials and publications along with advocacy groups, business organizations, independent experts, and so on.

Officials appear at two points in the model: as sources of information and as consumers of partisan publications. Data reported above indicate the extent to which officials, operationally defined in several ways, serve as sources for partisan publications. Determining the extent to which officials themselves read and are influenced by partisan publications is beyond the scope of this study.

The websites of the *National Review* and *The Progressive*, discussed in Chapter 2, contain the claim that political elites are prominent among their subscribers. It seems likely that, at least on the national level, officials are well aware of publications such as the *National Review* and *The Progressive*, and recognize that they can provide them with politically relevant information and perspectives usually not available for mainstream media and other conventional sources. Such material can include fresh, detailed analyses of enduring social issues, discussions of emerging trends in the political culture, and delineations of critical approaches to existing and proposed public policies.

Partisan publications such as the *National Review* and *The Progressive* offer citizens perspectives on parties, candidates, and issues that actively encourage partisanship and political engagement. They contain what Gans calls "explanatory journalism" and "participating news."[40] The former provides information on why things are as they are and what shores up the status quo; the latter provides information on the basis of which people can decide which political and other strategies might lead to reforms they seek.

The public can relate their personal experiences and perspectives to the partisan press. Such material can be used in the publications' discussions of public opinion and as dramatic support for the positions on social issues they advocate. (Ordinary citizens comprised 20.84 percent of *Progressive* sources on poverty.) Finally, as in the three other models, the electorate chooses officials who they believe will advocate social policies favorable to their own interests.

Content analysis of publications such as the *National Review* and *The Progressive* can provide insight into the role information sources play in constructing partisan accounts of social issues. Findings bear directly on the frequently discussed topic of the role of information sources in the creation of "media bias." The pattern of information sources used by explicitly partisan newsmagazines appears to be significantly different from that described in studies of their more mainstream counterparts. In particular, official sources often are not "primary definers" of social issues. Both of the partisan publications examined here used official sources much less extensively than mainstream publications as described by Sigal.[41]

Changes occurring since Sigal's study may have resulted in subsequent reduction in the mainstream media's use of official sources. First, the public lost some confidence in government and business.[42] This loss diminished the value of extensive use of government and business sources in the media's effort to assure the public of their "objectivity." Second, after 1980, the balance of hard news to soft news (items with no public policy content) in the media shifted decidedly toward soft news.[43] This lessened the need for the types of materials official sources could provide. This shift, coupled with reduced trust in government and business, "affected the quality of press-government relations in that the journalistic tone of the news during this time became more negative and cynical with journalists introducing their own voices into stories, often at the expense of direct quotes from the political sources they cover."[44]

Third, historically, organizations such as trade unions and environmental groups have been politically marginalized and have had to resort to the "politics of spectacle" to be considered by the mainstream media. However, such groups have developed new sophisticated techniques for securing coverage, thereby limiting the role of conventional news sources.[45]

In the context of partisan newsmagazines, official sources do not appear to have the consistently conservative influence often attributed to them in previous studies. It was hypothesized that a conservative publication such as the *National Review* would use official sources at least as frequently as do mainstream publications. In addition, liberal publications like *The Progressive* were expected to use official sources less extensively. These hypotheses were not supported. In fact, in its broadest definition, official sources were more commonly used by *The Progressive* than by the *National Review*.

The data presented in this chapter has several limitations. First, different partisan publications, such as the *Weekly Standard*, the *American Spectator*, the *Nation*, and the *New Republic*, may use sources differently in their coverage of crime, the environment, gender, and poverty. Second, the types of sources, and especially the use of official sources, may vary across issues not covered in this study. Official sources may be cited more frequently in coverage of education, healthcare, or racism than the issue areas selected for this analysis. This study does suggest, however, that understanding the role of sources in establishing "media bias," as it is popularly understood, requires an examination of not only how many official sources are cited in a given article, but what these officials are saying.

The common use of oppositional sources in the partisan publications examined in this study indicates that simply counting liberal and conservative sources is insufficient to determine the political bias or balance of a particular item or publication. Such sources can be employed in ways that advance a partisan perspective rather than mediate bias. The finding that partisan publications tend to rely more heavily on neutral than on ideologically supportive sources also suggests that, in analyzing media bias, attention should be paid more to the ways in which information is used than to the sources from which it is obtained.

Notes

1. Leo Sigal, *Reporters and Officials: The Organization and Politics of Newsmaking* (Lexington, MA: D. C. Heath, 1973).

2. Richard V. Erickson, Patricia Baranek, and Janet B. L. Chan, *Representing Order: Crime, Law, and Justice in the News Media* (Toronto: University of Toronto Press, 1989); Mark Fishman, "Crime Waves as Ideology," *Social Problems* 25, no. 5 (June 1978): 631–543; Herbert Gans, *Deciding What's News: A Study of CBS Evening News, NBC Nightly News, Newsweek and Time* (New York: Pantheon Books, 1979); James A. Holstein and Jaber F. Gubrium, *The Self We Live By: Narrative Identity in a Postmodern World* (New York: Oxford University Press, 2000).

3. Michael Schudson, "Deadlines, Datelines, and History," in *Reading the News*, eds. Karl Manoff and Michael Schudson (New York: Pantheon, 1986), 81.

4. Erickson, Baranek, and Chan, *Representing Order*; Gaye Tuchman, *Making News: A Study in the Construction of Reality* (New York: Free Press, 1978).

5. Stuart Hall, "The Rediscovery of 'Ideology:' Return of the Repressed in Media Studies," in *Culture, Society and the Media*, eds. Michael Gurevitch, Janet Woollacott, Tony Bennett, and James Curran (New York: Routledge, 1982), 56–90; Shanto Iyengar and Donald Kinder, *News That Matters: Television and American Opinion* (Chicago: University of Chicago Press, 1987).

6. Daniel C. Hallin, *The "Uncensored War": The Media and Vietnam* (Berkeley: University of California Press, 1986).

7. Edward S. Herman and Noam Chomsky, *Manufacturing Consent: The Political Economy of the Mass Media* (New York: Pantheon, 1988), 169.

8. Todd Gitlin, *The Whole World Is Watching* (Berkeley: University of California Press, 1980).

9. Doris Graber, *Processing the News: How People Tame the Information Tide* (New York: Longman, 1984), 327.

10. John J. Fialka, *Hotel Warriors: Covering the Gulf War* (Baltimore: John Hopkins University Press, 1992); Douglas Kellner, *The Persian Gulf TV War* (Boulder, CO: Westview, 1992); John R. MacArthur, *Second Front: Censorship and Propaganda in the Gulf War* (New York: Hill and Wang, 1992).

11. Bethami A. Dobkin, *Tales of Terror: Television News and the Construction of the Terrorist Threat* (New York: Praeger, 1992); Edward S. Herman and Gerry O'Sullivan, *The "Terrorism" Industry: The Experts and the Institutions That Shape Our View of Terror* (New York: Pantheon Books, 1989); Robert G. Picard, *Media Portrayals of Terrorism: Functions and Meaning of News Coverage* (Ames: Iowa State University Press, 1993).

12. David Miller, "The Propaganda Machine," in *Tell Me Lies: Propaganda and Media Distortion in the Attack on Iraq*, ed. David Miller (London: Pluto, 2004), 80–99.

13. Katherine Beckett, "Media Depictions of Drug Abuse: The Impact of Official Sources," *Research in Political Sociology* 7 (1995): 161–182; Ray Surette, *Media, Crime and Criminal Justice: Images and Realities* (Belmont, CA: West/Wadsworth, 1998).

14. Peter M. Sandman, David B. Sachsman, Michael R. Greenberg, and Michael Gochfield, *Environmental Risk and the Press* (New Brunswick, N.J.: Transaction Press, 1987).

15. William A. Gamson and Andre Modigliani, "The Changing Culture of Affirmative Action," *Research in Political Sociology* 3 (1987): 137–177.

16. William A. Gamson and Kathryn E. Lasch, "The Political Culture of Social Welfare Policy," in *Evaluating the Welfare State: Social and Political Perspectives*, eds. Shimon B. Spiro and Ephraim Yuchtman-Yaar (New York; Academic Press, 1983), 397–415.

17. Robin Brown, "Clausewitz in the Age of CNN: Rethinking the Military-Media Relationship," in *Framing Terrorism: The News Media, the Government and the Public*, eds. Pipa Norris, Montague Kern, and Marion R. Just (New York: Routledge, 2003), 43–58.

18. Herbert Strentz, *News Reporters and News Sources* (Ames: Iowa State University Press, 1989).

19. Ben Bagdikian, *The Media Monopoly*, 6th ed. (Boston: Beacon Press, 2004); Robert McChesney, *The Problem with Media: U. S. Communication Politics in the 21st Century* (New York: Monthly Review Press, 2004); Charlotte Ryan, *Prime Time Activism: Media Strategies for Grassroots Organizing* (Boston: South End Press, 1991); Lawrence C. Soley, *The News Shapers: The Sources Who Explain the News* (New York: Praeger, 1992); Strentz, *News Reporters and News Sources*; Tuchman, *Making News*.

20. Philip Schlesinger, "Rethinking the Sociology of Journalism: Source Strategies and the Limits of Media-Centrism," in *Public Communication: The New Imperatives—Future Directions for Media Research*, ed. Marjorie Ferguson (Newbury Park, CA: Sage, 1990), 61–83; Tuchman, *Making News*.

21. Herbert Gans, *Democracy and the News* (New York: Random House, 2003): 46.

22. W. Lance Bennett, "Gate Keeping and Press-Government Relations: A Multigated Model," in *Handbook of Political Communication Research*, ed. Linda L. Kaid (Mahwah, NJ: Lawrence Erlbaum Associates, 2004), 285.

23. John Dewey, *The Public and Its Problems* (New York: Henry Holt, 1927).

24. Bagdikian, *The Media Monopoly*; David Croteau and William Hoynes, *The Business of Media: Corporate Media and the Public Interest* (New York: Oxford University Press, 2001).

25. W. Lance Bennett, *News: The Politics of Illusion*, 5th ed. (New York: Longman, 2003); Joseph N. Capella and Kathleen H. Jamieson, *Spiral of Cynicism: The Press and the Public Good* (New York: Oxford University Press, 1997); Gans, *Deciding What's News*.

26. Bagdikian, *The Media Monopoly*.

27. Richard L. Kaplan, *Politics and the American Press: The Rise of Objectivity, 1865–1920* (New York: Cambridge University Press, 2002); Jeffrey Pasley, *The Tyranny of Printers: Newspaper Politics in the Early American Republic* (Charlottesville: University of Virginia Press, 2001).

28. Davis Merritt, *Public Journalism and Public Life: Why Telling the News Is Not Enough* (New York: Lawrence Erlbaum Associates, 1998); Carmen Sirianni and Lewis Friedland, *Civic Innovation in America: Community Empowerment, Public Policy and the Movement for Civic Renewal* (Berkeley: University of California Press, 2001).

29. W. Lance Bennett and Robert M. Entman, "Mediated Politics," in *Mediated Politics: Communication in the Future of Democracy*, eds. W. Lance Bennett and Robert

M. Entman (Cambridge, England: Cambridge University Press, 2001), 1–32; Peter Dahlgren, "The Internet and the Democratization of Civic Culture," *Political Communication* 17 (2000): 335–340; Oscar H. Gandy Jr., "Dividing Practices: Segmentation and Targeting in the Emerging Public Sphere," in *Mediated Politics: Communication in the Future of Democracy*, eds. W. Lance Bennett and Robert M. Entman (Cambridge, England: Cambridge University Press, 2001), 141–159.

30. Sigal, *Reporters and Officials.*

31. Beckett, "Media Depictons of Drug Abuse," 162.

32. Sigal, *Reporters and Officials.*

33. Sigal, *Reporters and Officials.*

34. Beckett, "Media Depictions of Drug Abuse"; Surette, *Media, Crime and Criminal Justice: Images and Realities*; Sandman et al., *Environmental Risk and the Press.*

35. David Barstow and Robin Stein, "Is It News or Public Relations? Under Bush, Lines Are Blurry," *New York Times*, March 13, 2005, A1, A18–19; Christopher Lee, "Administration Rejects Ruling on PR Videos. GAO Called Tapes Illegal Propaganda," *Washington Post*, March 15, 2005, A21.

36. George Howland Jr., "The New Outlaws," *The Progressive* (May 1994), 33.

37. "The New Outlaws," 34.

38. Tom Bethell, "'They Had a Dream': The Politics of Welfare Reform," *National Review* (August 23, 2003), 33.

39. Sigal, *Reporters and Officials.*

40. Gans, *Democracy and the News*, 90–100.

41. Sigal, *Reporters and Officials.*

42. Seymor M. Lipset and William S. Schneider, *The Confidence Gap: Business, Labor, and Government in the Public Mind* (New York: Free Press, 1983).

43. Thomas E. Peterson, "Doing Well and Doing Good: How Soft News and Critical Journalism Are Shrinking the News Audience and Weakening Democracy—and What News Outlets Can Do about It," Cambridge, MA: Harvard University, Jan Shorenstein Center on Press, Politics and Public Policy, Kennedy School of Government 2000 Faculty Research Working Paper Series, #RWP01-001.

44. Bennett, "Gate Keeping and Press-Government Relations," 287.

45. Paul Manning, *News and News Sources: A Critical Introduction* (Thousand Oaks: Sage, 2001).

Chapter 6

Assessing the Role of Historical Context in Media Bias

In the concluding section of Chapter 4, we emphasized the overwhelming consistency in the levels of bias of coverage for each of the four newsmagazines over the four issue areas examined during the twenty-five-year period for this study. Chapter 4 also provided some initial comparisons in relative coverage among the four publications, finding that while there were differences between partisan and mainstream newsmagazines in the emphasis placed on the four selected issue areas, no significant differences were found in "emphasis" between *Time* and *Newsweek* overall. Previous research has indicated that the amount of coverage given to a particular social issue waxes and wanes over time.[1] In addition, the relative emphasis on particular issues during certain periods is argued to be a sign of selection bias on the part of media outlets.[2] Earlier research has pointed to the importance of measuring this relative emphasis over time on coverage of issues and its relationship to media bias in general. For example, Bernard Goldberg and Christopher Hewitt both point out that coverage of homelessness was more extensive and more critical during Republican administrations.[3]

While it is impossible to identify everything of public importance the media do not cover,[4] it is possible to examine how coverage of particular issues changes over time and across publications. Here two related issues will be examined: the impact of presidential administration on the content of coverage of crime, the environment, gender, and poverty in *Time, Newsweek*, the *National Review*, and *The Progressive*, and how coverage differs as a result of significant political, historical, or social events which result in "dense" coverage of the four issue areas within these media outlets between 1975 and 2000. For example, does coverage of the environment change based on which party controls the White House or during periods when environmental issues are covered more heavily (due to significant historical, social, or political events such as the partial core meltdown at Three Mile Island in 1979)? This chapter examines the impact of social and political contexts in the relative emphasis placed on issue areas (measured in number of articles) and on the level of bias of coverage of issue areas over the period of study.

Presidential Administrations and Media Bias

Democratic versus Republican Administrations

Research on the coverage of political candidates and political officeholders suggests that the media often are biased toward or against individual political leaders and their policies.[5] Conservative writer Bernard Goldberg claims that presidential administrations have an impact on coverage of particular social issues.[6] For example, Goldberg argues that coverage of homelessness peaked during the Reagan and Bush administrations, declined while Clinton held office, and climbed again when George W. Bush took office. He blames a liberal media critical of Republican administrations for these shifts in coverage.

A series of t-tests comparing bias scores in Democratic and Republican administrations found no significant differences (at $p<.05$) in the bias level of coverage for any of the issue areas examined in this study. Table 6.1 reports the mean adjusted bias scores for each issue area during Democratic and Republican administrations and overall for each publication. The party affiliation of the sitting president had no impact on the bias level in coverage of any of the issue areas or for the overall bias level of each publication. We did not assess variations in subtopics within our issue areas (such as abortion, women's rights, sexual harassment, or divorce within the issue are of gender), but any such variations were not significant enough or consistent enough to result in changes in overall bias within an issue area. Our findings do not support the arguments made by Goldberg and Hewitt that presidential administration has a strong impact on media coverage for the issue areas and publications examined here.

Table 6.1 Mean Adjusted Bias Scores for Democratic and Republican Administrations

	National Review	*The Progressive*	*Time*	*Newsweek*
Crime	+.3862	-.5427	-.0505	+.1503
Democratic	+.3190	-.6311	-.1067	+.0477
Republican	+.4367	-.5847	-.0161	+.2265
Environment	+.6100	-.6174	-.2220	-.2129
Democratic	+.6472	-.6384	-.2210	-.1550
Republican	+.5745	-.6014	-.2224	-.2592
Gender	+.6722	-.6020	-.3672	-.1897
Democratic	+.6878	-.5935	-.4188	-.0743
Republican	+.6493	-.6085	-.3528	-.2832
Poverty	+.6710	-.6077	-.1625	-.0352
Democratic	+.6888	-.6841	-.3417	+.1409
Republican	+.6531	-.5553	-.1289	-.1320
Total	+.6098	-.6049	-.2284	-.0864
Democratic	+.6283	-.6311	-.2457	-.0444
Republican	+.5893	-.5847	-.2284	-.1179

Assessing the Impact of Individual Presidents

While our analysis did not find differences based on party affiliation, it is possible that a media outlet may exhibit bias against the policies or positions of a sitting president on a particular social or political issue. Therefore, in addition to examining the impact of party affiliation, the impact of individual presidential administrations was also analyzed. There is some support for this hypothesis based on ANOVA tests comparing mean adjusted bias scores across presidential administrations. The results of this analysis are found in Table 6.2. Coverage of the environment and poverty in the *National Review* changed significantly based on presidential administration. For the environment, adjusted bias score values peaked during the Ford administration (Mean abs = +.7000, *N*=2) and was lowest during the Carter administration (Mean abs = .0000, N=1). The *National Review*'s coverage of poverty reached its most conservative mean adjusted bias scores during the Ford and Carter administrations (Mean abs = +1.000, N=2) and its least conservative during the Reagan administration (Mean abs = +.5037, N=7). It is important to note, however, that this "low value" is still strongly biased and much more conservative than any of the mean adjusted bias score values obtained from *Time* and *Newsweek*.

Time's coverage of crime and poverty also varied significantly by presidential administration. Mean adjusted bias scores for poverty articles in *Time* ranged from -.5000 (N=1) during the Carter administration to -.0247 (N=12) during the Reagan administration. For coverage of crime, these values ranged from a mean adjusted bias score of -.1206 (N=9) during the Carter administration to a mean adjusted bias score of +.1101 (N=16) during Reagan's administration. While these values were significantly different, the high and low mean adjusted bias score values still lie within the "balanced" range (-.20 to +.20) as defined in Chapter 4. While mean adjusted bias scores changed significantly, *Time*'s coverage of these issue areas remained relatively "balanced" regardless of presidential administration.

Table 6.2 ANOVA Values for Differences among Mean Adjusted Bias Scores for Individual Presidential Administrations

	National Review	The Progressive	Time	Newsweek
Crime	0.406	1.356	3.364*	0.903
Environment	5.215**	1.467	1.874	0.941
Gender	1.391	0.185	0.143	1.660
Poverty	4.309**	0.725	5.031*	1.271

*p<.05
**p<.001

A series of t-tests comparing mean adjusted bias levels of each presidential administration against all other administrations combined identifies several instances where coverage varied significantly based on who was president (see Table 6.3). For example, *Time*'s coverage of all issues combined was significantly more conservative (t=2.108, df=241, p<.05) during the Reagan administration. Much of this is due to *Time*'s significantly more conservative coverage of poverty (t=3.81, df=17, p<.01) and crime (t=3.71, df=56, p<.001) during the Reagan years. In fact, mean adjusted bias scores for crime articles during this period were the only instance where the mean adjusted bias scores crossed into a positive (conservative) value (Mean abs = +.101), although they remained in the "balanced" category. *Newsweek* coverage of gender issues was more conservative during the Clinton administration (Mean abs = +.0355) than during other administrations (combined Mean abs = -.2855), representing the only significant shift in bias scores for the newsmagazine and the only significant shift in bias scores for the issue area of gender.

Table 6.3 T-tests Values for Differences between Adjusted Bias Scores for Each President (against adjusted bias score for All Other administrations combined)

	Time	*Newsweek*	*National Review*	*The Progressive*
Crime	Reagan (3.707***)			
Environment			Clinton (2.098*) Reagan (-2.434*) Carter (3.059**)	
Gender		Clinton (2.619*)		
Poverty	Reagan (3.811**) Bush (-2.660**)		Reagan (-2.310*) Carter (2.267*) Ford (2.267*)	
Overall	Reagan (2.108*)			Bush (2.010*)

*p<.05
**p<.01
***p<.001

The National Review's coverage seemed to vary most by presidential administration, where three significant shifts occurred in the newsmagazine's coverage of the environment and poverty. Interestingly, both shifts occurred during the Reagan administration, in coverage of the environment (Mean abs Reagan administration = +.3269, Mean abs other administrations combined = +.6313) and poverty (Mean abs Reagan administration = +.5037, Mean abs other administrations combined = +.7045), resulting in significantly less conservative coverage than those found during other administrations. The remaining shifts occurred during Democratic administrations, but these shifts were less connected to party affiliation, as discussed previously, than to individual presidencies.

The Progressive was the only newsmagazine included in the study which did not significantly alter coverage of any of the four issue areas in connection with an individual presidential administration. *The Progressive*'s overall coverage of the four issue areas combined was least liberal during the Bush administration (Mean abs Bush administration = -.5264, Mean abs other administrations combined = -.6203), but this shift in bias was not mirrored in any of the four individual issue areas examined.

While all four newsmagazines registered significant shifts in coverage bias scores based on presidential administration, no consistent pattern was found in these shifts among the four newsmagazines. For example, *Time* became more conservative in its coverage of poverty during the Reagan administration (Mean abs Reagan administration = -.0247, Mean abs other administrations combined = -.3988), while the *National Review*'s coverage (discussed previously) became less conservative during the same period. This lack of consistency fails to lend support to any argument (such as that discussed in Chapter 2) about systematic bias across the media industry more generally. Specifically focusing on putatively non-partisan publications, we find that shifts in coverage within *Time* and *Newsweek* were not associated with either issue area or presidential administration. The two publications varied in the issue areas where shifts occurred over the period of study. *Time* experienced shifts in coverage of crime and poverty while *Newsweek* coverage shifted for gender coverage only. In addition, shifts in coverage during individual presidential administration were inconsistent. For instance, the presence of a Republican in the White House did not result consistently in coverage that was more conservative (greater alignment with sitting president) or liberal (in opposition to sitting president). *Time*'s coverage was more conservative in two instances (crime and poverty) during the Reagan administration and more liberal in another (poverty during the Bush administration).

Issue "Emphasis" and Presidential Administrations

Bias in coverage has been measured not only in terms of coverage content associated with a particular president and his party affiliation (as previously discussed), but also in terms of the amount of attention given to a particular issue area during a presidential administration. This can be seen as a form of the "selection bias" such as that discussed by Goldberg,[7] as well as a form of bias through agenda setting.[8] For the articles examined in this study, party affiliation of the sitting president was not associated (based on Chi-Square analysis) with issue coverage (emphasis) for any of the issue areas covered by any the four newsmagazines. For example, gender issues were no more likely to be empha-sized during a Republican than a Democratic presidency.

Table 6.4 Frequencies of Articles by Topic Area and Presidential Adminis-tration for Each Publication

	Ford	Carter	Reagan	Bush	Clinton
***Time*[a]**					
Crime	5	9	16	15	13
Environment	10	11	31	17	10
Gender	11	16	36	21	3
Poverty	0	1	12	4	2
Total	26	37	95	57	28
***Newsweek*[b]**					
Crime	3	7	20	12	19
Environment	9	12	19	12	20
Gender	16	10	12	9	20
Poverty	4	1	14	2	10
Total	32	30	65	35	69
***National Review*[c]**					
Crime	2	2	9	9	13
Environment	2	1	3	17	20
Gender	3	4	16	15	46
Poverty	2	2	7	12	19
Total	9	9	35	53	98
***The Progressive*[d]**					
Crime	1	0	3	6	10
Environment	11	36	35	13	9
Gender	0	8	10	15	11
Poverty	5	3	7	4	8
Total	17	47	55	38	38

[a] x^2=20.987, df=12, p=.051; Cramer's V= .170; λ=.064, p=.011
[b] x^2=20.859, df=12, p=.052; Cramer's V= .173; λ = n.s.
[c] n.s.
[d] x^2=19.297, df=12, p<.001; Cramer's V= .290; λ = n.s.

Presidential administration was a slightly better predictor of issue emphasis, however. Table 6.4 provides an overview of frequencies for issue coverage (em-phasis) based on individual presidential administrations. *Progressive* coverage of the issue areas was significantly associated (at p<.001) with presidential administration. *Time* and *Newsweek* showed nearly significant associations (at $p<.05$) between frequency of issue coverage and presidential administration. For each of these newsmagazines, resulting values represent a moderate association between issue area and presidential administration (based on Cramer's V scores).

Some of the associations reported may be connected to different lengths of administrations, which were not controlled for in the analysis. For example, fifteen crime-related articles were published in *Time* during the four years of the Bush administration while only thirteen appeared during Clinton's two terms in the White House.

Comparing Issue Emphasis between One-Term and Two-Term Presidencies

When single and two-term presidents are compared to each other, few additional significant differences in emphasis emerge. In Table 6.5, the Ford administration was removed from the statistical analysis in order to make comparisons between the entire periods of each presidency. The period of study, 1975 to 2000, included only two years of Ford's four years in office. What results are two comparisons: between the single-term Carter and Bush administrations and between the two-term Reagan and Clinton administrations. There were no significant associations in issue emphasis for the *National Review* and *The Progressive* for either presidential pairing. In addition, findings indicate no significant associations for *Time*'s coverage for one-term presidential administrations.

Consistent patterns of coverage within this model may be interpreted as evidence that party affiliation plays a role in coverage. For example, if there are significant associations in coverage emphasis for both sets of presidential pairings, this would likely be due to a difference between Republican and Democratic administrations rather than a difference based on presidencies, controlling for length of term. While issue emphasis was significantly associated with presidential administration in *The Progressive*, these associations are not consistent in terms of party affiliation. There were nearly three times as many articles on the environment during the Carter administration as during the Bush administration. However, the association is reversed when comparing issue emphasis for the environment during the Reagan and Clinton administrations. Only nine articles appeared in *The Progressive* dealing with environmental issues during Clinton's administration compared to thirty-six articles while Reagan was in office. Further, coverage of gender was more extensive during the Bush administration (compared to Carter), but occurred with similar frequencies during the Reagan and Clinton administrations.

Table 6.5 Significant Associations in Issue Emphasis for One-Term and Two-Term Presidential Administrations

	One-Term		Two-Term	
	Carter	Bush	Reagan	Clinton
Time[a]				
Crime			16	13
Environment			31	10
Gender			36	3
Poverty			12	2
Total			95	28
The Progressive[b]				
Crime	0	6	3	10
Environment	36	13	35	9
Gender	8	15	10	11
Poverty	3	4	7	8
Total	47	38	55	38

[a] $x^2=13.702$, $df=3$, $p<.01$; Cramer's $V=.334$
[b] One-Term $x^2=18.322$, $df=3$, $p<.001$; Cramer's $V=.464$; Two-Term [b] $x^2=16.698$, $df=3$, $p<.01$; Cramer's $V=.424$

Time magazine's coverage of the four issue areas was significantly associated with presidential administration during the two-term presidencies of Reagan and Clinton. All four issue areas were covered far more extensively (in terms of numbers of articles) during the Reagan administration. In addition, Table 6.3 indicates that coverage during Reagan's administration was more conservative overall and more conservative in its coverage of crime and poverty in particular during this time period. This may lend some support to the arguments made by Hewitt and Goldberg that emphasize changes over time, but it is not clear that "emphasis" alone constitutes bias nor should it be assumed that the association is due entirely to presidential administration and not other factors, such as significant social, political, or economic events relevant to the issues studied. An event or series of events may increase the amount of coverage of a particular issue during a period of time quite apart from who serves in the White House. It should also not be assumed that heavy coverage is equivalent to biased coverage. The following section deals with one such alternative explanation: examining if bias level differs during periods of dense coverage.

Periods of Dense Coverage

For this analysis, "dense coverage" is defined as a five-year period within which at least thirty percent of all articles on a topic within a publication appear. This occurred ten times during the study (see Table 6.6). These dense periods of coverage can be connected to landmark court cases, social and political events, natural and man-made disasters, consequential legislation, and so on. For example, three periods of dense coverage were identified for the environment: 1977 to 1981(*The Progressive*), 1984 to 1988 (*Time*), and 1992 to 1996 (the *National Review*). These periods correspond to the occurrence of several significant environmental events. Between 1977 and 1981, the United States Department of Energy was created by President Carter (1977), the Soil and Water Conservation Act was passed (1977), toxic waste was discovered on a site once owned by Hooker Chemical and Plastics Corporation which was later developed into a residential community at Love Canal near Niagara Falls, New York (1978), and a partial meltdown occurred of a nuclear reactor at the Three Mile Island nuclear power plant (1979). The period from 1984 to 1988 includes the Bhopal (1984) and Chernobyl (1986) disasters and the first meeting of the Intergovernmental Panel on Global Climate Change (1988). Between 1992 and 1996, the first Earth Summit was held (1992) and major flooding occurred along the Missouri and Mississippi River Valleys (1993).

The occurrence of a number of events helps account for the heavy coverage of gender issues by the *National Review* and *Newsweek* between 1995 and 1999 as well. These include: success by the Christian Right in influencing Republican Party opposition to abortion rights; announcement of Pope John Paul II's encyclical opposing abortion, birth control, and in-vitro fertilization; rejection of President Clinton's nominee for Surgeon General largely for his outspoken support for legal abortion; termination of an Affirmative Action program in California requiring consideration of sex as well as race, religion, ethnicity, and national origin in the admission of students to colleges and universities; the legal struggle of women to gain admission to the all-male cadet corps of the Citadel; President Clinton's veto of a bill that would have banned so-called "partial-birth abortions:" several bombings of abortion clinics; and the discovery of sexual harassment throughout the army. Likewise, dense coverage on issues related to poverty by *Time* during the mid-1980s correspond to a period of economic recession, increasing poverty rates, a housing crisis among lower income Americans as subsidized housing established during the Johnson administration reverted to private ownership, welfare reform proposals to establish workfare, and the larger Reagan administration rhetoric about "welfare queens" scamming the system.

Table 6.6 T-test Analysis for Dense Issue Area Coverage by Publication

Newsmagazine/ Topic	Period of Dense Coverage	# of articles (% of total)
Time		
Gender	1975–1979	27 (31%)
Gender	1985–1989	30 (34%)
Environment	1984–1988	25 (32%)
Poverty[a]	1983–1987	11 (57%)
Newsweek		
Crime	1985–1989	20 (33%)
Gender[b]	1995–1999	20 (30%)
National Review		
Environment	1992–1996	23(53%)
Gender[c]	1995–1999	42 (50%)
Poverty	1992–1996	21 (50%)
The Progressive		
Environment	1977–1981	21(50%)

Note: t-test values compare Mean abs score for dense period to Mean abs score for all other years in sample.
[a] $t=2.162$, $df=17$, $p<.05$
[b] $t=2.619$, $df=65$, $p<.05$
[c] $t=2.232$, $df=82$, $p<.05$

In general, periods of dense coverage resulted in more conservative coverage from *Newsweek*, more liberal coverage from *Time* (with the exception of poverty discussed later), and more partisan coverage in the *National Review* and *The Progressive*. However, only three periods of dense coverage for the four newsmagazines examined resulted in significantly different bias levels compared to coverage during other years. In each of these three cases, coverage was significantly more conservative (less liberal) during the period of dense coverage.

Newsweek's coverage of gender issues were significantly more conservative (Dense Mean abs= +.0355) between 1995 and 1999 compared to the earlier years included in the study (Mean abs for remaining years = -.2855). *Time*'s coverage of poverty was significantly more conservative (Dense Mean abs= -.0572; Mean abs for remaining years = -.3073) between 1983 and 1987, during which more than 50 percent of all articles on poverty in the newsmagazine appeared. Finally, the *National Review*'s coverage of gender from 1995 to 1999 was also significantly more conservative than preceding years (Dense Mean abs= +.7331; Mean abs for remaining years = +.6113). Half of all *National Review* articles on gender appeared during this time.

Much of the variation in "emphasis" found in Table 6.4 based on presidential administration is explained more fully through an examination of coverage density surrounding significant social and political events. For example, in the previous discussion it was noted that *Newsweek*'s coverage of gender issues was significantly more conservative during the Clinton administration. Further analysis based on coverage density indicates that this difference is more likely a result of significant social and legal events occurring between 1995 and 1999 than to a bias on the part of *Newsweek* and its contributors toward President Bill Clinton.

The occurrence of a single or series of "significant" events may not always increase the amount of coverage (emphasis) in the media generally. Individual publications may increase coverage while others do not. For example, the series of significant environmental events which occurred between 1977 and 1981 impacted the density of coverage in only one publication, *The Progressive*, and this density of coverage did not result in significantly different coverage (in terms of bias level). In addition, only the *National Review* seems to have reported more heavily on poverty issues during the early part of Clinton's administration, when what would become the Personal Responsibility and Work Reconciliation Act of 1996 was drafted, debated, and signed. In fact, there was only one overlapping period where dense coverage was found for more than one publication. In this case (coverage of gender between 1995 and 1999 in *Newsweek* and the *National Review*), this dense period was associated with significantly more conservative coverage (based on Mean abs scores) in both publications. It should be noted that our analysis only included articles at least one page in length which discussed at least three of the four dimensions for analysis. This may have resulted in undercounting the total number of articles on a topic during a particular time period.

Discussion

Analysis from Chapter 4 indicated that there was an impressive consistency in the coverage of crime, the environment, gender, and poverty in *Time*, *Newsweek*, the *National Review*, and *The Progressive* during the twenty-five year period between 1975 and 2000. Additional analysis in this chapter provides a more nuanced examination of that consistency. While significant social, political, and economic events can alter the bias level of coverage, its impact seems to be limited to particular issues in particular publications during particular periods of time. Likewise, coverage, in terms of both bias and emphasis, was not strongly affected by presidential administration or the party affiliation of the president.

In their coverage of these four issue areas over the period of study, it seems that *Time, Newsweek,* the *National Review,* and *The Progressive* were little affected by larger social and political forces. The amount of attention given to an issue (emphasis) also had little effect on levels of bias for these four publications. In their coverage of particular issue areas, some significant variations were observed based on presidential administration, but these individual variations do not support claims of a deliberate or sustained bias against either Republicans or Democrats by either of the newsmagazines that represent mainstream media included in this study.

The stability of news media perspectives over time can provide the public with a sense of order and predictability in the political world. Despite dramatic events and different administrations, social issues will continue to seem potentially responsive to courses of action determine by institutionalized means of democratic political participation. Other ways in which news media serve political democracy is the subject of our final chapter.

Notes

1. Christopher Hewitt, "Estimating the Number of Homeless: Media Misrepresentation of an Urban Problem," *Journal of Urban Affairs* 18, no. 3 (1996): 431–477; Stephen Hilgartner and Charles L. Bosh, "The Rise and Fall of Social Problems: A Public Arenas Model," *American Journal of Sociology* 94, no. 1 (1988): 53–78.

2. Herbert Gans, *Deciding What's News: A Study of CBS Evening News, NBC Nightly News, Newsweek, and Time* (New York: Pantheon Books, 1979); W. Lance Bennett, *News: The Politics of Illusion* (New York: Longman, 2003); C. Richard Hofstetter and T. F. Buss, "Bias in Television News Coverage of Political Events: A Methodological Analysis," *Journal of Broadcasting* 22 (1978): 517–530; David M. White, "The Gate-Keeper: A Case Study in the Selection of News," *Journalism Quarterly* 27 (1950): 383–390.

3. Bernard Goldberg, *Bias: A CBS Insider Exposes How the Media Distort the News* (Washington, DC: Regnery Publishing, Inc., 2002); Hewitt, "Estimating the Number of Homeless."

4. Dave D'Alessio and Mike Allen, "Media Bias in Presidential Elections: A Meta-Analysis," *Journal of Communication* 50, no. 4 (2000): 133–156.

5. Adam J. Schiffer, "Assessing Partisan Bias in Political News: The Case(s) of Local Senate Election Coverage," *Political Communication* 23, no. 1 (January–March 2006): 23–39; David W. Brady and Jonathan Ma, "Newspapers' Labeling of Politicians Reveals a Liberal Bias," in *Media Bias,* ed. Stuart Kallen (San Diego: Greenhaven Press, 2004), 13–16; Dennis T. Lowry and Jon A. Shidler, "The Sound Bites, the Biters, and the Bitten: An Analysis of Network TV News Bias in Campaign '92," *Journalism & Mass Communication Quarterly* 72, no. 1 (Spring 1995): 33–44; Guido H. Stempel III and John W. Windhauser, "Coverage by the Prestige Press of the 1988 Presidential Campaign," *Journalism Quarterly* 55, no. 4 (Winter 1989): 894–896, 919.

6. Goldberg, *Bias.*

7. Goldberg, *Bias*.

8. Tony Atwater, "Network Evening News Coverage of the TWA Hostage Crisis," *Journalism Quarterly* 64, no. 2 (Summer/Autumn 1987):520–525; Sabine Wilhelm, "Coverage of the War in Iraq: Frame Choice in American and German National Newspapers," *Journal of Intercultural Communication* no. 10 (December 2005): 1–11; Dimitri Williams, "Synergy Bias: Conglomerates and Promotion in the News" *Journal of Broadcasting and Electronic Media* 46, no. 3(September 2002): 453–472.

Chapter 7

Have Our Media Been Serving Democracy in Their Coverage of Domestic Social Issues?

Defining *democracy* is the necessary point of departure for discussing the question raised in this concluding chapter. To this end, we draw upon sociologist Edward Shils's classic analysis of the concept. Next, attention is given to identifying some of the ways in which newsmagazine coverage of social issues can contribute to the viability and vitality of democracy defined in this particular way. In light of the analysis, we then review our data to evaluate *Time*, *Newsweek*, the *National Review*, and *The Progressive* discussions of the selected social issues. Finally, we consider the possibility that media bias, as we have conceptualized it, might be functional for political democracy. Perhaps, complaints about media bias, by ardent conservatives and liberals alike, have given not only the news media, but bias itself, a worse reputation than either deserves.

Defining *Democracy*

Sociologist Edward Shils succinctly identified the defining characteristics of a political democracy. It is a regime of civilian rule, with representative institutions and public liberties.[1]

Democracy involves civilian rule in at least two senses. The first is that, in a democratic system, all adults, regardless of class, are citizens and eligible participants in the political process. In a democracy, popular participation is emphasized and there is, in principle, equal right of access to government. Democracy also involves civilian rule in the sense that political decisions have to be justified publicly. Those outside the formal authority structure have some influence over the formulation and enactment of policy.

Democracy involves representative institutions in the sense that the authority to govern is derived from election by citizens. In complex societies, democracy is expressed in the competitive struggle among political elites who must seek, find, and maintain support from those they govern by at least appearing to represent their interests. The decisions political elites make must take into account citizen preferences.

Finally, in Shils's view, democracy involves the maintenance of public liberties in the sense that citizens have certain rights, such as the rights of free communication and free assembly, which the state must respect. The state has limited authority based on uncoerced agreements. Violence, intimidation, and fraud are barred in principle and the rights of minorities are guaranteed in principle.

Serving Democracy

News media can and do alert the public to conditions and events that violate widely shared social values. Reports of crimes, acts of discrimination, environmental pollution, and homelessness serve as examples. Accounts can create public awareness and stir public sentiment but, in themselves, lack political significance. News media serve democracy when they present such events and conditions as instances of social issues, that is, as widely shared problems that are amenable to political solution and for which public officials can be held accountable. Such narratives can help make citizens aware of their interests and to the means to realize them through the exercise of their political rights. Some knowledge about politics is essential if citizens are to discover their real interests and take effective advantage of the civic opportunities afforded them.[2]

The newsmagazine articles included in this research concerned enduring social issues. This may generally distinguish newsmagazine reports from related items appearing in newspapers and the electronic media. Those are more likely to be the basis for Lance Bennett's complaint that:

> If there is a single most important flaw in American news style, it is the over-whelmingly tendency to downplay the big social, economic or political picture in favor of the human trials, tragedies, and triumphs that sit at the surface of events.[3]

Attracting Public Attention to Social Issues

The amount and prominence of media coverage of a social issue influences the public ranking of the personal importance of that issue.[4] Extensive media coverage can set an agenda for officials by suggesting that it will be perceived by the public as a crisis that merits governmental attention.[5] Assuming elites' perception of such public concern, their subsequent positive response is an indicator of the operation of civilian rule and the vitality of representative institutions. On the other hand, when media overlook, underreport, or self-censor issue coverage, the public is unlikely to ask for official action, and elites will not be evaluated by the public on the basis of how well their policies served their social, economic, cultural, ideological, or other interests by their response to that issue. Under these circumstances, the sector of the public aware of and interested in the issue, even if it is a numerical majority, is unlikely to have its concerns represented.

Even assuming that it is a sensible question, there may be no clear way to determine how many articles, over a given period of time, a newsmagazine must publish in order to make a social issue salient to the public. However, the topic of amount of coverage can be approached by considering the relative frequencies with which a news organization presents items on various social issues. In this study, a newsmagazine will be considered to have given inadequate attention to a social issue if it devoted a significantly smaller number of articles to that issue than it did to the other issues with which it was compared.

Data in Table 4.1 bear on the question of whether the mainstream newsmagazines tended to pay relatively little attention to any of the enduring social issues. While *Time* and *Newsweek* devoted approximately equal proportions of their articles to crime, environmental, and gender issues, the data do show that they addressed the topic of poverty far less frequently. Such relatively scant coverage occurred during a twenty-five-year period in which the annual number of Americans whose incomes fell below the government's official poverty level ranged from 27 to 39 million people. As we have conceptualized it, limited coverage is not a defining characteristic of ideological bias. However, the question of ideological bias aside, the mainstream media did not serve democracy well when they called little attention to the plight of America's most needy. Little coverage of the topic of poverty did not alert the public or political elites to the serious needs of a vast number of fellow citizens, or promote some consideration of political responses that would represent their interests.

Both the *National Review* and *The Progressive* explicitly claim that public opinion leaders and political elites are among their regular readers. Relatively little discussion of a social problem by a partisan news organization not only diminishes its ability to call the problem to public attention, but also its ability to shape popular and elite debate on the topic. This, in turn, reduces its influence on the formation of public policy.

Data in Table 4.1 also show that the *National Review* devoted a larger number and proportion of its articles to the issue of poverty than did any of the other publications. In this sense, the magazine did more to alert the public to the problem than did the mainstream media. By way of contract, *The Progressive* presented a relatively small proportion of its articles to poverty (13.8 percent), particularly when compared to its coverage of environmental issues (53.3 percent). We find *The Progressive*'s relatively scant attention to poverty surprising, given our belief that concern for the poor is generally understood as a core feature of the liberal viewpoint.

Informing the Public about Social Issues

To serve popular democracy, (as opposed to the elite-based democracy advocated by writers such as Neuman, Schattschneider, and Schumpeter),[6] news media must do more than alert the public to existing social issues. They also must provide citizens with information about those issues. The requisite contents, quality, and quantity of that information have been a topic of long normative and empirical debate.[7] So too has the question of whether the American public has much interest in acquiring such information.[8]

Rather than attempting to address these long-standing questions, we will proceed on the basis of two assumptions. First, mainstream media are serving political democracy when they offer the public factual information about the costs, causes, and possible solutions that define various existing social issues and do so in an unbiased manner as operationally defined in this study. Second, partisan media are serving popular democracy when they consistently offer the public factual information about the costs, causes, and possible solutions that define various existing social issues from a coherent perspective that represents an alternative to that offered by the mainstream media. Prosaic as this may be, we conceptualize the material presented by the partisan media as a component of the "marketplace of ideas" in which the conflicting viewpoints that make the social issues political are representative and subsequently are they evaluated by political elites and by the public.

How well did *Time* and *Newsweek*, our representatives of mainstream media, serve democracy? Figures 4.1, 4.2, 4.3, and 4.4 clearly show that over time and for all issues, the adjusted bias scores of the two newsmagazines fell between those of the *National Review* and *The Progressive*. Data in Table 4.3 show that the overall mean adjusted bias scores of *Time* (-.228) and *Newsweek* (-.086) were vastly different from those of the explicitly partisan publications which were used as points of comparison (the *National Review* +.610, *The Progressive* -.605). We interpret these findings as indicating that the mainstream media were consistently informing the public by providing relatively unbiased accounts of important social issues and, in this sense, supporting democracy.

If attention is focused on the proportion of the magazine articles that were "balanced," then the findings could be interpreted as supporting a different conclusion. Table 4.2 shows that "only" 44 percent of *Time*'s articles were classified as "balanced," while the corresponding figure for *Newsweek* was an even smaller 23 percent. It is far from clear, however, that the higher the overall proportion of "balanced" articles a newsmagazine publishes, the more informative it is and therefore the better it serves democracy. Reporting on some issues might better serve the public interest if media do not attempt to offer balanced presentations. As Bennett and Serrin put it:

What, for example, is the point of the construction of a two-sided debate about global warming when one side consists overwhelmingly of scientists who have little scholarly doubt or disagreement, and the other side consists primarily of politicians and business interests who have quite another agenda fuelling their skepticism? The flip side of this normative dilemma is the problem of what watchdogs should do when one side of an issue is dominated by spin from a media-savvy source with high social standing and opponents have failed for whatever reasons to mount an equally effective press relations campaign. All too often, the watchdog retreats, and what is reported as the public record goes unchallenged in the news.[9]

If attention is focused on the overall distribution of the articles assigned to the conservative and liberal categories, as shown in Table 4.2, then conservatives are likely to be displeased, particularly with *Time*, which had only 5.8 percent of its articles generally supporting their ideological perspective and almost half of their articles classifying as liberal. On the other hand, liberals are not likely to agree that *Newsweek* had well informed the public on social issues when, as Table 4.2 also shows, almost one third of its articles on the selected topics classified as conservative. Conservatives and liberals alike probably would see these decontextualized findings as unambiguous confirmation of their belief in the existence of media bias. Those who have a firm ideological commitment tend to view the media as hostile to their perspectives and to embrace those data that appear to confirm their belief.

How well did the *National Review* and *The Progressive,* our representatives of partisan alternatives to the mainstream media, serve democracy? As noted above, the newsmagazines' overall bias scores differed significantly from those of *Time* and *Newsweek*. Table 4.2 shows that, overall, 93.1 percent of *National Review* articles were classified as conservative, while an almost identical 92.8 percent of *Progressive* articles were considered liberal. Similarly, data in Table 4.3 show that, overall, the mean adjusted bias score for the *National Review* was +.610 and the corresponding score for *The Progressive* was -.605 (the apparent exception to maintaining ideological consistency was the *National Review*'s reporting on the issue of crime which was discussed in Chapter 4). Figures 4.1, 4.2, 4.3, and 4.4 graphically display the distance between partisan (biased) and mainstream media. Each publication consistently provided information supporting one side of the public debates concerning crime, the environment, gender, and poverty, thereby turning these concerns into political issues to be resolved by the public and their representative political elites through democratic processes. As political scientist Murray Edelman observed:

> The character of problems leaders, and enemies that makes them political is precisely that controversy over their meanings is not resolved. Whether poverty originates in the inadequacies of its victims or in the pathologies of social institutions, whether a leader's actions are beneficial or damaging to the policy, whether a foreign, racial, religious, or ethnic group is an enemy or a desirable ally, typify the questions that persist indefinitely and remain controversial in their time. The debates over such questions constitute politics and catalyze po-

litical action. There is no politics respecting matters that evoke a consensus about the pertinent facts, their meanings, and the rational course of action.[10]

Herbert Gans's classic study of *CBS Evening News*, *NBC Nightly News*, *Time*, and *Newsweek* identified eight clusters of values that have shaped mainstream media news presentations.[11] Three of these value clusters are of particular importance here: "altruistic democracy," "responsible capitalism," and "individualism." Conservative and liberal perspectives differ fundamentally in their understanding of how these concepts apply to the present realities of the American political economy. Our operational definitions of conservative and liberal positions on the four domestic social issues reflect these differences.

The conservative viewpoint sees America's free market system as serving the public interest, promoting general economic prosperity, and supporting democracy. The outlook focuses on the agency of individual actors to change political, economic, and social conditions. The liberal perspective sees America's free market system as serving private interests, producing unreasonable profits, and sometimes the exploitation of workers and consumers. The position identifies political and institutional forces as the agents of social change. The conflicts of groups over various domestic social issues that constitute much of American political life, stem from different understandings of the issues. These are based largely on information provided by the American media system that includes conservative and liberal as well as mainstream news organizations.

"What we are seeing (when we encounter the news) is not a neutral body of information, but rather information gathered and presented to illustrate a way of seeing the world based on certain values and favorable to certain courses of action."[12] In this sense, all news is "biased." Mainstream and partisan media differ in the extent to which they consistently and intentionally provide more support to an ideological perspective in their accounts of enduring social issues. They do this through their narratives concerning the issues' costs, causes, and potential solutions. Conceptualized in this way, bias does not involve consideration of the empirical truth or falsity of the claims that together constitute their narratives.

It is unlikely that any long established, leading newsmagazine, whether mainstream or partisan, would knowingly publish claims that are empirically false. If such a publication were detected violating journalistic ethics in this way, competitors, media watchdog organizations, and political communication researchers, among others, would call the credibility of the publication into question and undermine public understanding of its contents as "news." As Anthony Smith observed, "Credibility in the minds of the audience is the *sine qua non* of news. All else is either propaganda or entertainment."[13] Perhaps this is one reason why those who complain most vociferously about media bias tend to be viewed more as entertainers than as serious media analysts.

All news organizations do not maintain equally high levels of accuracy in their reporting. This was illustrated by a study of public misperceptions of matters related to the war in Iraq. Data showed that those who relied on Fox television news as their main source of political information tended to be significantly more likely than those who routinely relied on other news organizations, particularly print media and NPR/PBS, to have misperceptions of the war. Their erroneous beliefs included: evidence of links between Iraq and al Qaeda had been found; weapons of mass destruction had been found in Iraq; world public opinion approved of the United States going to war with Iraq.[14] Democracy is subverted by dissemination of misinformation. Misrepresentation of political conditions and events can create the appearance of rational democracy while discouraging critical evaluation of public policy.[15]

Some Positive Functions of Media Bias

In the view developed in this book, to label a media account of a social issue "biased" is not to render a judgment about the truth or falsity of any aspect of the account nor to make an unfavorable evaluation of the conditions, actors or policies the account supports through its specification of costs, causes, and solutions. Assuming, for reasons cited above, that the biased accounts of mainstream media nevertheless strongly tend to be factually correct, there are several ways in which they can perform positive functions.

First, as Bennett and Serrin argued in their analysis of media coverage of global warming, discussed earlier in this chapter, it is not always in the public interest to present "balanced accounts" of social issues.[16] Their position might be taken regarding reporting on additional topics such as particular welfare legislation or some efforts at eliminating gender discrimination in the workplace.

Second, encountering biased reports could lead some to reconsider their own previously unquestioned understanding of the costs, causes, and possible solutions to a social issue or issues. To the extent that cognition influences political behavior, such learning could promote change in patterns of political participation, such as issue-based voting, more in line with the interest of the actors.

Third, encountering biased reports could produce in others greater clarity and certainty in their own beliefs through their improved understanding of an alternative perspective. It is a commonplace observation that understanding of what one has rejected produces greater appreciation of what one has accepted.

Fourth, biased accounts can represent the views of those generally lacking social resources and the ability to define social issues for the mass public. Such reports can rest on as much empirical evidence as more familiar perspectives that are socially accepted as uncontested representations of social reality. An article presenting a poor black woman's understanding of the costs, causes, and solutions to poverty can serve as an example.

Fifth, ironically, biased media accounts can promote social unity by presenting definitions of social issues that, as a result of their bias, correspond to the perspectives on those issues that are widely held by the public. It is a sociological truism that shared understanding of the social world promotes societal integration.

The first three functions of media bias support civilian rule by increasing the likelihood that patterns of civic participation will reflect not only enlightened self-interest, but also improved understanding of what serves public needs. The fourth function supports public liberties by giving voice to minorities that might otherwise be overlooked and unintentionally denied their social and political rights. It would be difficult to estimate the extent to which media bias performs each of these four functions. However, our data do bear on the question of whether conditions do occur in which media bias can promote consensus on the nature of and possible solutions to some social issues and thereby increase social and political integration and stability. Discussion of this topic leads to our concluding consideration of the very meaning of "media bias."

Media Bias?

The use of two leading newsmagazines' coverage of four social issues provided eight cases in which media bias could be examined. Data in Table 4.3, presenting mean adjusted bias scores, showed no evidence of conservative bias in any of the eight cases. However, they did indicate liberal bias in the cases of *Time* (-.222) and *Newsweek* (-.213) coverage of environmental issues and *Time* (-.367) articles on social problems related to gender. *Time* and *Newsweek* mean adjusted bias scores for their coverage of environmental issues barely fall outside the range of scores operationally defined as "balanced" (+.200 to -.200). *Time*'s liberal reporting on gender issues is the one reasonably clear case of media bias identified through the use of the measure developed in this study. In all three cases, the level of liberal bias of *Time* and *Newsweek* is far from that found in *The Progressive*, (environment = -.617, gender = -.602). Nevertheless, biased coverage has been identified and merits further discussion.

Public opinion on environmental issues has long tended to be liberal in the sense in which the term is used in this book. Dunlap and Scarce's examination of trends in polls concerning public attitudes toward the environment concluded that, by the early 1990s, public support for efforts at solving environmental problems had persisted and had risen in subsequent years. The study revealed not only an increasing likelihood of citizens to consider environmental problems serious and a threat to "human well-being" but also a growing tendency to believe that the federal government should take action in both expenditure and legislation to protect the environment.[17]

The overall liberal bias of *Time* and *Newsweek,* however slight, was consistent with public opinion. Such correspondence can perform the fifth function of media bias noted above—promoting social solidarity. Mainstream media and the public tend to agree that the government should have serious environmental concern, particularly as environmental matters affect public health, and should initiate effective regulatory policies. Given these data reporting public opinion on environmental issues, it seems unlikely that citizens would tend to consider mainstream media coverage of environmental issues, as analyzed in this study, to be "biased." Public perception of biased coverage of an issue is more likely a consequence of the public's stand on the issue than it is a reaction to characteristics of media messages about the issue such as the sources of information on which the coverage is based.[18]

There is evidence that the public tends to maintain a generally liberal perspective on gender issues, and that it has become more pronounced over the past three decades. A study by Huddy, Neely, and Lafay reports that, in 1970, 40 percent of women and 44 percent of men favored efforts to "strengthen and change women's status" in society. By the 1990s, between two-thirds and three-quarters of men and women reported "very favorable" or "mostly favorable" opinions of the women's movement.[19] Mason and Lu report a significant increase between 1977 and 1985 in pro-feminist views of the wife and mother roles in all socio-demographic subgroups in the population.[20] Poll data reviewed by Simon and Landis show that between 1972 and 1989, support for the participation of women in the non-domestic labor market increased, as had the proportion of those favoring equal pay for men and women, and the proportion of these supporting efforts to improve the status of women. They also found increased support for the liberal position that divorce is an acceptable solution to a marriage that is not working, and a reduction of support for the traditional division of labor between husbands and wives.[21] Finally, data show that while Americans are divided over the issue of abortion, a majority continues to believe that abortion should remain legal.[22] Given these data reporting public opinion on gender issues, it seems unlikely that citizens would tend to consider mainstream media coverage of gender issues, as analyzed in this study, to be "biased."

A search of data points in Figures 4.1–4.4 can locate *Time* and *Newsweek* articles in each of the four issue areas that are more conservative than some published in the *National Review*, and other articles in each of the four issue areas that are more liberal than some appearing in *The Progressive*. Several of these items might be cited in arguments presenting the "Liberal Media" thesis, while others might be used by those advancing the "Conservative Media" perspective. Such is the nature of anecdotal evidence.

Our analysis of *Time* and *Newsweek* coverage of crime and poverty finds no evidence of overall ideological bias. Both mainstream newsmagazines had liberally biased scores on environmental issues. However, their adjusted mean bias scores were barely outside the range of balanced coverage, were significantly less liberal than *Progressive* coverage of the issue, and were similar to the views of the public on environmental issues as reflected in public opinion polls.

Data presented in this book provide little evidence to support the "Liberal Media" thesis. The one reasonably clear case of ideological bias, *Time*'s coverage of gender issues, would not seem to provide much of a basis for conservative angst about the "Liberal Media." If, by some measure, owners of media organizations are conservative and do have some control over media content, then the findings of our study might be interpreted as providing specificity to the position that "The media are only as liberal as the conservative businesses that own them."

Notes

1. Edward Shils, *Political Development in the New States* (The Hague: Mouton, 1960), 51–60.
2. Michael X. Delli Carpini and Scott Keeter, *What Americans Know about Politics and Why It Matters* (New Haven: Yale University Press, 1996).
3. W. Lance Bennett, *News: the Politics of Illusion.* 5th Edition (New York: Addison, Wesley, Longman, 2003), 54.
4. Shanto Iyengar and Donald R. Kinder, *News That Matters* (Chicago: University of Chicago Press, 1987); Maxwell McCombs and Donlad L. Shaw, "The Agenda-Setting Function of the Mass Media," *Public Opinion Quarterly* 36 (1972): 176–185.
5. Leon Sigal, *Reporters and Officials: The Organization and Politics of News Making* (Lexington, MA: D. C. Heath, 1973).
6. W. Russell Neuman, *The Paradox of Mass Politics: Knowledge and Opinions in the American Electorate* (Cambridge: Harvard University Press, 1986); E. E. Schattsschneider, *The Semisovereign People: A Realist's View of Democracy in America* (New York: Holt, 1960); Joseph A. Schumpter, *Capitalism, Socialism and Democracy* (New York: Harper and Row, 1942).
7. Phillip Converse, "Popular Representation and the Distribution of Information," in *Information and Democratic Processes*, eds. John A. Ferejohn and James H. Kulinkski (Urbana: University of Illinois Press, 1990), 131–158; V. O. Key Jr., *The Responsible Electorate: Rationality in Presidential Voting 1936–1960.* (New York: Vintage, 1966); Samuel Popkin, *The Reasoning Voter: Communication and Persuasion in Presidential Campaigns* (Chicago: University of Chicago Press, 1991).
8. Robert M. Entman, *Democracy without Citizens: Media and the Decay of American Politics* (New York: Oxford University Press, 1989).
9. W. Lance Bennett and William Serrin, "The Watchdog Role," in *The Institutions of Democracy: The Press*, eds. Geneva Overholser and Katherine Hall Jamieson (New York: Oxford University Press, 2005).
10. Murray Edelman, *Constructing the Political Spectacle* (Chicago: University of Chicago Press, 1988).
11. Herbert Gans, *Deciding What's News* (New York: Random House, 1979).
12. Anthony Smith, *The Shadow in the Cave: The Broadcaster, His Audience and the State* (Urbana: University of Illinois Press, 1973), 101.
13. Smith, *The Shadow in the Cave: The Broadcaster, His Audience and the State,* 109.
14. Steven Kull, Clay Ramsay, and Evan Lewis, "Misperceptions, the Media and the Iraq War," *Political Science Quarterly,* 118 (2003): 569–598.
15. Murray Edelman, *The Politics of Misinformation* (New York: Cambridge University Press, 2001).
16. Bennett and Serrin, "The Watchdog Role."
17. Riley E. Dunlap and Rik Scarce, "The Polls—Trends: Environmental Problems and Protection," *Public Opinion Quarterly,* 55 (1991): 651–672.
18. Albert C. Gunther, "Biased Press or Biased Public? Attitudes toward Media Coverage of Social Groups," *Public Opinion Quarterly* 56 (1992): 147–167.
19. Leonie Huddy, Frances K. Neely, and Marilyn R. Lafay, "The Polls—Trends: Support for the Women's Movement," *Public Opinion Quarterly* 64 (2000): 309–350.
20. Karen Oppenheim Mason and Yu-Hsia Lu, "Attitudes towards Familial Roles: Changes in the United States, 1977–1985," *Gender & Society* (1988): 39–57.

21. Rita J. Simon and Jean M. Landis, "The Polls—A Report: Women's and Men's Attitudes about a Woman's Place and Role," *Public Opinion Quarterly* 53 (1989): 265–276.

22. Greg Shaw, "The Polls—Trends: Abortions," *Public Opinion Quarterly* 67 (2003): 407–429.

Bibliography

Alterman, Eric. *What Liberal Media? The Truth about Bias and the News*. New York: Basic Books, 2003.

Alvarez, R. Michael, and Jonathan Nagler. "Economies, Issues and the Perot Candidacy: Voter Choice in the 1992 Presidential Election." *American Journal of Political Science* 39, no. 3 (August 1995): 714–744.

Annin, Peter, and Sharon Begly. "Great Lake Effect." *Newsweek* (July 5, 1999): 52–54.

Ashley, Laura, and Beth Olson. "Constructing Reality: Print Media's Framing of the Women's Movement, 1966 to 1986." *Journalism & Mass Communications Quarterly* 75, no. 2 (Summer 1998): 263–277.

Atwater, Tony. "Network Evening News Coverage of the TWA Hostage Crisis." *Journalism Quarterly* 64, no. 2 (Summer/Autumn 1987): 520–525.

Bagdikian, Ben H. *The Media Monopoly*. Boston: Beacon Press, 1992.

———. *The Media Monopoly*. Boston: Beacon Press, 2000.

Baldastry, Gerald. *The Commercialization of News in the Nineteenth Century*. Madison: University of Wisconsin Press, 1992.

Barnes, Samuel, and Max Kaase. *Political Action: Mass Participation in Five Western Democracies*. Beverly Hills, CA: Sage, 1979.

Barstow, David, and Robin Stein. "Is It News or Public Relations? Under Bush, Lines are Blurry." *The New York Times* (March 13, 2005): A1, A18–19.

Beck, Paul A. "Voters' Intermediation Environments in the 1988 Presidential Contest." *Public Opinion Quarterly* 55, no. 3 (Fall 1991): 371–394.

Beckett, Katherine. "Media Depictions of Drug Abuse: The Impact of Official Sources." *Research in Political Sociology* 7 (1995): 161–182.

Bennett, Stephen E., Staci L. Rhine, and Richard S. Flickinger. "Assessing Americans' Opinions about the News Media's Fairness in 1996 and 1998." *Political Communication* 18, no. 2 (April–June 2001):163–182.

Bennett, W. Lance. *News: The Politics of Illusion.* 5th Edition. New York: Longman, 2003.

———. "Gate Keeping and Press-Government Relations: A Multigated Model." P. 285 in *Handbook of Political Communication Research,* edited by Linda L. Kaid. Mahwah, NJ: Lawrence Erlbaum Associates, Inc., 2004.

Bennett, W. Lance, and Robert M. Entman. "Mediated Politics." Pp. 1–32 in *Mediated Politics: Communication in the Future of Democracy,* edited by W. Lance Bennett and Robert M. Entman. Cambridge, England: Cambridge University Press, 2001.

Berelson, Bernard, Paul Lazarsfeld, and William McPhee. *Voting.* Chicago: University of Chicago Press, 1954.

Berryhill, Dale A. *The Media Hates Conservatives: How It Controls the Flow of Information.* Lafayette, LA: Huntington House Publishers, 1994.

Bethell, Tom. "They Had a Dream: The Politics of Welfare Reform." *National Review* (August 23, 2003): 33.

Bozell, L. Brent, III. *Weapons of Mass Distortion: The Coming Meltdown of the Liberal Media.* New York: Three Rivers Press, 2005.

Bozell, L. Brent, III, and Brent H. Baker, eds. *And That's the Way It Isn't: A Reference Guide to Media Bias.* Alexandria, VA: Media Research Center, 1990.

Brady, David W. and Jonathan Ma. "Newspapers' Labeling of Politicians Reveals a Liberal Bias." Pp. 13–16 in *Media Bias,* edited by Stuart Kallen. San Diego: Greenhaven Press, 2004.

Brophy-Baermann, Michelle, and Andrew J. Bloeser. "Stealthy Wealth: The Untold Story of Welfare Privatization." *Harvard International Journal of Press/Politics* 11, no. 3 (2006): 89–112.

Brown, Robin. "Clausewitz in the Age of CNN: Rethinking the Military-Media Relationship." Pp. 43–58 in *Framing Terrorism: The News Media, the Government and the Public,* edited by Pipa Norris, Montague Kern, and Marion R. Just. New York: Routledge, 2003.

Buchanan, Pat. "The Media Have a Liberal Bias." In *Media Bias,* edited by Stuart Kallen, 10–13. San Diego: Greenhaven Press, 2004.

Buckley, William H., Jr. *God and Man at Yale.* Chicago: Regnery, 1951.

Buckley, William H., Jr., and Brent Bozell. *McCarthy and His Enemies.* Chicago: Regnery, 1954.

Capella, Joseph N., and Kathleen H. Jamieson. *Spiral of Cynicism: The Press and the Public Good.* New York: Oxford University Press, 1997.

Chibnall, Steven. *Law and Order News.* London: Tavistock, 1974.

Cirino, Robert. *Don't Blame the People: How the News Media Use Bias, Distortion, and Censorship to Manipulate Public Opinion.* Los Angeles: Diversity Press, 1971.

Cocks, Jay. "How Long Till Equality?" *Time* (July 12, 1982): 29.

Coffey, Philip J. "A Quantitative Measure of Bias in Reporting of Political News." *Journalism Quarterly* 75, no. 3 (Autumn 1975): 551–553.

Cohen, Adam, and Hilary Hylton. "Who Should Still Be on Welfare?" *Time* (August 16, 1999): 22–28.

Coleman, James W., and Donald R. Cressey. *Social Problems.* 3rd edition. New York: Harper & Row, 1990.

Columbia Journalism Review. "Who Owns What?" http://www.cjr/resources/ (accessed October 9, 2006).

Conniff, Ruth. "Cutting the Lifeline, The Real Welfare Fraud." *The Progressive* (February 1992): 25–31.

Coulter, Ann. *Slander: Liberal Lies about the American Right.* New York: Crown Publishers, 2002.

Craig, Robert L. "Business Advertising and the Social Control of News." *Journal of Communication Inquiry* 28, no. 3 (July 2004): 233–252.

Croteau, David. "Challenging the 'Liberal Media' Claim." *Extra* July/August 1998, 4–5.

Croteau, David, and William Hoynes. *By Invitation Only: How the Media Limit Political Debates.* Monroe, ME: Common Courage Press, 1994.

———. *The Business of Media: Corporate Media and the Public Interest.* Thousand Oaks, CA: Pine Forge, 2001.

D'Alessio, Dave, and Mike Allen. "Media Bias in Presidential Elections: A Meta-Analysis." *Journal of Communication* 50, no. 4 (Autumn 2000):133–156.

Dahlgren, Peter. "The Inernet and the Democratization of Civic Culture." *Political Communication* 17 (March): 335–340.

Dalton, Russell, Paul A. Beck, and Robert Huckfeldt. "Partisan Cures and the Media: Information Flows in the 1992 Presidential Election." *The American Political Science Review* 92, no. 1 (March 1998): 111–126.

Dalton, Russell, Paul Beck, Robert Huckfeldt, and William Koetzel. "A Test of Media Centered *Agenda Setting:* Newspaper Context and Public Interests in a Presidential Election." *Political Communication* 15 (1998): 463–481.

Day, Samuel H., Jr. "Edwin Knoll and the H-Bomb Case." *The Progressive* (January 1999): 25.

Day, Samuel H., Jr., and William Stief. "On the 'Objective Press'." *The Progressive* (January 1999): 23–25.

Dewey, John. *The Public and Its Problems.* New York: Henry Holt, 1927.

Dickson, Sandra. "Understanding Media Bias: The Press and the U.S. Invasion of Panama." *Journalism Quarterly* 71, no. 4 (Winter 1994): 809–819.

Dobkin, Bethami A. *Tales of Terror: Television News and the Construction of the Terrorist Threat.* New York: Praeger, 1992.

Donovan, Hedley. "Coming to Terms with Viet Nam." *Time Magazine* (June 14, 1971): 30.

Dreier, Peter. "How the Media Compound Urban Problems." *Journal of Urban Affairs* 27, no. 2 (2005): 193–201.

Edelman, Murray. *Constructing the Political Spectacle.* Chicago: University of Chicago Press, 1988.

Eitzen, D. Stanley with Maxine Baca Zinn. *Social Problems.* 3rd edition. Boston: Allyn & Bacon, 1986.

———. *Social Problems.* 7th edition. Boston: Allyn & Bacon, 1997.

Elliot, Osborn. "A Time for Advocacy." *Newsweek* (Nov. 20, 1967): 32.

Entman, Robert M. "Television, Democratic Theory and the Visual Construction of Poverty." *Research in Political Sociology* 7 (1995): 139–159.

———. *Projections of Power: Framing News, Public Opinion, and U.S. Foreign Policy.* Chicago: University of Chicago Press, 2004.

Entman, Robert M., and Andrew Rojecki. "Freezing Out the Public." *Political Communication* 10, no. 2 (April–June 1993).

Erickson, Richard V., Patricia Baranek, and Janet B.L. Chan. *Representing Order: Crime, Law and Justice in the News Media.* Toronto: University of Toronto Press, 1989.

Farley, John E. *American Social Problems: An Institutional Analysis.* Englewood Cliffs, NJ: Prentice Hall, 1987.

Feagin, Joe R., and Clairece Booher Feagin. *Social Problems, A Critical Power-Conflict Perspective.* 3rd edition. Englewood Cliffs, NJ: Prentice Hall, 1990.

Fialka, John J. *Hotel Warriors: Covering the Gulf War.* Baltimore: John Hopkins University Press, 1992.

Fishman, Mark. "Crime Waves as Ideology." *Social Problems* 25, no. 5 (June 1978): 531–543.

Fraker, Susan, and Evert Clark. "Environment: Double Header." *Newsweek* (April 26, 1976): 32.

Gamson, William A., David Croteau, William Hoynes, and Theodore Sasson. "Media Images and the Social Construction of Reality." *Annual Review of Sociology* 18 (1992): 373–393.

Gamson, William A., and Katherine E. Lasch. "The Political Culture of Social Welfare Policy." Pp. 397–415 in *Evaluating the Welfare State: Social and Political Perspectives,* edited by Shimon E. Spiro and Ephraim Yuchtman-Yaar. New York: Academic Press, 1983.

Gamson, William A., and Andre Modigliani. "The Changing Culture of Affirmative Action." *Research in Political Sociology* 3 (1989): 137–177.

Gamson, William A., and Gadi Wolfsfeld. "Movements and Media as Interacting Systems." *The Annals of the American Academy of Political and Social Science,* no. 528 (1993): 114–125.

Gandy, Oscar H., Jr. "Dividing Practices: Segmentation and Targeting in the Emerfing Public Sphere." Pp. 141–159 in *Mediated Politics: Communication in the Future of Democracy,* edited by W. Lance Bennett and Robert M. Entman. Cambridge, England: Cambridge University Press, 2001.

Gans, Herbert. *Deciding What's News: A Study of CBS Evening News, NBC Nightly News, Newsweek and Time.* New York: Pantheon Books, 1979.

———. "Are U.S. Journalists Dangerously Liberal?" *Columbia Journalism Review* 24, no. 4 (November/December 1985): 31–33.

———. *Democracy and the News.* New York: Random House, 2003.

Gibbs, Nancy, and Cathy Booth. "Working Harder, Getting Nowhere." *Time* (July 3, 1995): 17–18.

Gitlin, Todd. *The Whole World Is Watching.* Berkeley: University of California Press, 1980.

Goldberg, Bernard. *Bias: A CBS Insider Exposes How the Media Distort the News.* Washington, DC: Regnery Publishing, Inc., 2002.

Goodale, James C. "Born Classified—*The Progressive Magazine* Case." *New York Law Journal* (March 23, 1979): 1–7.

Goodman, Peter. "What Vietnam Did to Us." *Newsweek* (Dec. 14, 1981): 49.

Graber, Doris A. *Processing the News: How People Tame the Information Tide.* New York: Longman, 1984.

———. *Mass Media and American Politics.* 6th edition. Washington, DC: Congressional Quarterly Press, 2002.

Groseclose, Tim, and Jeffrey Milyo. "A Measure of Media Bias." *The Quarterly Journal of Economics* 70, no. 4 (November 2005): 1192–1237.

Gross, Bertram. "Deeply Concerned about the Welfare of the Iraqi People: The Sanctions Regime against Iraq in the *New York Times* (1966-98)." *Journalism Studies* 3, no. 1 (Feb. 2002): 83–99.

Gunther, Albert C. "Biased Press or Biased Public: Attitudes toward Media Coverage of Social Groups." *The Public Opinion Quarterly* 56, no. 2 (Summer 1992): 147–167.

Gunther, Albert C., and Stella Chih-Yun Chia. "Predicting Pluralistic Ignorance: The Hostile Media Perception and Its Consequences." *Journalism & Mass Communication Quarterly* 79, no. 4 (Winter 2001): 688–701.

Haas, Tanni, and Linda Steiner. "Fear of Corporate Colonization in Journalism Reviewers' Critiques of Public Journalism." *Journalism Studies* 4, no. 3 (August 2002): 325–341.

Hall, Stuart. "The Rediscovery of 'Ideology': Return of the Repressed in Media Studies." Pp. 56–90 in *Culture, Society and the Media*, edited by Michael Gurevitch, Janet Woollacott, Tony Bennett and James Curran. New York: Routledge, 1982.

Hall, Stuart, Charles Critcher, Tony Jefferson, John Clarke, and Brian Roberts. *Policing the Crisis: Mugging, the State and Law and Order*. New York: Holmes and Meier 1978.

Hallin, Daniel C. *"The Uncensored War": The Media and Vietnam*. Berkeley: University of California Press. 1986.

Hart, Peter, and Julie Hollar. "Fear & Favor 2004—FAIR's Fifth Annual Report How Power Shapes the News." *Extra*. March/April 2005. http://www.fair.org/index.php?page=2486 (accessed May 24, 2007).

Hartsgaard, Mark. *On Bended Knee: The Press and the Reagan Presidency*. New York: Farrar, Strauss, Giroux, 1989.

Hawkins, Virgil. "The Other Side of the CNN Factor: The Media and Conflict." *Journalism Studies* 3, no. 2 (May 2002): 225–240.

Herman, Edward S., and Noam Chomsky. *Manufacturing Consent: The Political Economy of the Mass Media*. New York: Pantheon Books, 1988.

Herman, Edward S., and Gerry O'Sullivan. *The "Terrorism" Industry: The Experts and the Institutions That Shape our View of Terror*. New York: Pantheon Books, 1989.

Herzstein, Robert Edwin. *Henry R. Luce, Time, and the American Crusade in Asia*. New York: Cambridge University Press, 2005.

Hewitt, Christopher. "Estimating the Number of Homeless: Media Misrepresentation of an Urban Problem." *Journal of Urban Affairs* 18, no. 3 (1996): 431–447.

Hickey, Neil. "Money Lust: How Pressure for Profit Is Perverting Journalism." *Columbia Journalism Review* 18, no. 2 (July/August 1998): 32.

Hilgartner, Stephen, and Charles L. Bosh. "The Rise and Fall of Social Problems: A Public Arenas Model." *American Journal of Sociology* 94, no. 1 (1988): 53–78.

Hofstetter, C. Richard. *Bias in the News: Network Television Coverage of the 1972 Election Campaign*. Columbus: Ohio State University Press, 1976.

Holstein, James A., and Jaber F. Gubrium. *The Self We Live By: Narrative Identity in a Postmodern World*. New York: Oxford University Press, 2000.

Horton, Paul B., and Gerald R. Leslie. *The Sociology of Social Problems*. 6th edition. Englewood Cliffs, NJ: Prentice Hall, 1978.

Howland, George Jr. "The New Outlaws." *The Progressive* 58, no. 5 (1994): 33.

Iyengar, Shanto. "Television News and Citizen Explanation of National Affairs." *American Political Science Review* 80, no. 3 (September 1988): 815–831.

Iyengar, Shanto, and Donald Kinder. *News That Matters: Television and American Opinion.* Chicago: University of Chicago Press, 1987.

Jensen, Carl. *20 Years of Censored News.* New York: Seven Stories Press, 1997.

Johnstone, John W. C., Edward J. Slawski, and William W. Bowman. *The News People: A Sociological Portrait of American Journalists and Their Work.* Urbana: University of Illinois Press, 1976.

Just, Marion R., Ann N. Crigler, Dean E. Alger, and Timothy E. Cook. *Crosstalk: Citizens, Candidates, and the Media in a Presidential Campaign.* Chicago: University of Chicago Press, 1996.

Just, Marion, Ann Crigler, and Tami Buhr. "Voice Substance, and Cynicism in Presidential Campaign Media." *Political Communication* 16, no. 1 (1999): 25–43.

Kaplan, Richard L. *Politics and the American Press: The Rise of Objectivity, 1865–1920.* New York: Cambridge University Press, 2002.

Kellner, Douglas. *The Persian Gulf TV War.* Boulder, CO: Westview, 1992.

Kensicki, Linda J. "No Cure for What Ails Us: The Media-Constructed Disconnect between Social Problems and Possible Solutions." *Journalism & Mass Communication Quarterly* 81, no. 2 (2004): 53–73.

Kirkpatrick, Daniel D. "National Review Founder to Leave Stage." *The New York Times* (June 29, 2004): Section A, 18.

Klein, Joe. "Monumental Callousness." *Newsweek* (August 12, 1996): 45.

Knoll, Edwin. "Just to the Left: Seventy-Five Years but Who's Counting?" *The Progressive* (July 4, 1984): 4.

Kornblum, William, and Joseph Julian. *Social Problems.* 8th edition. Englewood Cliffs, NJ: Prentice Hall, 1995.

Lacayo, Richard. "Law and Order." *Time* (June 15, 1996): 51.

Lang, Kurt, and Gladys Engel Lang. "Noam Chomsky and the Manufacture of Consent for American Foreign Policy." *Political Communication* 21, no. 1 (November 2004): 94.

Lee, Christopher. "Administration Rejects Ruling on PR Videos: GAO Called Tapes Illegal Propaganda." *The Washington Post* (March 15, 2005): A21.

Lee, Martin A., and Norman Solomon. *Unreliable Sources: A Guide to Detecting Bias in News Media.* New York: Lyle Stuart, 1990.

Lee, Tien-Tsung. "The Liberal Media Myth Revisited: An Examination of Factors Influencing Perceptions of Media Bias." *Journal of Broadcasting & Electronic Media* 49, no. 1 (March 2005): 543–64.

Lenz, Richard. *Symbols, the News Magazines, and Martin Luther King.* Baton Rouge: Louisiana State University Press, 1990.

Lepre, Carolyn R., Kim Walsh-Childer, and Jean C. Chance. "Newspaper Coverage Portrays Managed Care Negatively." *Newspaper Research Journal* 24, no. 2 (2003): 6–21.

Lichter, S. Robert, Stanley Rothman, and Linda S. Lichter. *The Media Elite.* Bethesda, MD: Adler & Adler, 1986.

Lieberman, Trudy. *Slanting the Story: The Forces That Shape the News.* New York: New Press, 2000.

Lipset, Seymor M., and William S. Schneider. *The Confidence Gap: Business, Labor, and Government in the Public Mind.* New York: Free Press, 1983.

Lott, John R., Jr. *The Bias against Guns: Why Almost Everything You've Heard about Gun Control Is Wrong.* Washington, DC: Regnery Publishing, Inc., 2003.

Lowry, Dennis T., and Jon A. Shidler. "The Sound Bites, the Biters, and the Bitten: An Analysis of Network TV News Bias in Campaign '92." *Journalism & Mass Communication Quarterly* 72, no. 1 (Spring 1995): 33–44.

Luther, Catherine, and Mark Miller. "Framing of the 2003 U.S–Iraq War Demonstrations: An Analysis of News and Partisan Texts." *Journalism & Mass Communication Quarterly* 82, no. 1 (2005): 78–96.

MacArthur. John R. *Second Front: Censorship and Propaganda in the Gulf War.* New York: Hill and Wang, 1992.

McAdam, Douglas. *Political Process and the Development of Black Insurgency, 1930–1970.* Chicago: University of Chicago Press, 1982.

McChesney, Robert. *The Problem with Media: U.S. Communication Politics in the 21st Century.* New York: Monthly Review Press, 2004.

Manning, Paul. *News and News Sources: A Critical Introduction.* Thousand Oaks: Sage, 2001.

Mason, Laurie, and Clifford Nass. "How Partisan and Non-Partisan Readers Perceive Political Foes and Newspaper Bias." *Journalism Quarterly* 66, no. 3 (Autumn 1989): 564–570, 778.

Merritt, Davis. *Public Journalism and Public Life: Why Telling the News Is Not Enough.* New York: Lawrence Erlbaum Associates, 1998.

Miller, David. "The Propaganda machine." Pp. 80–99 in *Tell Me Lies: Propaganda and Media Distortion in the Attack on Iraq,* edited by David Miller. London: Pluto, 2004.

Monroe Mendelsohn Research, Inc. "The Mendelsohn Affluent Survey." http://www.mmrsurveys.com/MendelsohnAffluentSurvey.htm (accessed May 29, 2007).

Monroe Mendelsohn Research, Inc. "The Summary Report of Selected Findings for 2006." http://www.mmrsurveys.com/data/Survey_2006.pdf (accessed May 29, 2007).

Morgan, David. *The Flacks of Washington: Government Information and the Public Agenda.* New York: Greenwood Press, 1986.

Morrow, Lance. "The Time of Our Lives." *Time* (March 9, 1998): 84–91.

Murphy, Janet L. "An Analysis of Political Bias in Evening Network News during the 1996 Presidential Campaigns." PhD diss., The University of Oklahoma, 1998. Retrieved from Dissertation Abstracts May 23, 2007.

Nash, George. *The Conservative Intellectual Movement in America since 1945.* New York: Basic Books, 1976.

"*Newsweek* U.S. Mendelsohn Affluent Profile," *Newsweek* Media Kit online. http://www.newsweekmediakit.com/newsite/pdf/us_mmr.pdf (accessed May 29, 2007).

"*Newsweek*: A History of Growth and Innovation," *Newsweek* Media Kit online. http://www.newsweekmediakit.com/newsite/us/about/history.shtml (accessed June 5, 2007).

"New Federal War on Drugs." *Newsweek* (May 11, 1981): 27.

Nichols, John. "Portrait of the Founder, Fighting Bob LaFollette." *The Progressive* (January 1999): 10–14.

Nimmo, Dan D. *Newsgathering in Washington: A Study in Political Communication.* New York: Atherton Press, 1964.

Nimmo, Dan, and James Combs. *Subliminal Politics.* Englewood Cliffs, NJ: Prentice Hall, 1983.

Niven, David. "A Fair Test of Media Bias: Party, Race and Gender in Coverage of the 1992 House Baking Scandal." *Polity* 36, no. 4 (July 2004): 637–649.

———. "Bolstering an Illusory Majority: The Effects of the Media's Portrayal of Death Penalty Support." *Social Science Quarterly* 83, no. 2 (September 2002): 671–689.

———. "Objective Evidence on Media Bias: Newspaper Coverage of Congressional Party Switchers." *Journalism & Mass Communication Quarterly* 80, no. 2 (Summer 2003): 311–326.

———. "Partisan Bias in the Media? A New Test." *Social Science Quarterly* 80, no. 4 (December 1999): 847–857.

Noyes, Rich. "The Media Are Biased against Conservative Economic Policies." Pp. 23–28 in *Media Bias*, edited by Stuart Kallen. San Diego: Greenhaven Press, 2004.

Ogan, Christine L., Charlene J. Brown, and David H. Weaver. "Characteristics of Managers of Selected Daily Newspapers." *Journalism Quarterly* 56, no. 3 (Winter 1979): 803–809.

Olasky, Marvin. *The Press and Abortion, 1838–1988.* Hillsdale, N. J.: Lawrence Erlbaum Associates, 1988.

———. *Prodigal Press: The Anti-Christian Bias of the American News Media.* Westchester, IL: Crossway, 1988.

Paletz, David L. *The Media in American Politics.* New York: Longman, 2002.

Parenti, Michael. *Inventing Reality: The Politics of the Mass Media.* New York: St. Martin's Press, 1986.

Pasley, Jeffrey. *The Tyranny of Printers: Newspaper Politics in the Early American Republic.* Charlottesville: University of Virginia Press, 2001.

Patterson, Thomas E. *The Mass Media Election: How Americans Choose Their President.* New York: Praeger, 1980.

Patterson, Thomas. *Out of Order.* New York: Knopf, 1993.

Patterson, Thomas E., and Wolfgang Donsbach. "News Decisions: Journalists as Partisan Actors." *Political Communication*, 13 no. 4 (October–December 1996): 455–468.

Patterson, Thomas E., and Robert D. McClure. *The Unseeing Eye: The Myth of Television Power in National Elections.* New York: G. P. Putnam's Sons, 1976.

Perry, John, and Erna Perry. *Face to Face: The Individual and Social Problems.* Boston: Little Brown, 1976.

Peterson, Theodore. *Magazine in the Twentieth Century.* Urbana: University of Illinois Press, 1964.

Peterson, Thomas E., "Doing Well and Doing Good: How Soft News and Critical Journalism Are Shrinking the News Audience and Weakening Democracy—and What News Outlets Can Do about It," Cambridge, MA; Harvard University, Jan Shorenstein Center on Press, Politics and Public Policy, Kennedy School of Government 2000 Faculty Research Working Paper Series, #RWP01-001.

Pew Research Center for the People and the Press. "America's Place in the World 2005: An Investigation of the Attitudes of American Opinion Leaders and the American Public about International Affairs." http://people-press.org/reports/pdf/263.pdf (accessed May 18, 2007).

Pew Research Center for the People and the Press. "How Journalists See Journalists in 2004." http://people-press.org/reports/pdf/214.pdf (accessed May 18, 2007).

Picard, Robert G. *Media Portrayals of Terrorism: Functions and Meaning of News Coverage*. Ames: Iowa Sate University Press, 1993.

Project for Excellence in Journalism. "The State of the News Media 2007: An Annual Report on American Journalism." 2007. http://www.stateofthemedia.org/2007/narrative_magazines_audience.asp?cat=2&media=8 (accessed May 29, 2007).

Qualter, Terence. *Opinion Control in the Democracies*. New York: St. Martin's Press, 1985.

Reasons, Charles E., and William D. Perdue. *The Ideology of Social Problems*. Sherman Oaks, CA: Alfred Publishing, 1981.

Rosten, Leo. *The Washington Correspondents*. New York: Harcourt Brace, 1937.

Rothman, Stanley, and Amy E. Black. "Media and Business Elites: Still in Conflict?" *Public Interest* no. 143 (Spring 2001): 72–86.

Rothschild, Mathew. "Ninety Years of Stubborn Sound." *The Progressive* (January 1999): 4.

Rusher, William A. *The Coming Battle for the Media: Curbing the Power of the Media Elite*. New York: William Morrow and Company, Inc., 1988.

Ryan, Charlotte. *Prime Time Activism: Media Strategies for Grassroots Organizing*. Boston: South End Press, 1991.

Salholz, Eloise, Ann McDaniel, Patrick King, Nadine Joseph, Gregory Cerio, and Ginny Carroll. "The Battle over Abortion." *Newsweek* (May 1, 1989): 28–32.

Sandman, Peter M., David B. Sachsman, Michael R. Greenberg, and Michael Gochfield. *Environmental Risk and the Press*. New Brunswick, N.J.: Transaction Press, 1987.

Schechter, Danny. "ABC News Was Biased Against the U.S. War in Iraq." Pp. 70-77 in *Media Bias*, edited by Stuart Kallen. San Diego: Greenhaven Press, 2004.

Schudson, Michael. "Deadlines, Datelines, and History." P. 81 in *Reading the News*, edited by Karl Manoff and Michael Schudson. New York: Pantheon, 1986.

Shields, Todd G. "Network News Construction of Homelessness: 1980–1993." *Communication Review* 4, no. 2 (2001): 193–218.

Schiffer, Adam J. "Assessing Partisan Bias in Political News: The Case(s) of Local Senate Election Coverage." *Political Communication* 23, no. 1 (January–March 2006): 23–39.

Schlesinger, Philip. "Rethinking the Sociology of Journalism: Source Strategies and the Limits of Media Centrism." In *Public Communication: The New Imperatives*, edited by Marjorie Ferguson, 61–83. Thousand Oaks, CA: Sage, 1990.

———. *Media State and Nation: Political Violence and Collective Identities*. Newbury Park, CA: Sage, 1991.

Sigal, Leo. *Reporters and Officials: The Organization and Politics of Newsmaking*. Lexington, MA: Heath, 1973.

Sirianni, Carmen, and Lewis Friedland. *Civic Innovation in America: Community Empowerment, Public Policy and the Movement for Civic Renewal*. Berkeley: University of California Press, 2001.

Snow, David A., E. Burke Rochford Jr., Steven K. Worden, and Robert D. Benford. "Frame Alignment Processes, Micro Mobilization and Movement Participation." *American Sociological Review* 51, no. 4 (August 1986): 464–481.

Soley, Lawrence C. *The News Shapers: The Sources Who Explain the News*. New York: Praeger, 1992.

Soley, Lawrence. "The Power of the Press Has a Price." *Extra* (July/August 1997). http://www.fair.org/index.php?page=1387 (accessed May 24, 2007).

Solomon, Norman. *The Habits of Highly Deceptive Media: Decoding Spin and Lies in Mainstream News*. Monroe, ME: Common Courage Press, 1999.

Sparrow, Bartholomew. *Uncertain Guardians: The News Media as a Political Institution*. Baltimore: Johns Hopkins University Press, 1999.

Steele, Janet E. "Experts and the Operational Bias of Television News: The Case of the Persian Gulf War." *Journalism & Mass Communication Quarterly* 72, no. 4 (Winter 1995): 799–812.

Stempel, Guido H., III, and John W. Windhauser. "Coverage by the Prestige Press of the 1988 Presidential Campaign." *Journalism Quarterly* 66, no. 4 (Winter 1989): 894–896, 919.

Stevenson, Robert L., and Mark T. Greene. "A Reconsideration of Bias in the News." *Journalism Quarterly* 51, no. 1 (1980): 115–121.

Stone, Deborah. "Causal Stories and the Formation of Policy Agendas." *Political Science Quarterly* 104, no. 2 (Summer 1989): 281–300.

Strentz, Herbert. *News Reporters and News Sources*. Ames: Iowa State University Press, 1989.

Sullivan, Thomas, Kenrick Thompson, Richard Wright, George Gross, and Dale Spady. *Social Problems, Divergent Perspectives*. New York: John Wiley & Sons, 1980.

Surette, Ray. *Media, Crime and Criminal Justice: Images and Realities*. Belmont, CA: West/Wadsworth, 1998.

Sutter, Daniel. "An Indirect Test of the Liberal Media Thesis Using Newsmagazine Circulation." Unpublished Manuscript. University of Oklahoma.

Tebbel, John, and Mary Ellen Zuckerman. *The Magazine in America*. New York: Oxford University Press, 1991.

"The War on Drugs Is Lost." *National Review* (February 1996): 34.

Tilly, Charles. *Why? What Happens When People Give Reasons . . . Why*. Princeton, NJ: Princeton University Press, 2006.

Time Magazine. "The Crime Wave." (June 30, 1975): 10–14.

Time, Inc., "2006 MRI: Time U.S. Audience Profile." http://www.time.com/time/mediakit/1/us/timemagazine/audience/mri/index.html (accessed May 29, 2007).

Tuchman, Gaye. *Making News: A Study in the Construction of Reality*. New York: Free Press, 1978.

Turque, Bill, and Anne Underwood. "A New Line against Crime." *Newsweek* (August 27, 1990): 36.

Vallone, Robert. P., Lee Ross, and Mark R. Lepper. "The Hostile Media Phenomenon: Biased Perceptions and Perceptions of Media Bias in Coverage of the Beirut Massacre." *Journal of Personality and Social Psychology* 48, no. 3 (1985): 577–585.

Watts, Mark D., David Domke, Dhavan Shah, and David P. Fan. "Elite Cues and Media Bias in Presidential Campaigns: Explaining Public Perceptions of a Liberal Press." *Communication Research* 26, no. 2 (April 1999): 144–175.

Weaver, David H., and G. Cleveland Wilhoit. *The American Journalist*. Bloomington, University of Indiana Press, 1986.

Weaver, David H., Randal A. Beam, Bonnie J. Browlee, Paul S. Voakes, and G. Cleveland Wilhoit. *The American Journalist in the 21st Century: U.S. News People and the Dawn of a New Millennium.* Mahwah, N.J.: Lawrence Erlbaum Associates, Inc., 2007.

Weiss, Carol H. "What America's Leaders Read." *The Public Opinion Quarterly* 38, no. 1 (Spring 1974): 1–22.

Welch, Michael, Melissa Fenwick, and Meredith Roberts. "Primary Definitions of Crime and Moral Panic: A Content Analysis of Experts' Quotes in Feature Newspaper Articles on Crime." *Journal of Research in Crime and Delinquency* 34, no. 4 (November 1997): 474–494.

Wells, Chris. "Newsweek (a Fact) Is the New Hot Book (an Opinion)." *Esquire* (November, 1969): 155. Quoted in Alan Nourie and Barbara Nourie, *American Mass Market Magazines* (Westport, CT: Greenwood Press, 1990): 314.

White, David M. "The Gate Keeper: A Case Study in the Selection of News." *Journalism Quarterly* 27 (1950): 383–390.

Whitney, D. Charles, Marilyn Fritzler, Steven Jones, Sharon Mazzarella, and Lana Rakow. "Geographic and Source Bias in Network Television News 1982–1984." *Journal of Broadcasting and Electronic Media* 33, no. 2 (1989):159–174.

Wilhelm, Sabine. "Coverage of the War in Iraq: Frame Choice in American and German National Newspapers." *Journal of Intercultural Communication*, no. 10 (December 2005): 1–11.

Wilhoit, G. Cleveland, and David H. Weaver. *The American Journalists: A Portrait of U.S. News People and Their Work.* 2nd edition. Bloomington: Indiana University Press, 1991.

Will, George F. "The Cold War among Women." *Newsweek* (June 26, 1978): 100.

Williams, Dimitrie. "Synergy Bias: Conglomerates and Promotion in the News." *Journal of Broadcasting and Electronic Media* 46, no. 3 (September 2002): 453–472.

Woodward, Bob. *Five Presidents and the Legacy of Watergate.* New York: Simon & Schuster, 1999.

Woodward, Kenneth L. "Hymns, Hers and Theirs." *Newsweek* (February 12, 1996): 75.

Zaller, John, and Dennis Chiu. "Government's Little Helper: U.S. Press Coverage of Foreign Policy Crises, 1945–1991." *Political Communication* 13, no. 4 (October–December 1996): 385–405.

Index

Abortion, xv, 5, 6, 7, 50, 53, 54, 61, 62,
    64, 65, 66, 67, 80, 87, 89, 101, 114,
    122, 135; "partial birth abortions,"
    89, 122
Accuracy in the Media, 11
Adjusted Bias Score (ABS), defined,
    63-64; examples for computation of,
    64-67
Advocacy groups, 33, 56, 58, 97, 98,
    99, 100, 101, 106
AFDC, 33, 34
AIDS, 6
al Qaeda, 133
Alger, Dean E., xiv, 90
"All Things Considered," 28
Allen, Mike, xiv, 8, 90, 113
Alterman, Eric, xiii, 8, 43, 44
Alvarez, R. Michael, 33
American Conservative, 32
American Enterprise Institute, 15
American Journalism Review, 14
American Life League, 53
American Online (AOL), 28, 37, 44
American Prospect, 32

American Spectator, 32, 108
Americans for Democratic Action
    (ADA), 7
Ammunition, 38
Annin, Peter, 79
Ashland Oil, 13
Ashley, Laura, 8
Astor, Vincent, 37
Atlanta, GA, 30, 103
Atwater, Tony, 118

Baca Zinn, Maxine, 51
Bagdikian, Ben H., 8, 12, 14, 44, 95, 96
Baker, Brent H., 1, 2, 3, 4, 5, 6
"balanced" coverage, 39, 74, 76, 90,
    131, 133, 134, 136
Baldastry, Gerald, 10, 16
Balkans, 87
Baltimore News, 35
Banfield, Edward, 31
Baranek, Patricia, 53, 94
Barnes, Samuel, 29
Barstow, David, 103
Beam, Randal A., 2, 3

Beck, Paul A., xiii, 9
Beckett, Katherine, 53, 95, 96, 101
Begly, Sharon, 79
Benford, Robert D., 17
Bennett, Stephen E., 9, 49
Bennett, W. Lance, 95, 96, 107, 113,
    128, 130-1, 133
Berelson, Bernard, 16
Berryhill, Dale A., xiii
Bethell, Tom, 106
Bhopal, 122
Black, Amy E., 3
Bloeser, Andrew J., 12
Blumenthal, Sidney, 3
Booher Feagin, Clairece, 51
Book-of-the-Month-Club, 44
Booth, Cathy, 81
Bosh, Charles L., 113
Bowman, William W., 2
Bozell, L. Brent III, 1, 2, 3, 4, 5, 6, 40
Brady, David W., 4, 5, 114
Brookings Institution, 5, 15
Brophy-Baermann, Michelle, 12
Browlee, Bonnie J., 2, 3
Brown, Charlene J., 2
Brown, Robin, 95
Buchannon, Pat, 3
Buckley, Jr. William F., 40, 41
Buhr, Tami, 17
Bush Administration, 5, 114, 117, 118,
    120, 121
Bush, George H. W., 5
Bush, George W., 3, 5, 33, 115

Cambodia, 12
Capella, Joseph N., 96
capital punishment, 90
Carroll, Ginny, 80
Carter Administration, 41, 116, 117,
    119, 120, 121
Carter, Jimmy, 122
CBS Evening News, 132
censorship, 44
Center for Reproductive Law and
    Policy, 53, 66
Center for Strategic and International
    Studies, 15
Cerio, Gregory, 80

Chan, Janet B.L., 53, 94
Chance, Jean C., 12
Cheney, Richard, 14
Chernobyl, 122
Chia, Stella Chih-Yun, 9
Chibnall, Steven, 53
Chicago, IL, 30
China, 15, 37
Chiu, Dennis, 8, 12
Christian Right, 122
Christianity, bias against, 6-7
Cirino, Robert, 8
Clark, Evert, 79
Clark, Ramsey, 31
Clarke, John, 53
Clinton Administration, 3, 5, 62, 117,
    124
Clinton, Bill, 3, 5, 7, 33, 114
Cocks, Jay, 80, 81
Coffey, Philip J., 8
Cohen, Adam, 74
Cold War, the, 37, 38
Coleman, James W., 51
Columbia Journalism Review, 12, 13
Combs, James, xvi
Conniff, Ruth, 33, 34, 35
Conscience of a Conservative, 40
"conservative media," 16, 135;
    evidence of conservative media bias,
    xiii, 9-17; reactions to evidence of,
    17-18
"conservative," defining, xiv-xv
Converse, Phillip, 130
Cook, Timothy E., xiv, 90
Coulter, Ann, 1, 3
Craig, Robert L., 8
credibility, xviii, 132
Cressey, Donald R., 51
Crigler, Ann N., xiv, 17, 90
crime, 6, 7, 13, 30-31, 50, 51, 54-55,
    56, 58-59, 72, 73, 86, 129, 130, 131,
    135; conservative and liberal
    positions on, 58-59; discussion of
    solutions in the coverage of, 86-88,
    89-90; impact of dramatic events on
    the coverage of, 123, 124; media
    coverage of, 6, 13, 30-31, 55, 56;
    National Review coverage of, 75,

76-77, 82, 117, 119, 124, 129;
Newsweek coverage of, 77-79, 82,
117, 119, 123, 124, 135; presidential
administrations and the coverage of,
115, 116, 117, 118, 119, 120, 121,
123, 124; *Progressive* coverage of,
77, 82, 117, 119, 121, 124; *Time*
coverage of, 30-31, 77-79, 82, 116,
117, 118, 119, 120, 121, 124, 129,
135; use of sources in the coverage
of, 95, 97, 98, 99, 101-102, 104, 105,
108
Critcher, Charles, 53
Cronkite, Walter, 4
Croteau, David, xiii, 8, 10, 12, 14, 15,
44, 56, 88, 96
Cuomo, Mario, 106

D'Alessio, Dave, xiv, 8, 9, 90, 113
Dahlgren, Peter, 96
Dalton, Russell, xiii, 9
Davis, Patricia, 33
Day, Samuel H., Jr., 42
decontextualized news, 16
Delli Carpini, Michael X., 128
democracy, xix, 11, 32, 41, 43, 44, 93,
96, 97, 106, 127, 128, 129, 130, 131,
132, 133; defining, 127-128
dense coverage, 121-125
Detroit, MI, 30, 38
Dewey, John, 96
Dickson, Sandra, 8
Disney Corporation, 12
Dobkin, Bethami A, 95
Dole, Bob, 5, 7, 58
Domke, David, xiii, 9
Donaldson, Sam, 14, 15
Donovan, Hadley, 36, 37
Donsbach, Wolfgang, 8
Dreier, Peter, 56, 87
Drug Enforcement Administration
(DEA), 78
Duke, David, 33
Dulles, John Foster, 36
Dunlap, Riley E., 134

Eagle Forum, 53, 61
Earth Summit, 122

eBay, 37
Edelman, Murray, xvi, 52, 54, 55, 131-
132, 133
Eisenhower Administration, 36
Eitzen, D. Stanley, 51
El Salvador, 11
Elektra Records, 37
Elliot, Osborn, 39
Ellis, Rose, 33
Engel Lang, Gladys, 17, 18
Entman, Robert M., 28, 37, 55, 86, 96,
130
environment, 5, 13, 15, 50, 51, 54, 71,
72, 73, 75, 77, 78, 79, 81, 83, 86, 87,
124, 129, 131; conservative and
liberal positions on, 60-61;
discussion of solutions in the
coverage of, 86, 87, 88; impact of
dramatic events on the coverage of,
122, 123, 124; media coverage of,
13, 15, 54, 55, 95; public opinion
towards, 134; *National Review*
coverage of, 40, 71, 72, 73, 77, 81,
83, 97, 98, 102, 104, 105, 115, 117,
119, 122, 123; *Newsweek* coverage
of, 72, 73, 78, 79, 83, 87, 115, 116,
117, 119, 134; presidential
administrations and the coverage of,
115, 116, 117, 119, 120, 121;
Progressive coverage of, 71, 72, 73,
75, 77, 83, 97, 99, 102, 104, 105,
115, 116, 117, 119, 120, 121, 122,
123, 124, 135; *Time* coverage of, 72,
73, 78, 79, 83, 86, 87, 116, 117, 119,
121, 122, 123; use of sources in the
coverage of, 97, 98, 99, 101, 102,
104, 105, 108, 115, 116
Equal Rights Amendment (ERA), xix
Erickson, Richard V., 53, 94
experts, 6, 14, 15, 56, 57, 79, 97, 98,
99, 100, 101, 105, 106
"explanatory journalism," 16, 107
Exxon, 13

Family Enrichment Center, 34
Fan, David P., xiii, 9
Farley, John E., 51
Feagin, Joe R., 51

Federal Bureau of Investigation (FBI), 78

Federal Family Support Act, 33

Feminism, 5, 50, 61, 62, 80, 87

Fenwick, Melissa, 8

Fialka, John J., 95

Fishman, Mark, 53, 94

"flack," 11

Flickinger, Richard S., 9, 49

Ford, Gerald, 30

Ford Administration, 30, 31, 115, 116, 117, 119, 120

Fortune Magazine, 36

Forum, 36

Fox television news, 132

Fraker, Susan, 79

Friedland, Lewis, 96

Friedman, Milton, 40

Fritzler, Marilyn, 53

Gamson, William A., 52, 53, 56, 87-88, 95

Gandy, Oscar H., Jr., 96

Gans, Herbert, 8, 27, 28, 31, 39-40, 53, 94, 95, 107, 113, 132

gay rights, 5, 7

Gaylin, William, 31

gender, 6, 7, 50, 51, 71, 114, 122, 131, 133, 1234; conservative and liberal positions on, 61-62; discussion of solutions in the coverage of, 87, 88; impact of dramatic events on the coverage of, 122, 123, 124, 125; media coverage of, 6, 17; *National Review* coverage of, 72, 73, 75, 77, 84, 87, 88, 89, 97, 98, 102, 103, 104, 105, 115, 116, 117, 119, 122, 123, 124; *Newsweek* coverage of, 72, 73, 75, 78, 80-81, 82, 84, 87, 88, 89, 115, 116, 117, 118, 119, 122, 123, 124; presidential administrations and the coverage of, 115, 116, 117, 118, 119, 120, 121; *Progressive* coverage of, 72, 73, 75, 77, 84, 87, 88, 89, 97, 99, 102, 103, 104, 105, 115, 116, 117, 119, 120, 121, 124; public opinion towards, 135; *Time* coverage of, 72, 73, 75, 78, 80-81, 84, 87, 88,

89, 115, 116, 117, 119, 121, 123, 134; use of sources in the coverage of, 97, 98, 101, 102, 103, 104, 105

General Accounting Office, 13

General Electric, 12, 60

Gibbs, Nancy, 81

Gingrich, Newt, 15

Gitlin, Todd, xvi, 36, 53, 95

global warming, 131, 133

Gochfield, Michael, 95

God and Man at Yale, 40

Goldberg, Bernard, xiii, 1, 3, 4, 5, 6, 113, 114, 118

Goldwater, Barry, 40

Goodale, James C., 42

Goodman, Peter, 39

Graber, Doris, 16, 30, 95

Graham, Katherine, 38, 39

Granada, 86

Grandy, Fred, 74

Greenberg, Michael R., 95

Greene, Mark T., xiii

Greenfield, Meg, 86

Groseclose, Tim, 7

Gross, Bertram, 12

Gross, George, 51

Guatemala, 11

Gubrium, Jaber F., 94

gun control, 5, 6, 59, 77, 87, 90, 105

Gunther, Albert C., 9, 134

Haas, Tanni, 14

Hacker, Frederick, 31

Hadden, Briton, 35, 36

Hall, Stuart, 52, 53, 94

Hallin, Daniel C., 36, 94

Hart, Peter, 8

Hartsgaard, Mark, xiii, 14

Hatch, Orrin, 15

Hawkins, Virgil, 14

HBO Home Video, 37

health care issues, 12

Heinz, John, 31

Heritage Foundation, 5

Herman, Edward S., xiii, xiv, 10-11, 95

Herzstein, Robert Edwin, 36

Hewitt, Christopher, 5, 6, 113, 114, 121

Hickey, Neil, 51

Hightower, Jim, 13
Hilgartner, Stephen, 113
Hofstetter, C. Richard, xiv, 90, 113
Hollar, Julie, 8
Holstein, James A., 94
homelessness, 5, 12, 54, 63, 103, 113, 114, 128
Hooker Chemical and Plastics Corporation, 122
horse race coverage, 9
Horton, Paul B., 51
"hostile media effect," 9
Houston, TX, 30
Howland, George Jr., 103
Hoynes, William, xiii, 10, 12, 14, 15, 44, 56, 87-88, 96
Huckfeldt, Robert, xiii, 9
Huddy, Leonie, 135
Human Events, 32
Hyde, Henry, 15
Hylton, Hilary, 74

In These Times, 32
incumbents, advantages of, 10
Institute for Policy Studies, 14
Intercoder reliability, 68
Intergovernmental Panel on Global Climate Change, 122
Internal Revenue Service (IRS), 78
International Paper, 13
Iraq, 3, 12, 95, 132
Iyengar, Shanto, 52, 94, 128

Jamieson, Kathleen H., 96
Jefferson, Tony, 53
Jensen, Carl, 13
John Birch Society, 3
Johnstone, John W. C., 2
Jones, Steven, 53
Joseph, Nadine, 80
journalists, xiii, xiv, 1, 2, 3, 4, 5, 6, 7, 8, 14, 15, 17, 18, 27, 28, 30, 31, 35, 37, 43, 44, 53, 79, 95, 96, 108; ideology of, 2-4; for *Time* and *Newsweek*, 28
"Judgment Calls," 86
Julian, Joseph, 51
Just, Marion J., xiv, 17, 90

Kaase, Max, 29
Kaplan, Richard L., 10, 96
Katz, Michael, 63, 106
Keeter, Scott, 128
Kellner, Douglas, 95
Kensicki, Linda J., 56
Key, V. O., Jr., 130
Kinder, Donald, 94, 128
King, Patrick, 80
Kirk, Russell, 40
Kirkpatrick, Daniel D., 41
Kissinger, Henry, 44
Klein, Joe, 81, 86
Knoll, Edwin, 42
Koetzel, William, xiii
Kornblum, William, 51
Kosovo, 12
Kull, Steven, 133

Lacayo, Richard, 78
Lafay, Marilyn R., 135
LaFollette's Weekly, 41
Landis, Jean M., 135
Lang, Kurt, 17, 18
Laos, 12
Lasch, Katherine E., 52
Lazarsfeld, Paul, 16
"Learnfare" program, 33
Lee, Christopher, 103
Lee, Martin A., 8, 14, 15
Lee, Tien-Tsung, 9
Lenz, Richard, 37
Lepper, Mark R., 9
Lepre, Carolyn R., 12
Leslie, Gerald R., 51
Lewis, Evan, 133
"liberal media," 135; evidence of liberal media bias, xiii, 2-7; reactions to evidence of, 8-9
"liberal," defining, xiv-xv
Libya, 86
Lichter, Linda S., xiii, 2, 3, 4, 5, 7, 8
Lichter, S. Robert, xiii, 2, 3, 4, 5, 7, 8
Lieberman, Joe, 7
Lieberman, Trudy, 53
Limbaugh, Rush, 13
Lipset, Seymour M., 31, 107
Literary Digest, 36, 38

Little, Brown and Company, 29, 37, 44
Los Angeles Times, 28, 65
Los Angeles, CA, 30, 38
Losing Ground, 106
Lott, John R., Jr., 5, 6
Love Canal, 122
Lowry, Dennis T., 4, 114
Luce, Henry, 35, 36, 37, 38, 39, 43
Luther, Catherine, 12
Lynch, Bill, 103

Ma, Jonathan, 4, 5, 114
MacArthur, John R., 95
Mack, Katrina, 33
Manning, Paul, 108
"market model" of media, 10
Marshall, George, 41
Martyn, Thomas J. C., 37
Mason, Laurie, 9
Mattick, Han, 31
Mazzarella, Sharon, 53
McAdam, Douglas, 53
McCarthy and His Enemies, 40
McCarthy, Joseph, 40, 41
McChesney, Robert, 95
McClure, Robert D., 90
McCombs, Maxwell, 128
McDaniel, Ann, 80
McGovern, George, 3
McNeil Lehrer News Hour, 15
McPhee, William, 16
media bias, and public opinion, 6, 134; and truth, xviii; complaints about xiii, 1-7, 9-16; defining, xiv-xv, 49-50; media bias, positive functions of, 133-135; measuring, 63-67;
Media Institute, 11
Media Research Center (MRC), 4
Medicaid, 56
Merritt, Davis, 96
Merton, Robert, 31
Miller, David, 95
Miller, Mark, 12
Miller, Walter, 31
Milyo, Jeffrey, 7
Modigliani, Andre, 95
Moley, Raymond, 38
Money Magazine, 37

Morgan, David, 53
"Morning Edition," 28
Morris, Norman, 31
Morrow, Lance, 37
Mother Jones, 32
Moynihan, Patrick, 106
"multiperspectival news," 31
Murphy, Janet L., 5
"My Turn," 40, 41

Nabisco, 13
Nader, Ralph, 13
NAFTA, 8
Nagler, Jonathon, 33
Nash, George, 40
Nass, Clifford, 9
Nation, 32, 108
National Abortion and Reproduction Rights Action League (NARAL), 53
National Organization for Women (NOW), 53
National Review, xiv, xvii, xviii, 27, 32, 33, 35, 40, 41, 50, 53, 64, 65, 67, 71, 72, 73, 74, 75, 76, 77, 81, 82, 83, 84, 85, 88, 89, 90, 93, 97, 98, 100, 102, 103, 104, 105, 106, 107, 108, 114, 115, 116, 117, 119, 120, 123, 124, 127, 129, 130, 131, 135; changing position on drugs in, 76-77; history of, 40-41; readership, 32; use of sources in, 97-98; See also crime, environment, gender, poverty
National Right to Life, 53
NBC Nightly News, 132
Neely, Frances K., 135
Neuman, W. Russell, 130
New Deal, 36, 40
New York Times, 3, 5, 6, 7, 12, 13, 15, 28, 30, 44, 57, 94
news, xvi, 136; social construction of, xviii; political role of, xviii
News Corporation Limited, 12
Newsweek, xiv, xvii, xviii, 7, 27, 28, 29, 30, 31, 32, 35, 37, 38, 39, 40, 42, 43, 44, 45, 50, 51, 71, 72, 73, 74, 75, 76, 77, 78, 79, 80, 81, 82, 83, 84, 85, 86, 87, 88, 89, 90, 113, 114, 115, 116, 117, 118, 119, 120, 122, 123,

124, 125, 129, 130, 131, 132, 134, 135; criticisms of, 42-45; history of, 37-40; readership, 28-29; See also crime, environment, gender, poverty
Newsworthiness, xiv, 6
Nicaragua, 11
Nichols, John, 41
Nightline, 15
Nimmo, Dan D., xvi, 53
Niven, David, 8, 9
Nixon Administration, 43
Nixon, Richard, 43
Noyes, Rich, 5
NPR/PBS, 132
Nuclear Regulatory Commission, 13

Ogan, Christine L., 2
Ohlin, Lloyd, 31
Olasky, Marvin, 5, 6, 7
Olson, Beth, 8
"ordinary citizens," 103
O'Sullivan, Gerry, 95

Paletz, David L., 12, 28, 55
Parenti, Michael, 14
Pasley, Jeffrey, 10, 96
Patterson, Thomas E., xiv, 8, 16, 90
Pentagon, 13, 28, 94
Perdue, William D., 51
Perry, Erna, 51
Perry, John, 51
Personal Responsibility and Work Reconciliation Act, 81, 124
Peterson, Theodore, 36, 107
Picard, Robert G., 95
Pillsbury, 13
Planned Parenthood, 53, 66, 80
Poland, 12
political democracy, xix, 41, 43, 96, 106, 125, 127, 130
Pope John Paul II, 122
Popkin, Samuel, 130
poverty, 31, 32, 34, 50, 51, 54, 55, 56, 71, 74, 85, 86, 89, 90, 129, 131; conservative and liberal positions on, 63; discussion of solutions in the coverage of, 56, 86, 87, 88, 89, 133; impact of dramatic events on the

coverage of, 122, 123, 124, 125; limited coverage of, 71-72; media coverage of, 54-55; *National Review* coverage of, 72, 73, 75, 77, 85, 87, 88, 97, 98, 102, 105, 115, 116, 117, 118, 119, 123, 124, 129; *Newsweek* coverage of, 72, 73, 75, 78, 81, 85, 87, 88, 89, 115, 116, 117, 118, 119, 135; presidential administrations and the coverage of, 115, 116, 117, 118, 119, 121; *Progressive* coverage of, 32, 33, 72, 73, 75, 77, 85, 87, 88, 99, 102, 103, 105, 107, 115, 116, 117, 119, 121, 129; *Time* coverage of, 72, 73, 74, 75, 78, 81, 85, 87, 88, 115, 116, 117, 118, 119, 121, 122, 123, 135; use of sources in the coverage of, 74, 97, 98, 99, 101, 102, 103, 104, 105, 107
"primary definers," 53, 94, 95, 107
Progressive Party, 41
Progressive, xiv, xvii, xviii, 27, 32, 33, 34, 35, 41, 42, 50, 53, 64, 66, 67, 71, 72, 73, 74, 75, 76, 77, 82, 83, 84, 85, 86, 87, 88, 89, 93, 97, 99, 100, 102, 103, 104, 105, 107, 108, 114, 115, 116, 117, 118, 119, 120, 121, 122, 123, 124, 125, 127, 129, 130, 131, 134, 135; history of, 41-32; readership, 41-42; use of sources in, 97, 99; See also crime, environment, gender, poverty
Project Censored, 13
Project Success, 34
Pro-Life Action League, 53
Propaganda, 11, 12, 17, 102, 132
"Public Lives," 86
public service announcements, 12
Purdue University, 50

Qualter, Terence, 10

Racism/racial discrimination, 5
Rakow, Lana, 53
Ralston-Purina, 13
Ramsay, Clay, 133
Rather, Dan, 15

Reagan administration, 13, 41, 60, 114,
    116, 117, 118, 119, 120, 121, 122
Reagan, Ronald, 5, 6, 78
Reasons, Charles E., 51
Rhine, Staci L., 9, 49
Roberts, Brian, 53
Roberts, Meredith, 8
Rochford, Jr., E. Burke, 17
Roe v. Wade, 53, 87
Rojecki, Andrew, 37
Rosenthal, Jack, 3
Ross, Lee, 9
Ross, Thomas, 3
Rosten, Leo, 3
Rothman, Stanley, xiii, 2, 3, 4, 5, 7, 8
Rothschild, Mathew, 41
Rusher, William A., 1, 5, 43
Russia, 37, 41
Ryan, Charlotte, 95

Sachsman, David B., 95
Salholz, Eloise, 80
Samuelson, Robert, 86
Sandman, Peter M., 95
Sasson, Theodore, 56, 87
Saxbe, William, 31
Scarce, Rik, 134
Schaffley, Phyllis, 5
Schattschneider, E. E., 130
Schechter, Danny, 8
Schiffer, Adam J., 4, 114
Schlesinger, Philip, xiv, 53, 95
Schneider, William S., 107
Schudson, Michael, 94
Schumpter, Joseph A., 130
Seagram Corporation, 13
Serrin, William, 130-1, 133
Sexual harassment, 87, 101, 114
Shah, Dhavan, xiii, 9
Shaw, Donald L., 128
Shaw, Greg, 135
Shidler, Jon A., 4, 114
Shields, Todd G., 12
Shils, Edward, 127
Sigal, Leo, xvi, 8, 53, 93, 94, 95, 96,
    97, 100, 106, 107, 129
Simon, Rita J., 135
Sirianni, Carmen, 96

Slawski, Edward J., 2
Smith, Anthony, 132
Snow, David A., 17
Soil and Water Conservation Act, 122
Soley, Lawrence C., 8, 95
Solomon, Norman, 8, 14, 15
Somalia, 86
Sony Telecommunications, 12
Sources of news, xiii, xvi, 8, 9, 11, 14-
    18, 30, 31, 34, 35, 36, 37, 50, 52, 53-
    54, 78, 93-108, 134; categories of,
    56-58, 97-100; classifying as liberal
    or conservative, 56-58; media bias
    and, 14-16, 50, 74, 134; official
    sources, 30, 100-103, 108;
    oppositional sources, 105-106, 108;
    source alignment, 104-105
Spady, Dale, 51
Sparrow, Bartholomew, 16, 43
Stainbrook, Edward, 31
Steele, Janet E., 8
Stein, Robin, 103
Steiner, Linda, 14
Stempel III, Guido H., 4, 114
Stevenson, Robert L., xiii
Stief, William, 42
Stone, Deborah, 54
Strentz, Herbert, 95
Sullivan, Louis, 33
Sullivan, Thomas, 51
Surette, Ray, 95
Sutter, Daniel, 7, 43

Talbot, Strobe, 3
"Taxpayer Protection Act," 33
Tebbel, John, 35, 36, 38
Telecommunications Act, 1996, 12
Texaco, 13
Thomas, Detrick, 103
Thompson, Kenrick, 51
Thompson, Tommy, 33
Three Mile Island, xviii, 89, 114, 122
Tilly, Charles, 31
Time Warner, 29, 37, 44
Time, xiv, xvii, xviii, 3, 7, 27, 28, 29,
    30, 31, 32, 35, 36, 37, 38, 39, 40, 42,
    43, 44, 45, 50, 51, 71, 72, 73, 74, 75,
    76, 77, 78, 79, 80, 81, 82, 83, 84, 85,

86, 87, 88, 89, 90, 113, 114, 115,
116, 117, 118, 119, 120, 121, 122,
123, 124, 125, 127, 129, 130, 131,
132, 133, 135; criticisms of, 42-45;
history of, 35-37; readership, 28-29;
See also crime, environment, gender,
poverty
Today, 37, 38
Tribe, Laurence, 4
Truman, Harry, 41
Tuchman, Gaye, 8, 94

U.S. News and World Report, 7, 28
Union of Concerned Scientists, 13
United Nations, 12
United States Department of Energy,
122
United Technologies, 13

Vallone, Robert. P., 9
Viacom, 12
Vietnam, 12, 36, 37, 39, 41, 94
Vietnam War, 35, 94
Voakes, Paul S., 2, 3
Vorenberg, James, 31

Wall Street Journal, 16, 30
Wallace, Janice, 33
Walsh-Childer, Kim, 12
"war on terrorism," 3
Warner Brothers Recreational
Enterprises, 37
Warner Brothers Studios, 29
Washington Post Co., 30, 38, 42, 44
Washington Post, 5, 42, 43, 65, 80, 94
Watergate, 37, 41
Watts, Mark D., xiii, 9
Weaver, David H., 2, 3, 4, 28
Weekly Standard, 21, 108
Weiss, Carol H., 29, 43
Welch, Michel, 8
"welfare queens," 123
Welfare reform legislation, xix, 35
welfare reform, 12, 33, 34, 35, 74, 81,
89, 122
Wells, Chris, 38
Westinghouse, 12
Weyerhauser, 13

White, David M., 113
Whitney, D. Charles, 53
Wilhelm, Sabine, 118
Wilhoit, G. Cleveland, 2, 3, 4, 28
Will, George, 13, 80
Williams, Dimitri, 118
Wilson, James Q., 31
Windhauser, John W., 4, 114
Wolfgang, Marvin, 31
Wolfsfeld, Gadi, 53
Women's movement, 50, 61, 101, 135
women's rights, 4, 5, 6, 114
Woodward, Bob, 37
Woodward, Kenneth, 80, 81
Worden, Steven K., 17
World Policy Institute, 15
Wright, Richard, 51

YAHOO, 28
Yale University, 35, 41
Yudowitz, Bernard, 31

Zaller, John, 8, 12
Zuckerman, Mary Ellen, 35, 36, 38

About the Authors

Tawnya J. Adkins Covert is associate professor of sociology at Western Illinois University. She holds a PhD and MS in Sociology from Purdue University and BA in sociology from Marshall University. Her research has been published in journals such as *Mass Communication and Society*, *The Sociological Quarterly*, *Social Science Quarterly*, and *Journal of Consumer Culture*.

Philo C. Wasburn is professor of sociology at Purdue University. He holds a PhD in sociology from Cornell University, and an MA and BA in philosophy from the University of Michigan. He is the author of *Political Sociology: Approaches, Concepts, Hypotheses*; *Broadcasting Propaganda: International Radio Broadcasting and the Construction of Political Reality;* and *The Social Construction of International News*.